Equity and Science
Education Reform

Equity and Science Education Reform

Sharon J. Lynch
The George Washington University

LAWRENCE ERLBAUM ASSOCIATES, PUBLISHERS
2000   Mahwah, New Jersey   London

Lawrence Erlbaum Associates, Inc., Publishers
10 Industrial Avenue
Mahwah, NJ 07430

Cover design by Kathryn Houghtaling Lacey

Cover photo by Barbara Kinney.

Special thanks to the students from Colonel E. Brooke Lee Middle School
who posed for the cover photo—Jessica Mina, Catherine Newman,
Christina Panizales, Christy Portillo, Andrew Schulder, and Jennifer Slack
—wonderful models who are in no way connected to the students whose
stories are told in this book. Lee Middle School is a positive example of a
place where education reform for all is a reality because of leaders like
Stephen Bedford and Charles Askew and their talented and progressive
teaching staff.

Library of Congress Cataloging-in-Publication Data

Lynch, Sharon J.
Equity and Science Education Reform /
Sharon J. Lynch.
p.   cm.
Includes bibliographical references and index.
ISBN 0-8058-3248-3 (cloth : alk. Paper)
ISBN 0-8058-3249-1 (pbk. : alk. paper)
1. Science–study and teaching–United States.
2. Educational equalization–United States. I. Title.
LB1585.3.L96   2000
507.1—dc21   99-38080
                                                  CIP

Books published by Lawrence Erlbaum Associates are printed
on acid-free paper, and their bindings are chosen for strength
and durability.

Printed in the United States of America
10 9 8 7 6 5 4 3 2

For Tereska,
all of the Elenas of the United States,
and for
Rabi Smith (1984–1999).

Contents

Foreword

Walter G. Secada
University of Wisconsin–Madison

Sharon Lynch has performed a major service to science and equity educators with this volume in which she makes four major contributions to the field. First, she has assembled an incredible amount of information from a wide range of outlets and placed that information in a single place. Drawing from large national data sets, her work is also informed by data from smaller, more focused studies. As I look at the various charts, tables, and figures, I am struck by the parallels in trends that can be found across different data sets and across different equity groups.

What is more, her organizing of these data sets position educators to pose more subtle questions. For example, can the same social-class trends in achievement be found across all subgroups equally strongly for girls and boys? Or alternatively, is social class a more powerful predictor of achievement and of learning for boys of one ethnic group than it is for girls of that group? If, in fact, social class, ethnicity, and gender interact in different ways, then it suggests that some very powerful and complex social forces are at work. Future work in equity for science education will need to identify those forces, try to better understand them, and help us to overcome them.

Second, this book demonstrates how concerns for equity are complexly situated in concerns for the life chances of people. Through the Elena story, Sharon provides powerful evidence that equity is deeply rooted in an ethos of *caring* for other people. There is a real sense in which, without caring, equity concerns lose their human dimensions and become little more than intellectual exercise. The passions which are aroused on all sides of equity

ix

debates are inextricably linked to the fact that, as people, we have a responsibility to care for one another.

As implicit in the achievement data found in this book, equity is also related to our beliefs about the nature of equality and that people should be
treated equally. In informal interactions with one another, and in the can-
ons of law, we believe that all people should be given an equal chance to
better themselves, to lead productive lives, and to contribute to our society.

Ideas about equity also find their roots in our ideas about social justice.
What is inequitable is unjust; and equity is an effort to return the scales of
justice to their rightful balance. Sometimes, we rely on comparing people
and groups to one another in an effort to determine what is fair. Yet also,
ideas about justice and fairness come into play when we encounter situations that are shocking to the conscience. Even if everyone in a school district were to be treated the same, most people would agree that placing
students in a dangerous learning environment is simply unfair (to say nothing of its being ineffective).

Finally, equity is founded on our ideas of socially enlightened self-interest. That is, schools and the larger society can no longer afford to educate an
ever-shrinking sliver of their population while consigning an ever-increas-
ing proportion of students to the wreckage heap of failure. While *some* failure might be tolerable, social demands for a scientifically literate and
capable work force and voting public have rendered what is acceptable to be
a very small fraction of the total population.

Caring, equality, fairness, and self interest: equity lies at various intersec-
tions of these ideas. Yet somehow, as evidenced by Sharon Lynch's efforts in
this book, the whole is more complex than the sum of those parts.

This book's third major contribution to the field lies in how it zig-zags between the worlds of theory and practice. Theories about the nature of equity
and cultural differences inform the efforts that educators engage in. But
also, demographic data and evaluations of programs provide hard-nosed reality tests to those theories. By zig-zagging back and forth between the two
and refusing to sit comfortably in one or another camp, Sharon Lynch invites the reader to inquire about her or his own personal stance to theory
and practice. Some of us may spend more time in one or another world, but
it is at their intersection that the more interesting tensions get enacted and
that one finds room for some creative thinking and action.

Finally, this book treats its various topics with a sense of integrity. In an
effort to find parallels between gender and cultural differences, for instance,
one might be tempted to gloss over the work on the relationship of students'
worldviews to their various cultural backgrounds. This volume treats the
topic of worldviews in as positive a light as possible, while also suggesting
that there is something to be gained by thinking across categories.

I also think that readers should be careful to avoid some of the pitfalls, which this volume has managed to do admirably well. Often, we are tempted to treat demographic categories as givens. That is, once an individual is situated by her or his race, class, and the like, everything that there is to say about that person has been said. We have come a very long way from the days when this form of essentialism was accepted so unquestionably. A person's individual fate, even in the face of nearly insurmountable odds (as in the example of Elena), is not fixed. Rather, each individual is active in the construction of his or her life story. While social groups are convenient ways of tracking how society treats people who have certain physical or other characteristics, or who are born to different levels of wealth, there is much individual variation within those groups. Ethnic groups regulate their own membership and people change their patterns of self-identification across generations as well as within a single decade, or less.

A volume like this also raises more questions than it answers. That reflects the state of the art. While educators know quite a lot about how the current system operates, we are less clear on how to restructure that system to achieve equitable outcomes. I find our lack of definitive knowledge on how to restructure the system stimulating. Sharon Lynch's contributions to the field provide a foundation on which future efforts can build. I would hope that when Sharon attempts to revise this book in ten or fewer years, the field will have moved so much farther along that she will find so many answers to the questions that are found in her work and so many new ways of thinking about the issues that she has written about, that she will rethink and rewrite the entire book from the ground up. If that happens, then her efforts will have paid off handsomely, because the comprehensive survey of the field found in this book will have made those advances possible.

Preface

This is a volume for science educators, including idealists and exacting pragmatists, who are dedicated to exploring what it means to put into practice rallying cries like "science literacy for all," "equity and excellence," and "standards based reform." It acknowledges that those who work with diverse populations of K–12 students require something beyond good intentions and slogans. This volume takes a hard look at science education reform efforts and the issues it raises for learners who differ along gender, socioeconomic, ethnic, cultural, linguistic lines, or disability status. It invites the best thinking of the teachers, administrators, curriculum specialists, college and university science educators, and policymakers whose practices and decisions affect these students.

The need for a volume of this sort became evident in 1994 when the American Association for the Advancement of Sciences (AAAS) Project 2061 brought together a group of educators, including myself, to explore the equity implications of the science education reform and to write an *Equity Blueprint*. Although a wealth of information was available about some issues related to equity and science education reform (e.g., the literature on gender and science teaching and learning is well developed), in other areas, the solid research on effective practice was sparser than advocacy pieces recommending one view or intervention or another. Moreover, even the advocacy pieces tended to be written from a particular standpoint, that of special, multicultural, or ESL/bilingual education, or a specific ethnic group. There seemed to be a need to bring together these various views to better understand the scope of the equity issues facing science education reform. This volume draws on various research and practice perspectives to explore common themes, promising practices, and forces for change.

In the literature on education reform, discussions of how diverse learners are actually experiencing the reforms being enacted in schools are often relegated to a special "Equity" chapter or section of a work. At the same time, many educators have come to understand that equity issues are at the heart of the reform efforts, and are its most daunting challenges. This book is designed to be used in preservice science teacher education classes in tandem with the regular text or course readings. As a science teaching and learning topic is encountered, its equity implications should be simultaneously considered. Discussion of elements of science education reform that have positive or negative effects on diverse learners should be woven seamlessly into preservice instruction, rather than compartmentalized in a special section of a course.

The volume is also intended for professional development. Those who work first hand with the complex ethical, organizational, interpersonal, and epistemological quandaries raised by science education reform should find resources here for making informed choices. This wide audience includes not only science educators, but also teachers who work with students with disabilities or English language learners, curriculum specialists, administrators, and individuals who make and influence education policy—from concerned, activist parents to lawmakers. These readers will recognize many of the problems raised here and learn from how they are being addressed across the United States.

Drawing heavily from the education policy, equity, and science education research literature, the volume explores how the sociocultural contexts of the students' lives influence science education reform efforts. It contains stories about teachers, students, and science classrooms, some hopeful and some distressing, chosen to illustrate the complexity and contradictions of the reform. (These stories are true in the sense that all have been drawn from actual situations, but their contexts have been altered in order to preserve confidences, and pseudonyms are used.)

In the first chapter, the reader is invited to engage in a scenario that shows how difficult it can be for one student, a working class Latina child named Elena, to access an education that could lead her to science literacy. Chapter 1 also introduces an "equity schema," set in the context of standards-based reform. The equity schema provides a framework for understanding and perhaps resolving some of the equity issues in this volume. Chapters 2 and 3 provide statistics comparing those historically underserved by science education with those who have fared better. Reviewing the work of equity experts and theorists with a range of perspectives, the reader is led to understand the complexity of the causes underlying the achievement gaps, and the breadth of the equity issue. Chapter 4 explores a different sort of gap—the span between the worldviews of socioculturally diverse learners and the worldviews implicit in the science classrooms that these students occupy. Chapters 5 through 9 employ an equity perspective to examine various aspects of the reform such as curriculum, resource allocation, teaching, and assessment, highlighting problems as well as promising practices. Chapter 10 refocuses on individual students, and how the sociocultural–political forces within schools and without affect how children learn. Chapter 11 summarizes what is known about equity and science education reform, and suggests a research agenda to fill in the substantial gaps between rhetoric, beliefs, practice, and systematic inquiry.

This volume is intended to stimulate thinking and discussion about equity issues and science education reform, and to direct the reader to the research and policy base. As it developed, it became apparent that any one of the chapters could be expanded into a full-length book, which could be explored from any number of different perspectives. Consequently, I offer this work to fellow science educators less as a definitive work, than as a catalyst for thinking and to suggest changes in education policy and practices for diverse learners. For policymakers and researchers, the volume should raise questions about some of the assumptions of science education reform and the need to find better answers, if we are serious about our commitment to science literacy for all. Finally, I hope it persuades us to "listen to our better angels" when making educational decisions, large and small, on behalf of all our students.

ACKNOWLEDGMENTS

This volume arose from the work of the American Association for the Advancement of Science Project 2061 Equity Blueprint Committee. I especially appreciate the encouragement and support of the Project 2061 staff members: Jo Ellen Roseman, Andrew Ahlgren, James Rutherford, Gerry Kulm, Kathy Comfort, and Pat O'Connell-Ross. The Equity Blueprint committee included an outstanding group of educators whose individual and collective wisdom supplied the impetus for much of the thinking in this volume, and included Mary Atwater (University of Georgia), Jack Cawley (SUNY at Buffalo), Jacque Eccles (University of Michigan, Ann Arbor), Okhee Lee (University of Miami), co-chair Cora Marrett (University of Wisconsin–Madison and currently at University of Massachusetts, Amhearst), Doreen Rojas Medlin (Daugherty County Public Schools, Georgia), Walter Secada (University of Wisconsin–Madison), Greg Stefanich (University of

Northern Iowa), and Abbie Willetto. This volume owes many of its richer insights to these people, but in no way claims to represent their views, which are as diverse as the committee members themselves.

In addition, I am indebted to many friends and colleagues who reviewed drafts of chapters and gave encouragement and advice, especially Okhee Lee, Walter Secada, Senta Raizen, and other readers including Angela Benjamin, Rena Subotnik, Lynda Tredway, Juliana Taymans, Anna Chamot, and Peter Perenyi. My department chair, Jay Shotel, supplied the impetus to get this volume in publishable shape by providing the services of John Murdock, my doctoral student as well as tablemaker and figuremaker extraordinaire. I am indebted to the many preservice and inservice teachers who allowed me into their classrooms and whose insights and struggles prompted many of the discussions herein. I would also like to thank the other professional colleagues who made the time to discuss equity issues and whose contributions are acknowledged via the personal communications scattered throughout this book.

The time to do the writing and thinking for this book was the result of a sabbatical leave provided by The George Washington University and the support of a fellowship with the National Institute of Science Education (NISE)[1] at the University of Wisconsin–Madison. I would like to thank the co-directors of NISE–Andrew Porter and Senta Raizen–for this opportunity. Larry Suter of the NSF has been especially encouraging and helpful throughout this process, and I also appreciate the materials made available to me through Bernice Anderson of NSF. Any opinions, findings, or conclusions are those of the author and do not necessarily reflect the view of the people or the supporting agencies acknowledged herein.

I would like to thank my editor at LEA, Naomi Silverman, for her help and encouragement in all phases of the project. Naomi's calm good nature and fine management skills were indispensable for a first-time book author like myself. I also appreciate the timely assistance of the LEA publishing staff who were extremely patient, yet kept the work on schedule.

Last, I would like to thank my husband and daughter, Peter and Tereska Perenyi, for all of their patience and encouragement, and for putting up with the piles of paper and books on virtually every surface of our house over the last 2 years.

—Sharon J. Lynch

[1]Funded by a cooperative agreement between the National Science Foundation and the University of Wisconsin–Madison (Cooperative Agreement No. RED–9452971). At the University of Wisconsin–Madison, the NISE is housed in the Wisconsin Center for Education Research and is a collaborative effort of the College of Agricultural and Life Sciences, the School of Education, the College of Engineering, and the College of Letters and Science. The collaborative effort is also joined by the National Center for Improving Science Education in Washington, DC.

1

Science, Literacy, Social Justice, and Equity: Listening to Our Better Angels*

The world has changed in such a way that scientific literacy has become necessary for everyone, not just a privileged few; science education will have to change to make that possible. We are all responsible for the deplorable state of affairs in education, and **it will take us all to reform it.**

—*Science for All Americans*, American Association for the Advancement of Science, Project 2061 (1989, p. ix)

Imagination is more important than knowledge.

—Albert Einstein

Albert Einstein achieved his first insights into the theory of relativity by creating a thought experiment, a mind trip where he imagined himself in a spaceship hurtling through the far reaches of the universe, chasing a beam of light (Friedman & Donley, 1985). Philosopher John Rawls used a somewhat similar device in his groundbreaking book, A *Theory of Justice* (1971). He asks us to imagine the sort of rules we might create for a system of justice in a new society where our position as a member of that society was not known. Rather, all positions—in terms of wealth, power, ability, health, and so on—would be established completely at random. If this were the case, certainly the rules we would create to govern this society would be as fair and as equitable as we could make them because we would not know how we would be positioned given a random assignment of traits. Like Einstein's thought experiment, a change of perspective helps elucidate concepts of social justice.

---

*A phrase used by Abraham Lincoln in his second Inaugural Address.

This volume on equity and science education reform begins with a thought experiment. Each reader is invited to personally engage in an elaborate and extended scenario that has been designed to present a fundamental problem, perhaps *the* fundamental problem, of Grades K–12 school science in the United States today. The scenario is intentionally melodramatic and a bit fantastic. It has been chosen as a case of miseducation, undereducation, or of an education system that frequently fails to match its resources with what students need. It is about responsibility and education.

TAKING RESPONSIBILITY FOR EDUCATION: THE ELENA SCENARIO

Suppose that one day as you are making your way down a city street cluttered with construction barricades, a huge piece of scaffolding tears loose from the building above you and hurls thousands of pounds of cement and steel directly on your path. At the last instant, just as you are about to become an Occupation Safety and Health Administration (OSHA) fatality statistic, a worker flings himself at your body, driving you out of harm's way. Yet, in the process, the man himself is struck fatally by the falling debris. He lies crushed beneath the rubble and in his dying breath, he exacts a promise from you. It seems that he is the father of an 11-year-old girl, an only child. The child's mother is dead. He is her sole parent and her source of love, care, and financial support. He asks you to assure him that you will protect and watch over the child as she grows up. This man has just saved you from death. What more can you do but assure him as he dies that you will take care of the girl and that you understand the importance of the responsibility that you have been given in exchange for your life?

Now imagine this child and what she might be like. Suppose that she could be drawn at random from the entire pool of American 11-year-olds. She might be rich, poor, or middle class. She might live on an Indian reservation in South Dakota; in an apartment in central Los Angeles; in a grand house in Greenwich, Connecticut; on a farm in Ohio; or in a small city in Texas. She could be attractive or not, shy or outgoing, inquisitive and eager to learn or glued to a television set, someone easy for you to talk with and understand or someone whose life is totally alien to your experience. Envision as many possibilities as you can. For each child, think about the implications of your promise to the girl's dying father. Because you are a moral person, you know that your life has been unalterably changed. You must find a way to help this child no matter what, and you will not be relieved of this responsibility for years, perhaps until you can see her safely settled into a productive, safe, and happy adult life.

However, along with being an ethical human being, you are also reasonably intelligent and practical, and a bit selfish—in other words, typical. You understand that who this child is and how she is situated will determine what you must do to intervene on her behalf. The implications are staggering. If the man who has so courageously given his life for you is the owner of the construction company, your responsibilities will be considerably different than if he lives with his daughter in a shelter for homeless families. It is with great trepidation, therefore, that you seek out the child.

Now, from this pool of all 11-year-old girls living in the United States, imagine that the child for whom you are suddenly responsible is of lesser socioeconomic circumstances than you and is of a different ethnic group. Helping this child, as you have pledged to do, is bound to be a challenge and an adventure into an unfamiliar culture. You know that you must be open, sensitive, aware, and careful. The most fundamental worries come to mind. The worst comes to mind. Will she be healthy? Living in a drug house? Neglected? Will her circumstances be so dire that you will be obligated to become her legal guardian, taking care of a complete stranger, a child whom you may not even like?

You learn that her father, the man you owe your life, was an immigrant from Salvador and his daughter lives with her aunt, uncle, and cousins in a small apartment in an ethnic area of the city. The child's name is Elena. Preparing yourself for the worst, you visit her in her home and are vastly relieved to find a situation considerably brighter than what you feared. Elena is an attractive, friendly child. Although you cannot communicate freely because you speak no Spanish and the girl's English is rudimentary (the family speaks Spanish at home), she seems healthy, lively, and intelligent. Her aunt and uncle are often not at home because both work long hours in low-paying service jobs, but Elena's older cousins watch out for the younger children and care for them. Altogether it seems to be a warm, happy, and secure household, although one that struggles to stay above the poverty line. Yet, Elena has sufficient food, clothes, and health care, and most importantly, she is loved and cared for.

In short, you are off the hook in a major way. The most fundamental needs in this child's life are provided. Still, you have made your pledge to help her, and you must honor the commitment. You begin to get to know her. You take her for outings, buy her a present or two. She likes animals and spends hours making painstaking drawings of dogs and horses from library books that she cannot really read. She especially enjoys trips to the aquarium and zoo. At museums, she is inquisitive and eager to learn, although the explanations written in English are beyond her at this point. You wonder why. She has been in the country since she was 3 years old and has always gone to school in the city.

You ask to visit her school. The elementary school is a caring, safe place with a good principal who has found dedicated teachers for her students. Members of the community drop by to help, and the university regularly places student teachers there. However, classes are large, and there are too many children struggling to learn English, adjusting to a new country, or contending with home situations and poverty far more dire than Elena's. The children often have what seems to be odd, and sometimes serious, health problems—last year there was an outbreak of mumps, a childhood disease that you thought had been eradicated in the United States. Books, basic equipment, and supplies are scarce in this school, and the bathrooms are frequently broken, with even toilet paper in short supply. You begin to understand why a child as intelligent as Elena has not learned more.

Worse yet, in a year, Elena will leave the elementary school and enter the neighborhood middle school, located near a vacant lot where groups of loud men in various phases of intoxication spend their days, and where prostitution and drug sales are rampant. The walls of the middle school are festooned with gang signs, its playgrounds are littered with broken glass and worse. Police come and go. Half of the population of the school is poor, urban African American children, and the other half are children recently arrived from other countries, primarily Latin America, as well as some from Africa and Southeast Asia. The school is characterized by these language divisions, and the general education half of the teachers and students have little to do with the English as a second language (ESL) half, each group dispiritedly competing for scarce resources from a school district on the verge of insolvency. There is a high rate of teacher turnover, and at any time, a substantial proportion of the classrooms are occupied by uncertified teachers, most of whom are ill equipped to teach these children. The science teachers are among the least qualified and those who are certified often teach out of their area of science expertise. Science classrooms are nearly devoid of equipment. There are shelves loaded with donated computers, unused because the school has not been wired for them and will not be any time soon. There is almost no software, and most of the teachers are too unskilled or disheartened to tackle the job. Students, when they come to school at all, sit filling out worksheet after worksheet or copying from the blackboard notes that most neither understand nor care about. You worry that in this environment, Elena will join the ranks of high school dropouts and teenage mothers that stroll around the neighborhood with no jobs and few prospects.

Because you can change neither the school nor the neighborhood, you persuade Elena's aunt and uncle to consider moving their family to the suburbs where the public schools are reputably better. As immigrants from Salvador who have had little schooling themselves and who speak limited English, they are unaccustomed to the importance of parental advocacy for school children in the United States. You convince them that the educational opportunities for all of their children could improve if they relocate just a few miles to the suburbs. They know the area from the rapidly growing Spanish-speaking community there and agree to relocate. You assist them in finding an apartment in a neighborhood known for its good schools, as well as its very diverse student population. You help them move, breathing a sigh of relief that Elena is now in a place where she can get a better education.

In her new suburban middle school, Elena is placed in the third level of an ESL program. About 30% of the students in this school are in the ESL program or have recently completed it. Elena is in the highest level and will be expected to transition out next year. Now in sixth grade, Elena's English begins to improve, as does her reading. All of Elena's ESL teachers are certified and several speak Spanish. You begin to feel encouraged, as Elena begins to make rapid progress in English. Yet, other things nag at you. For instance, the science assignments that Elena brings home are really lists of vocabulary words and grammar exercises. Even worse, what science there is in them, is often incorrect or trivial, but Elena's ESL teacher readily admits that she knows little of science—too little to even make use of the laboratory and computers she has been provided. She must teach several academic subjects as well as various levels of ESL. Her affiliation is with the large ESL department, not science, social studies, or math departments, and she gets little assistance from the general education teachers who, in turn, complain about the numbers of children in their classes that do not speak English well.

Troubled that Elena is falling further behind in her various academic subjects each year, you worry that she will be ill equipped for high school— much less a career that will provide her with a decent living. The teachers assure you that things will change next year when Elena transitions into the mainstream of general education for most of her subjects.

In seventh grade, Elena takes life science with an experienced certified teacher who has volunteered to teach a small class designed to help students having difficulties. There are several students like Elena who have recently completed the ESL program, 10 general education students as well as 6 special education students with learning disabilities. The teacher has not had any special training in ESL methods or special education, but is a master teacher with a reputation for patience and innovation. In addition, the special education department has provided a full-time teaching aide for the class. At first blush, this arrangement seems generous, but the number of students with learning disabilities should have resulted in a full-time special education teacher to team teach the class, not just an aide. The school has not budgeted for such a team. Still, the science teacher tries his best to teach science for all, modifying his lesson plans and teaching techniques for this group. Especially successful is the hands-on activities and laboratory work that the students seem to enjoy and frequently understand. Yet, they struggle with the vocabulary lists he gives them to memorize, dread the frequent quizzes and tests, and do not grasp the complicated grading rubrics he provides for long-term projects. He is frustrated by the refusal of most of the students to do their homework—the result of the prevailing ethos among many students that only nerds take home books. It looks as if he must abandon his favorite long-term, creative assignments because too many of these students just do not seem to complete them, and he is under pressure from the administration to keep grades in the passing range.

When you and Elena sit down together for her homework (you have begun to tutor her twice each week), you see another problem: Elena frequently does not understand her homework assignments. Her aunt and uncle cannot help her and her older cousin is seldom home as he works long hours and is with his friends the rest of the time. Elena willingly does homework consisting of vocabulary words or worksheets requiring her to do word searches, simple matching, or filling in the blanks. Yet, the major concepts often go over her head because they are so embedded in trivia. She is seldom asked to think or reason on her own or to apply anything covered in the science classroom to her world. Elena, once so eager to learn about animals and so fascinated with museums, does not even seem to like life science.

Perhaps the local high school will be better? Its huge size (more than 2,500 students) allows the school officials to tout the school's ability to offer specialized classes for all kinds of students. After all, does it not house the school district's science and mathematics magnet program for academically talented students? Surely some of this excellence will trickle down to Elena's science classes, even though you now harbor no illusions about Elena's chances of joining the ranks of the academically talented, no matter how intelligent she seems to be.

A visit to the high school is anything but heartening. True, the magnet-school classes seem spectacular—great teaching, fantastic science labs, computers, and a special schedule with long time blocks for serious laboratory work. The students in these classes constantly win awards and scholarships for their work in science, mathematics, and technology. However, Elena is unlikely to experience any of this; as a matter of fact, a total stranger could walk into this building and determine with 100% accuracy the level of science class—magnet, honors, college preparatory, general track, or basic skills—by simply counting the number of African American and immigrant students in it. The level of the course is inversely proportional to the number of children of color, with the magnet program consisting mostly of White males and Asian American students of both sexes. Moreover, the expertise and energy level of the teachers often seems to reflect the track of the students that they are teaching— the general education science classes seem innervated and characterized by low expectations. You begin to understand the stigma that interest in science and mathematics carries for students of color, who seldom take any of the upper level classes—a fact that cannot be lost on anyone who enters the school.

You are worried. As a moral person, you cannot relax until you know that Elena has grown up, educated, with a decent job and income, and able to form healthy, close relationships with others. Fortunately, her situation in her family has provided an excellent prognosis for the latter, but you can see her education failing her in the other areas, areas in which you should be able to provide some help. Although Elena is intelligent and motivated, her schooling thus far has not seemed to level the playing field and her potential is not matched by the quality of her education.

There is one last chance for her in the public schools. The school system has a choice option that makes it easy for students of color to transfer to high schools that are predominantly White, which generally means affluent. There is a high school, reputed to have the best all-around program in the system, that may be a good match for Elena, and she is eligible because she is Salvadoran. You persuade Elena to accompany you for a visit to the school. After a long drive, you know you have arrived by the number of expensive and fashionable vehicles parked in the student lot. The school has a country club ambience, and the students attending the classes seem as eager to learn as they are attractively turned out. Virtually 100% of the students here go to college, and low-track classes have all but been eliminated because, the principal explains, more than 60% of the students have been identified as gifted and talented. The school has a stable teaching staff that prides itself on innovation, and these upper middle class students provide an excellent laboratory where teachers can try new techniques and methods. The latest effort is a thematic curriculum for ninth graders in which all of the subject disciplines are geared to explore various aspects of a single theme in an integrated fashion. The theme for the current semester is the U.S. economy and balancing the federal budget. It is high level teaching and learning, tied to real life, including a community service component that is a clothing drive for poor children who go to school in another area of the school district. The poor children's school happens to be the elementary school attended by Elena's little cousins, a fact not lost on Elena, who has looked uncomfortable from the moment she set foot inside this building.

You can see by the expression on Elena's face how spectacularly awful this latest idea of yours has been. It is true that Elena could ride the bus for 2 hours every day to attend this school, characterized by its highly motivated and well-to-do student population and she would not be the only Spanish-speaking student—there are the families of the Bolivian entrepreneur, the doctor from Cuba, the university professor from Honduras. There are other students of color, but initially, she would know no one there, be miles away from her home, and certainly one of the poorest (socioeconomically) students in the school. To attend this school, she would essentially have to give up her identity, or at least cordon it off from the reality of this affluent high school.

Discouraged, both of you make the long drive home. What to do? You have not given up, and neither has she. What would you do?

GENERALIZING ELENA

The school situations dramatized in the Elena scenario are not uncommon and may constitute the rule rather than the exception. Moreover, the case of Elena is not a limited example of a specific situation—how our educational system frequently fails students who are English language learners. Unfortunately, in addition to Hispanic children, there is an entire array of 11-year-olds in the United States—Black Americans, Native Americans/Alaskan Natives, as well as poor children and students with disabilities of any ethnicity, some rural students and many girls—who find the deck similarly stacked against them, especially in the areas of science, mathematics, and technology education.

It is no secret that in the United States, there is a prevalent stereotype of science as work done by middle-class White males, by Asian Americans, or by science nerds of any ethnicity or gender. When asked to draw a picture of a scientist, children most often respond with an elderly, bespectacled man in a white coat (National Science Foundation, 1994)— a bloodless, lonely type who beavers away in a sterile laboratory on arcane problems that only an elite portion of the general public might understand or care about. This unfortunate image is exactly the opposite of real science—a lively, human, and dynamic enterprise done by people of both sexes and all colors in research laboratories and schools, hospitals and garages, engineering firms and kitchens, forests and farms.

The primary purpose of this volume is to explore how school science education must change so that science is understandable, accessible, and perhaps even enjoyable to all students in Grades K–12. Since the late 1980s, the national reform efforts in science education (Goals 2000, American Association for the Advancement of Science Project 2061, National Research Council's National Science Education Standards, and National Science Teachers Association Scope, Sequence & Coordination) all have been in fundamental agreement about this goal. Moreover, both resolve and substantial incentive funding at the national (National Science Foundation, NSF, and the Department of Education), state, and local levels have resulted in attempts across the United States to systematically and systemically change how science is taught and learned in our schools. However, it must be admitted that progress has been slow and fitful (Lynch, 1997), with few limited examples of the sort of classroom environments that invite all students to engage in scientific habits of mind and activities envisioned by the reformers. Why is this goal of science literacy for all so difficult to achieve?

Science education comes with a special set of baggage that other subject areas, such as English, history, and even mathematics, do not carry because all students have been expected to achieve a degree of literacy in these subjects. In contrast, science has been viewed as the province of a privileged few. For example, some school systems have initiated science and mathematics magnet schools at the elementary level as a device to persuade middle-class White parents to keep their children in the public school system (Weldon, 1995). Others locate special science and mathematics programs for the gifted and talented primarily attended by White and Asian American children in disadvantaged schools to provide the appearance of integration, perhaps giving the children of color in that school an unintentional but clear message that science is not for them.

In U.S. high schools, only the most motivated and able 30% or 40% of students take physics or advanced science courses (NSF, 1994). Colleges and universities have used introductory science courses to separate the scientifically talented from the masses, an initiation rite designed to weed out all but the most persistent and dedicated—referred to as the *science pipeline*. These practices and others have led to a general impression that science is not for all, but only for the few who succeed in spite of the system, rather than because of it.

What if science literacy were considered as important and crucial as literacy in reading and writing? What if our schools produced adults who could participate intelligently and vigorously as citizens in complex decisions that require a sound and fundamental understanding of science? Wouldn't a scientifically literate workforce help the U.S. economy grow and prosper as the business community and policymakers predict? Wouldn't the complexion of science literally and metaphorically change if all students graduated from high school able to solve problems in their communities using scientific habits of mind, capable of taking good jobs requiring technical expertise without needing extensive further training, or pursuing formal education in the sciences?

This volume explores the implications of science education reform for various groups of students who presently:

- Are underrepresented in science classes and science related careers.
- Do not achieve highly in science.
- Have difficulty getting access to appropriate learning environments for science.
- May not match current stereotypes of a science sort of student.

DEFINING EQUITY

It is probably true that everyone has his or her own unique definition of *equity*, depending on personal experiences, gender, ethnicity, or socioeconomic background. It is a term that not only means different things to different people, but also a single individual may change its connotation in a single conversation. Apple (1995), referring to this phenomenon called *equity* a "sliding signifier" and Secada (1994a) described it as a "moving target." Increasingly, it seems that the equity mantle may be wrapped around any number of conflicting positions with a flourish of righteousness—affirmative action or its abolition, heterogeneous grouping or homogeneous grouping (tracking), school bussing or keeping children in their neighborhood schools. In a society troubled by pervasive and growing inequalities among its increasingly diverse groups, no education reform effort can succeed unless it directly addresses equity issues (Atwater, 1995; Marrett & Ziege, 1995).

Equity is defined, in general terms, as "the quality of being fair or impartial;" in legal terms, it means "the application of the dictates of conscience or the principles of natural justice to the settlement of controversies" that serves to supplement and remedy the limitations of the common law (*Webster's Encyclopedic Unabridged Dictionary of the English Language*, 1989). Thus, equity has to do with the law and its codified ordinances, yet goes beyond them. However, equity must also include the unwritten rules, unwritten justices, that operate in social arrangements to assure that the application of a law does not violate our notion of justice (Secada, 1994b). Rawls (1971) pointed out that justice is the first virtue of social institutions, as truth is to systems of thought. To Rawls, a *just institution* is one that distributes social goods such as rights, liberties, access to power, and opportunity equally among its participants.

For science education, then, *equity* may be defined as justice and something more—fairness. It seems possible for a situation to be legal but unfair and probable that views of fairness will vary with the individual perceiving the situation. Thus, it is useful to return to Rawls' original device—imagining what one might perceive as fair if one were unsure of what one's position in society might be.

Secada (1994c) identified six different conceptions of equity commonly used by educators and allowed that there may be even more. Kahle (1996) took these six conceptions and arranged them in a historical continuum. The second definition has been divided into two parts for this volume, for reasons that will become apparent:

1. *Equity* involves maximum return on the minimum investment—resources go to those most likely to succeed (post-Sputnik, c. 1957).

2a. *Equity* is the same treatment for everyone, equality of inputs (civil rights era, c. 1960s), so that,

2b. All students have an equal opportunity to meet and master standards, *equality of outcomes.*

3. *Equity* is concern for the whole child as an individual with unique educational, socioemotional and physical needs (women's movement, c. 1970s).

4. *Equity* as triage, that is, investing in students whose success or failure depends on their school experience (women's movement, c. 1970s).

5. *Equity* that compensates for social injustice for specific groups who have not received fair treatment (postmodern world and affirmative action, c. 1980s).

6. *Equity* as a safety net for individual differences, including alternative programs or other resources, so that if one program is ineffective for an individual student, other options are available (1990s).

Kahle (1996) favored the last definition because she saw it as being supported by the best current research and teaching practices. However, here we propose an operational definition of equity in the context of science education reform, one that lends itself to a systematic examination of the conditions of learning in education reform and that provides a basis for the analysis of factors that seem to contribute to equity issues. This definition of equity roughly corresponds respectively to Concepts 2a, 2b, and 6 in an equity schema, Fig. 1.1.

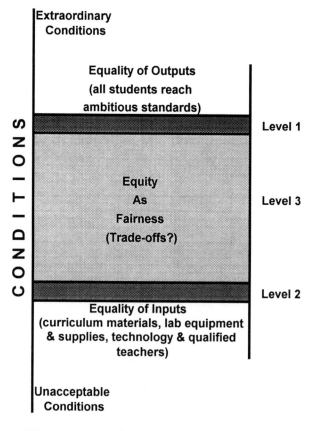

FIG. 1.1.   Equity schema for science education reform.

1. *Equality* of outputs—achievement of high standards such as the National Science Education Standards or the Project 2061 Benchmarks by all students (Level 1).
2. *Equality* of inputs, or the traditional level-playing-field connotation of equity (Level 2).
3. *Equity* as fairness and tradeoffs—the middle ground for thoughtful negotiation and decision making (Level 3).

Equality of Outputs

Equality of outputs (corresponding to Level 1 on the equity schema, Fig. 1.1, and Concept 2b) has to do with results, not inputs. It involves closing the science achievement gaps between various groups. (The groupings and nature of gaps are discussed in chaps. 2 and 3.) This does not mean that a realistic goal is for each and every student to achieve at exactly the same level and in the same manner. Rather, *equality* of outputs has been characterized as a distribution curve of student outcomes in science that roughly looks the same across groups—for example, as many high achievers among groups of Blacks as Whites, females as males, and so on (Marrett & Zeige, 1995).

However, in the world of science literacy for all, the traditional bell-shaped curve is replaced by something different. For science education reform, the primary equity goal is for all students to achieve a certain minimum threshold of science literacy, outcomes such as those in the National Science Education Standards (National Research Council, 1995) and Benchmarks (American Association for the Advancement of Science, 1992). These outcomes are, nonetheless, more ambitious, rigorous and deep than what is currently the norm in U.S. schools.

Many students are expected to go beyond these thresholds. The equity goal is for these more advanced students not to be concentrated in certain groups, but rather to be distributed evenly among ethnic and socioeconomic groups and by gender. Equality of outputs are reflected by achievement measures on assessments (yet to be developed) for these outputs. There is an implicit, long-term, but clearly definable goal that involves both closing achievement gaps while raising standards for all. This ultimately will result in equal representation of various groups in science-related careers at all levels.

So, the first test of educational equity in science education reform is to view a particular group of students (at the level of the state, the school district, and the school or individual classroom) and ask if they have achieved the outcomes set forth in the standards documents or a specific interpretation of the standards set by the individual state. This is Level 1 of the equity schema. Allowing for the unavoidable and annoying fact that at this time, there are no national assessments precisely aligned with the standards documents, if with indirect evidence from other assessments, the answer appears to be *yes*, our definition of equity has been satisfied. If, on the other hand, the answer is *no*, all students have not reached the ambitious thresholds (and state-level science assessments aligned with standards such as those developed in Maryland, Kentucky, and Michigan provide good evidence that this is true), then we must look for reasons for this. It seems logical to examine the conditions of learning—equality of inputs.

Equality of Inputs

It is probably true that the definition of equity that finds the most favor with the general public and has enjoyed the longest history of consensus is Concept 2a, equality of inputs, equal opportunity to learn, equal access (Marrett & Zeige, 1995). *Equality of educational opportunity* usually refers to efforts to ensure that diverse groups of learners, in aggregate, are treated equally (Secada, 1994a, 1995)—that all have a level playing field. This has most often meant concern for equal resources. In the context of science education, this may be manifested in equally good classroom facilities, materials, technology, curriculum, and teachers. It may mean equal access, an equal opportunity to take upper level classes, or equally encouraging treatment of students by teachers in classes.

The examination of Level 2, equality of inputs, across large educational agencies such as states and school districts, but also within schools, will be a major concern of this volume (chaps. 6 and 7 particularly deal with these issues). If it can be clearly established that within an educational unit, some students do not experience conditions of learning that are remotely equivalent to those of others and do not allow achievement of the outcomes set forth by the unit, then clearly the situation must be remedied by creating a decent minimum floor of resources across the system. Currently in the United States, no less than 37 states are in the midst of lawsuits challenging the fairness of unequal distribution of resources (Laguarda, Breckenridge, & Hightower, 1994).

However, within some school districts, particularly the more affluent ones, one may be able to find a fair distribution of resources from school to school, but still group and individual differences in science achievement persist, such that some students fall well below targeted outcomes. For example, what if some groups of students (some ethnic groups, students with disabilities, students who are learning to speak English) are not doing well in science, despite what appears to be equal opportunity to learn? If it is found that the school has really provided such students with an equal opportunity to learn (and what constitutes equal opportunity in a science classroom setting is discussed in detail in chaps. 6 and 7), then we turn to Level 3, equity as fairness and trade-offs.

Equity as Fairness: Making Trade-Offs

When school systems are in the position to provide basic good conditions in science education for all, or have gone well beyond the minimum, we can turn attention to conditions for groups of learners within the school. Consider, for example, Elena's seventh-grade, mainstream science class. She has a certified science teacher and an aide, but still some students are having difficulty. According to the state-level assessment, all of the students are not achieving the standards (equality of outputs). Although Elena's class was constructed to have more resources than most—a skilled teacher and an aide, access to good facilities and standard curriculum materials, and a smaller class size (equality of inputs and then some)— many students are having difficulties, especially those who are learning English and students with disabilities. Perhaps even more resources are needed—more instructional assistance or extra time allotted for tutoring, specialized professional development for the teacher, or new curriculum materials. Perhaps extant resources could be allocated differently or new more effective approaches to instruction developed. Yet, in a world of finite school financing and resources, it is clear that decision makers will have to eventually weigh trade-offs, balancing the needs of one group against another. Consequently, the teachers and administrators at the school must be asked to examine the situation in terms of fairness. Changes must be considered that will provide these students with a better opportunity to meet the science outcomes set by the state. This may include making a number of trade-offs in staffing patterns, class size, and expenditure of funds. It must be done within the school, weighing the best way to reach these students and the cost to other students. This is Level 3 of the equity schema, equity as fairness.

This progressive examination of equity issues based on science education reform principles is designed to take specific equity questions out of the morass of varying conceptions of equity and hand-wringing frustration and to propel them toward solution. Of course, the schema inevitably arrives at *fairness*, Level 3, a concept about which it is hard to find consensus. Yet, the steps prior to this may help to clarify issues and perhaps reduce some confusion.

Real equality of opportunity in school would give each Black American, White, Hispanic, Asian, or Native American student, male or female, from any economic stratum a fair chance at great success in science. *Science for all* means an education that would allow all these students to understand and use basic scientific habits of mind in their lives, jobs, and performance as citizens. Is this definition of equity in science education practically obtainable in the United States? Does equity in science education have a price tag that, literally and figuratively, Americans are willing to pay? Is the cost of ignoring equity issues likely to be even higher?

There are at least two rationales for making special efforts to include underrepresented groups in science education reform. One rationale for advancing equity is enlightened self-interest (Secada, 1991–1992). The assumption is that an initiative that aims for all K–12 students to achieve science literacy will have a direct payoff for the nation's economy in the form of a more technologically sophisticated workforce and greater prosperity for all (Secada, 1989). A second rationale is that equity in science learning reflects broader responsibility, embodied by the social justice model: the obligation to prepare all students to participate in a postindustrial society with an equal chance at attaining the accompanying social goods—rights, liberties, and access to power.

Just as equity in science education requires attending to economic issues and social justice, it also demands attending to what Delpit (1988) called an explicit education in the culture of power. *Science knowledge* includes an understanding of a system of shared meaning that requires access to the social knowledge (e.g., where to go to school and with whom to study, how to write and speak convincingly to other scientists, and so on) that facilitates access to scientific knowledge. This is crucial to an equity agenda because every system of knowledge has a cultural or social component, and inclusion or exclusion for an individual or a group may depend on it (Atwater, 1995; Bourdieu, 1977).

> Knowledge is central to power. Knowledge helps us envision the contours of our existence, what is desirable and what is possible, and what actions might bring about the possibilities. Knowledge helps us examine relationships between what is ethical and what is desirable; it widens our experiences; it provides analytic tools for thinking through questions, situations, and problems. Knowledge that empowers centers around the interests and aims of the prospective knower. Apart from the knower, knowledge has no intrinsic power. (Sleeter & Grant, 1991, p. 50)

If knowledge is so influential, then persons who understand science and who contribute to the science canon are truly powerful people (Atwater, 1995). Yet, knowledge of science is not randomly distributed across groups in American society.

What has this talk of power got to do with schooling and how a fourth grader, for instance, understands batteries and bulbs or how insects metamorphose? A pair of headlines on the front page of the *Washington Post* provides some explicit instruction. The first, "In Fairfax High Tech Equals Power" (Lipton, 1995), discussed how political power has shifted over the last 10 years from the hands of land developers to the hands of those in the software industries, making up 25% of the economy in Fairfax County, Virginia, the largest municipality in the Washington, DC metropolitan area. The 15 top power brokers listed in the article (mostly company CEOs) are White men (ascertained by phone calls to each firm, March 1996). Their local political agenda focuses on schools, roads, and the tax structure. In Fairfax County Public Schools, high-school students can, for example, learn astronomy by linking with the Berkeley Hall of Science, which transmits images of far-off galaxies via satellite and internet for the students to explore (Lynch & Thomas, 1995). Students' fingers fly over keyboards in their school's computer lab, processing and analyzing the data from distant stars, while conferring occasionally with astronomers on both coasts, as well as with students across the United States.

In contrast, the *Washington Post* provided a second article on the same page on that same day, "Daily Struggles, Distant Dreams" (Greene, 1995). It is about another group of White businessmen who have contributed to the "I Have a Dream" project involving a selected group of junior high school-age, poor, children (in this case, mostly African Americans) in Washington, DC who are guaranteed a paid college education if they graduate from high school. Despite this assurance, only half of the 70 program students have received their high school diplomas, the rest succumbing to violence, pregnancies, drug use, and the panoply of social ills afflicting our urban centers today. The urban school system is anything but an equalizer. In contrast to the computer-literate children in Fairfax County, DC students often learn science via an endless stream of worksheets in poorly equipped classrooms taught by overstressed, and sometimes underprepared teachers. Equity in science reform demands that this situation change.

It is fair to say that the distance in power between the world of high-tech CEOs and their children in Fairfax County, Virginia and the high school students in Washington, DC is vast, although the geographic distance is only the width of the Potomac River. The equity–power ramifications are staggering.

Which children have had an education in the culture of power, be it implicit or explicit? Which children have been excluded from the interlocking discussion of science, technology, economics, and politics, even before they have completed high school, despite some of the best intentions and an infusion of money to help them to succeed? Can science education reform provide direction to schools and communities that will allow children, all children, experiences that will give equitable access to the social knowledge of science education which, in turn, will bring them into the culture of power?

THE PUBLIC RESPONSE TO EQUITY
AND SCIENCE EDUCATION REFORM

The goals of science education reform are consistent with both the enlightened self-interest model and the justice model of equity. Science reform appeals to a broad array of interest groups and individuals. The business community, for example, has long been a strong supporter of science education reform, in order to produce a more scientifically, mathematically, and technologically competent workforce than currently exists. This rationale for equity in science is particularly convincing and appealing to many people, especially those associated with business, development, and some political areas, as well as those who want the simple but laudable assurance that our young people leave school sufficiently well-prepared to get decent jobs. However, a scientifically semiliterate public may be more interested in short-term political treats (i.e., tax cuts) and nostrums (i.e., school uniforms), rather than serious science education reform, although recently, education has occupied a loftier place in public attention span than usual. Policymakers and science educators should make clear the direct connections between science literacy for all and national–international economic health to parents, civic organizations, and business people. We need more examples of media (e.g., newspaper articles and films) that show children, all kinds of children, using scientific habits or mind, designing investigations on relevant issues, and using the tools of modern technology in K–12 classrooms. Such materials could be effective communicators of science education reform goals and could assist schools in obtaining the funds to achieve them. In short, we need to call in what Abraham Lincoln referred to as the better angels of our nature.

Yet, for those who have had less access to the culture of power in the United States and have less trust in the system, or those who are primarily concerned with the sociology and ethics of education, a different approach may be more convincing. Science education reform is appealing because it is also congruent with the social justice model. The conception of equity in science education is social justice that results in the distribution of education resources in a way that will empower all to participate in, contribute to, and reap the rewards of U.S. society. This, in turn, requires the acknowledgment of the relation among science knowledge, social activism, and political power. Talk of power tends to put many people off and makes others angry or defensive. So, we return to Elena who is relatively powerless and who must be empowered in a meaningful way through education (knowledgeable, politically involved, and economically self-sufficient) if the obligation to her is to be fulfilled.

In the Elena scenario, a fantastic situation was created—the death of Elena's father in return for your life and oath of support—in order to dramatize the bind that a moral person would feel if the responsibility for a child suddenly fell on his or her shoulders. The ineffectiveness of the school system, the number of children falling through the cracks, the failure of a discipline like science education to educate in a meaningful way—troubling before—would seem much more immediate and dire when the burden of a child's welfare falls directly on oneself. This is certainly the way that many parents feel when they see schools failing to prepare their children for life, while other children cruise along successfully. Yet, doesn't social justice, moral obligation, and the U.S. commitment to democracy and equality of opportunity demand that the Elenas of our schools are as much our responsibility as are our own children, even if we have no children?

ELENA AND EQUITY:
A SUMMARY AND A BEGINNING

What of Elena? Has her schooling in its various permutations, urban and suburban, been equitable? Were these school situations just and fair? Although one person's notion of fairness may differ radically from another's (Secada, 1994b), we can agree, however that in Elena's case, the urban and suburban schools were hardly equal in resources. Even in the suburban middle school, Elena's placement in ESL classes provided her with compensatory education in English, but was accompanied by low level and unequal instruction in science. Has she had equitable access to the culture of power? When Elena was urged to consider attending a school where all students have access to high status knowledge, she rejected the opportunity because the immediate social cost was too high for her. How many of us would respond differently, especially at age 14? Does equity demand that similar, high-level opportunities to learn science be provided in an environment that is comfortable, familiar, and friendly—one reaches her in her world rather than an unfamiliar and alien one?

As this volume proceeds, we return to the equity schema to guide our discussions. Science education reform is a vast and complex enterprise. Although we may be able to identify some problems, solutions are more elusive because they require attention to students as learners in their schools, homes, and communities. Students are becoming more diverse, the education system is hard to budge, and the teaching staff is getting older. In chapters 2 and 3, we get a brief overview of some of the indicators of equity in science education for various groups of diverse learners, considering gender, ethnicity, socioeconomic status (SES), as well as students who are learning English, have disabilities, or who live in urban or rural areas. In chapters 4 through 10, we more carefully examine schools, science education, and reform mandates and try to understand what must be done in order make science literacy for all a reality. We must also listen hard for those better angels of our nature to guide us through the perilous world of equity and science education reform.

2

Demographics and Trends
in Science Education

*He offered me more deer jerky, but I was too thirsty from the salty
meat, so I offered him a Pepsi instead. It's a little known fact that
Indians can be broken into two distinct groups: Pepsi tribes and Coke
tribes.*

—Sherman Alexie (1999, p. 101)

There is likely to be little disagreement among Americans about general
equity goals. Americans are committed to the principles of fairness, im-
partiality, and justice that lie at the heart of democracy. Yet, beyond
general areas of agreement are fundamental differences, many with broad
implications for education planning and practice, especially for science
education that has traditionally been looked on as the province of the
educated and intellectual elite. A commitment to equity exists alongside
clear evidence that some groups of Americans are more likely to participate
and be successful in science than others (Marrett & Ziege, 1995). Although
many of these differences are common knowledge, it is useful to examine
current statistics comparing especially those groups that have been bypassed by science education in the past. In some areas, substantial gains
have been made, pointing a way for success for groups that have seen less
progress. This discussion of the demographics of science education should
set the stage for the equity agenda that emerges from this volume.

There has been a concerted effort by the NSF and the U.S. Department of Education (USDOE) to chart the progress of underrepresented
groups in science. One excellent resource for the most up-to-date statis-

tics is *Women, Minorities, and Persons With Disabilities in Science and Engineering*, published biennially by the NSF. The 1994 edition is the source of many of the figures and tables in chapters 2 and 3 of this volume. Another excellent NSF resource is *Indicators for Science and Mathematics Education*.[1] These documents include compilations of information from large databases and national and international studies, and as such, may provide the most comprehensive view of the state of U.S. science education available.

Charting the science achievement of U.S. school children is no easy task, even for federal agencies, as the sources of decision-making power in the realm of K–12 science are concentrated primarily at the state level, secondarily at local school districts, and lastly at the federal level. In order to jump-start science education reform, federal agencies rely on their leadership skills, buoyed by federal incentive money (NSF's Systemic Initiatives and Eisenhower Funds from USDOE) for which states can apply. However, unlike the vast majority of industrialized countries, we have neither a national science curriculum nor mandated national assessments to guide the way. Attempts to achieve some uniformity and consensus on what children should know and be able to do, such as Goals 2000, National Council for Teachers of Mathematics (NCTM) Mathematics Standards, the National Research Council (NRC) National Science Education Standards, or Project 2061's Benchmarks for science, are subject to state-level approval for participation and implementation. These decisions are affected by who happens to be in control of the state political system at any particular time. There is evidence, however, that most of the states are changing their science curricula and assessments to correspond with the national science reform principles.

The National Assessment for Education Progress (NAEP), funded by Congress and administered by the Educational Testing Service (ETS), is the best assessment system available for a national overview of the state of K–12 science. However, it is only given every 4 years and some states choose not to participate—for instance, eight states and the District of Columbia opted out of the 1992 NAEP mathematics assessment (NSF, 1996a). Still, the NAEP is the most widely used indicator and is generally respected as it provides a longitudinal view of achievement in that it is given to children at ages 9, 13, and 17 (see Fig. 2.1). Moreover, with a scale ranging from 0 to 500, it measures science mastery at several levels—*basic* (200), *middle* (250 and 300) and *advanced* (350); see Fig.

---

[1]NSF publications such as these two are updated regularly. The most recent versions can be found on the NSF website. For a more geographically specific view, many states publish achievement results on their websites.

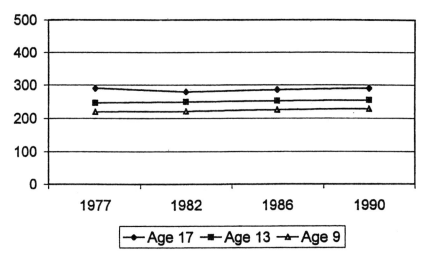

FIG. 2.1.   Average science score on a scale of 0 to 500 for students 9, 13, and 17 years old, 1977 to 1990. This exhibit repeats information presented in the 1993 Goals Report. From *Data Volume for the National Education Goals Report, Volume 1*, by National Education Goals Panel, 1994.

2.2. As the levels increase, the test questions require more reasoning and interpretive skills, as opposed to recall of science facts. Unlike the SAT and ACT, NAEPs are taken by the broad spectrum of students in a given state, not just the college-bound.

Achievement test scores are not the only indicators of equity in science education. Researchers can also make comparisons of the progress of various groups of students based on their rates of participation in science courses, the grades they are awarded, and their attitudes toward science. In order to fill in the picture of who is and is not involved in science, it is also crucial to examine the patterns of participation of various groups of students in college, graduate school, or in their chosen careers. Although the focus of science reform and the new standards has been on science literacy for all in the K–12 system, the "proof of the pudding" may be what children choose to do with science after they graduate from high school, where much of their participation is voluntary rather than mandated.

Some of the news is good. Student achievement in science in the United States, as measured by NAEP trends, has increased for students of every ethnicity and at every age since the 1970s (NSF, 1996a). Yet, gaps still exist in achievement and in opportunity to learn. Moreover, there are huge differences in the living conditions of U.S. children and their chance of living in nurturing, healthy, safe environments that can support learning. The discussion that follows provides examples of progress, but also points out problems specific to one group or another (e.g.,

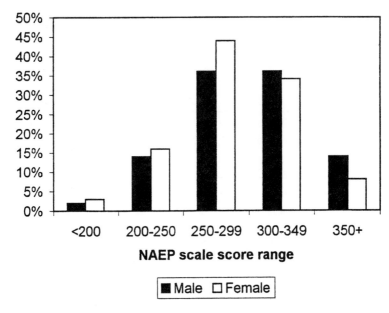

FIG. 2.2. Percentage of 12th grade students at each scale score range in science, by sex: 1990. *Note.* 200–249: Understands simple scientific principles; 250–299: Applies general scientific information; 300–349: Analyzes scientific procedures and data; 350+: Integrates specialized scientific information. From *Women, Minorities, and Persons With Disabilities in Science and Engineering* by NSF, 1994.

stereotyping, lack of resources, etc.). Most such instantiations, however, can be applied to more general issues that need to be addressed in the area of equity and science education reform.

The NSF report, *Women, Minorities, and Persons With Disabilities in Science and Engineering* (1994), makes an important point about reporting achievement data and making comparisons among groups. Although information about outcomes is a useful starting point for examining the role that K–12 education plays in the underrepresentation of various groups in science, mathematics, and engineering, analysis of important inputs—family resources, school characteristics, and opportunity to learn—is critical in order to understand the situation and to change it. That is a purpose of this volume.

GENDER

Women constitute about 50% of the population of the United States, about 46% of the labor force, and obtain about 55% of the bachelors' and masters' degrees as well as 43% of doctoral degrees. Tremendous progress has been made in women's participation rates in science and related fields. However, statistics gathered in the early 1990s indicate that females still make up only 22% of those in science and engineering occupations (NSF, 1994). Their distribution within science fields varies widely, comprising just 9% of engineers, but 50% of social scientists (see Table 2.1).

The differences between males and females in K–12 science and mathematics achievement, as measured by NAEP scores, have narrowed substantially from 1977 to 1992 and, in some instances, have disappeared altogether. Yet, a gap in the NAEP science scores of 12th-grade males and females persists and is especially evident at the highest level of science proficiency—350+ (see Fig. 2.2). One explanation for this gap is differential facility in the physical sciences of males and females, which

TABLE 2.1
Selected Characteristics by Sex

	Percentage Distribution		
Characteristic	Total	Male	Female
Total population, 1990 census	100.0	48.7	51.2
Persons 5–18 years old, October 1992	100.0	51.2	48.8
Persons 5–18 years old enrolled in school October 1992	100.0	51.4	48.6
Undergraduate enrollment, fall 1991	100.0	44.5	55.5
Bachelors' degrees, 1991	100.0	45.5	54.5
Science	100.0	49.7	50.3
Engineering	100.0	84.0	16.0
Other	100.0	40.0	60.0
Graduate enrollment, fall 1992[a]	100.0	46.4	53.6
Science	100.0	57.5	42.5
Engineering	100.0	85.5	14.5
Other	100.0	39.9	60.1
Masters' degrees, 1991	100.0	43.8	56.2
Science	100.0	45.2	54.8
Engineering	100.0	84.8	15.2
Other	100.0	40.3	59.7
Doctoral Degrees, 1992	100.0	56.5	43.4
Science	100.0	61.0	39.0
Engineering	100.0	87.0	12.9
Other	100.0	45.4	54.6
Civilian labor force, 1990	100.0	54.2	45.7
Scientists	100.0	63.1	36.9
Natural scientists	100.0	73.5	26.4
Math & computer scientists	100.0	64.6	35.4
Social Scientists	100.0	49.1	50.9
Engineers	100.0	90.9	9.1

Note.   Because of rounding, percentages may not add to 100. From *Women, Minorities, and Persons With Disabilities in Science and Engineering,* by NSF, 1994. [a]includes nonresident aliens.

in turn, may be related to differences in course-taking patterns (NSF, 1994). Perhaps due to increased high school graduation requirements in science, more girls than boys currently take high school biology and chemistry, but not physics (NSF, 1998). Yet, a 1994 NSF report noted that the most striking differences between boys and girls is not opportunity to learn science, but rather their attitudes toward it. Females like science less, see it as less important to their future, and are less confident about their abilities in it even when their achievements in it are the same as that of males (see Table 2.2). Only 2.8% of female high school students are likely to aspire to careers in science, math, and engineering, compared to 10% of their male peers. Explanations for this persistent pattern are discussed in depth in chapter 10.

Gender differences in science participation become more marked during the college years (Eccles, 1995). Although the percentage of bachelors' degrees awarded to women in the fields of engineering and physics has increased over the last 10 years, women are still underrepresented in these fields. For example, women earned only 16% of the bachelors' degrees in engineering, 32% of the degrees in the physical sciences, and

TABLE 2.2

Percentage of Public High School Seniors Citing Selected
Reasons for Not Taking a Mathematics or Science Course
in Their Senior Year, by Subject and Sex: 1989–1990

Subject and sex	Took all	Will not need	Did not like	Not do well	Advised not to	Wanted other	Avoid work	Sample size
Mathematics:								
Total	5	28	34	31	31	37	27	687
Male	7	31	27	28	26	33	27	297
Female	3	25	40	33	34	40	27	390
Science:								
Total	8	39	29	24	30	37	24	918
Male	9	42	22	24	26	31	21	412
Female	7	38	35	24	32	41	26	506

Note. The students were asked the following question:
"If you are not taking any science classes this semester, which of the following best indicate your reasons for this decision? (Mark all that apply.)
  —I have taken the highest level science course available here.
  —I will not need advanced science for what I plan to do in the future.
  —I do not like science.
  —I did not think that I would do well in more advanced science classes.
  —I was advised that I did not need to take more science.
  —There were other courses that I wanted to take.
  —I did not want to work that hard during my senior year."
From *Women, minorities, and persons with disabilities in science and engineering*, by NSF, 1994.

30% of the degrees in computer science in 1991. In contrast, 73% of the bachelors' degrees in psychology, 51% of the degrees in biological sciences, and 47% of the bachelors' degrees in mathematics went to women (NSF, 1994).

Some have argued that the underrepresentation of females in the sciences is a consequence of gender differences in aptitude. Proponents of this argument point to the consistent gender differences in performance on standardized tests in mathematics and the sciences, with the SAT mathematics scores of females lagging behind those of males by about 50 points. Yet, University of Michigan sociologist Eccles (1995) pointed out that although it is the case that females often do not perform as well as males on rigidly timed standardized tests of mathematics, it is unlikely that differences in test scores account fully for the gender differences in participation rates in science courses and careers. Even among populations of gifted and talented, where all of the females have the requisite abilities to do science and mathematics at high levels of achievement and where females receive as high or higher grades than males, gifted women still back away from science at rates that are similar to those of typical populations. It is likely that other factors such as social forces and personal beliefs (discussed throughout this volume) play a significant role in perpetuating these gender differences in the educational and vocational patterns in science.

Before concluding the topic of gender differences in science education, it should be noted that although the patterns discussed are accurate for the population overall, the national data may mask different trends for different ethnic or socioeconomic groups (Greenfield, 1996). Young Black males living in the cities, for instance, are frequently placed at risk educationally across the board, as well as in science, as evidenced by an increase in special programs designed to keep them safe and in school. Therefore, the picture is more complicated than the group statistics given in this chapter would lead one to believe. These complexities and patterns are revisited throughout this volume.

THE FIGMENT OF THE PIGMENT: RACE, ETHNICITY, OR SOMETHING ELSE?

Although race is treated as if it were a biological reality in this era of identity politics, race has been an obsolete concept among anthropologists since the 1950s (Wright, 1994). There has never been much agreement about how to determine racial groups. Three races or 300? Moreover, race as defined by the U.S. Census is a scientific and anthropological joke, according to demographer Hodgkinson (1995). For instance, since 1990, racial categories that appear on all forms authorized by the federal government allow four racial groups—American Indian/Alaskan Native, Asian/Pacific Islander, Black, and White. Yet, if the category *Mixed Race* is added in the next census in the year 2000, about 80% of Black Americans could claim it, as could most of the rest of us. Asian Americans and American Indians, two groups where intermarriage outside their respective groups is common, could disappear altogether from the demographic landscape. Stephen Jay Gould suggested that the term *race* be replaced by the notion of *biological cline*, a series of different characteristics within a population in an area that accounts for some of the diversity within the species (Wright, 1994). If race is a "figment of the pigment," why do we need to identify the race of people at all (Thernstrom, 1993)?

The American irony of the times is that we need the categories in order to eliminate them. Without knowing who the oppressed groups are, how can remedies be developed to avoid future oppression (Hodgkinson, 1995)? Perversely, racial categorization based on myth drives both prejudice and the programs designed to remedy it, such as school desegregation plans, affirmative action, college scholarships, and civil rights regulations for loans, housing, and jobs. To eliminate the categorization process would be to jeopardize Historically Black Colleges and tribal colleges, the Voting Rights Act, as well as set aside and entitlement programs. Advocates of various ethnic groups point out that many of the people who are now calling for a colorblind society are from the political wing that has an interest in undermining the progress and advantages currently accrued by non-Whites through affirmative action programs (Wright, 1994).

The statistics in this chapter have been collated by federal agencies on the basis of the racial categories provided in the 1990 U.S. Census, and this volume, by extension, adheres to them. However, because the term *race* seems to be scientifically empty, this volume follows the lead of the anthropologist, Ashley Montagu, who used the term *ethnic group*—self-perceived group membership in a population—which is much more accurate and less offensive. Yet, no matter what the term, two things are apparent: People from different ancestral backgrounds may have different behaviors based on their cultures; they may be discriminated against because of other people's perceptions about who they are and how they should be treated (Wright, 1994). With the process of labeling comes a heightened awareness of identity, even if that identity is almost wholly an artificial product of the process itself. A good example is the relatively recent term *Hispanic*, which has emerged since the 1970s. In the 1990 census, *Hispanic* was treated as an ethnic group. The National Council of La Raza has proposed that it be changed to a racial category in the 2000 census. If the government concurs, then the *Hispanic race* may include Spanish-speaking Blacks from the Caribbean, Whites from Argentina, mestizos from across Central and South America who, in turn, would be considered American Indians if they had happened to have originated in the United States, Brazilians who speak Portuguese, and some Mexican Americans who speak only English (Hodgkinson, 1995).

This labeling process is especially important to the discussion of equity in science education because it can create social cohesion and a heightened sense of group membership resulting in political clout. It also influences developing adolescents' notions of identity and where that leads in school and later life. Because science is seen largely as the realm of the White male (NSF, 1994), how students are labeled or label themselves affects them and their view of themselves in science classroom. Let us speculate. Mexican American students, according to the 1990 census, would have been placed in the Hispanic ethnic group and the White race. With a change in categorizing in the year 2000, these same children could be members of the Hispanic race and are non-White. If they become non-White, will this affect their chances of finding themselves, or placing themselves, in the science pipeline? As another example, since the 1940s, Asian Indians have been categorized as members of the Hindu race or as Whites and have currently come to rest in the Asian/Pacific Islander racial category. Has this improved their chances of becoming science or math whizzes? It seems silly, but then, perhaps not.

This volume avoids using the term *minority* because it gives offense to some as its root is *minor* and is not particularly elevating. It can be awkward and inaccurate, as in "the school was majority minority." The English language does not seem to provide a term that is both a precise and nonoffensive equivalent to "various diverse ethnic and other groups who may or may not be White." The term *people of color* is respectful, but incorrect because upon direct measurement, about 25% of the White population is darker in skin color than the lightest quarter of the Black population (Hodgkinson, 1995), an insight that casual observation will verify. Other terms commonly used—*nondominant, disadvantaged, at risk*— have pejorative connotations that make assumptions about ethnicity and advantage that may be untrue. Consequently, Americans struggle with a language that has not yet provided an encompassing term that is both accurate and positive in connotation, and use terms like *ethnic group, diverse learners,* and *underrepresented groups,* acknowledging that all are less than perfect.

Black Americans

The term *Black Americans* is used as an inclusive category because many Caribbeans and Africans identify themselves according to their country of origin or use this term and because this is the classification system used by the federal government (Atwater, 1995). Black Americans make up about 12% of the population, but received only 6% of the bachelors' degrees awarded from 1990 to 1992. Table 2.4 shows that Black Americans earned 6.5% of the science and 3.9% of the engineering undergraduate degrees, but only 2.6% and 1.9% of the doctorate degrees in these areas, respectively. These low rates of college and university graduation may be explained in part by the fact that college is expensive, and more Black Americans live in poverty than any other ethnic group (see Fig. 2.3). Alarmingly, this figure is rising for all ethnic groups (NSF, 1996a).

There are positive signs as well. A recent report issued by U.S. Census Bureau shows that for the first time, Black American students are graduating from high school at the same rate as Whites—87%—an indicator of social and economic well-being (Sanchez, 1996). However, a substantial proportion of these degrees are the result of young adults returning to school for equivalency degrees, not because these Black Americans have faired well in the typical high school system. In order to increase the chances for success in science at the college level, adequate prepara-

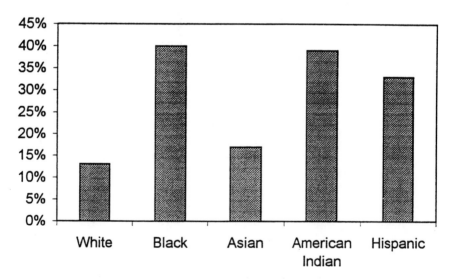

FIG. 2.3. Percentage of U.S. children under age 18 living in poverty, by race/ethnicity: 1990. From *Women, Minorities, and Persons With Disabilities in Science and Engineering* by NSF, 1994.

tion for Grades K–12 is very important. It is worrisome, then, that about one in three students in central city public schools, a generally weak link in the U.S. educational system, are Black Americans (Alsalam, Fischer, Ogle, & Smith, 1993).

Compared to other groups, Black American and Hispanic children have made the greatest gains in science on the NAEP, especially those at the lowest achievement levels. For instance, in 1977, only 29% of Black 13-year-olds scored at the 250 level on the NAEP mathematics assessment, but by 1992, that number rose to 51% (NSF, 1996a). In general, the NAEP science and mathematics scores of Black students are slowly but steadily improving, and the gap between achievement scores of Blacks and other groups of students is gradually narrowing—see Fig. 2.4.

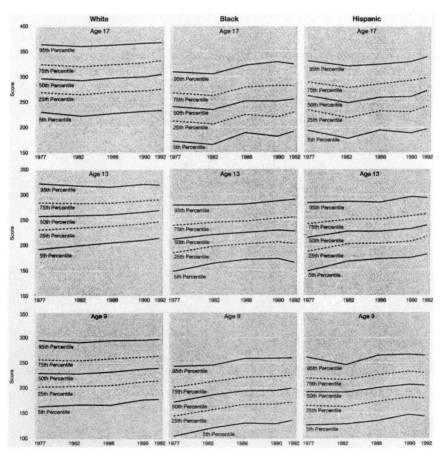

FIG. 2.4. NAEP mean science score percentile distributions: 1977 to 1992. From *Indicators of Science and Mathematics Education 1995* by NSF, 1996a.

However, a text on equity cannot afford to gloss over the tough issues. Table 2.3 shows that although few U.S. school children of any ethnicity are able to achieve at the highest levels on the science NAEP, the achievement of Black students in science, despite substantial gains since the 1970s, lags behind that of other groups. Continued and accelerated improvement of these scores is a clear target for achieving equity in science education. As with gender differences in achievement, if more Black American students took more science courses and more advanced science courses, achievement gaps would narrow. Figure 2.5 shows the gaps in course-taking among various ethnic groups.

In 1991, Black American students who graduated from college had a degree distribution in science roughly equivalent to that of their gradu-

TABLE 2.3

Average Science Proficiency and Percentage of Students at or
Above Four Proficiency Levels, by Grade and Race/Ethnicity: 1990

Grade and race/ethnicity	Average proficiency	Percentage of students at or above proficiency level			
		Level 200	Level 250	Level 300	Level 350
Grade 4:					
Asian	233	88	29	2	0
Hispanic	212	66	10	0	0
Black	205	58	5	0	0
White	242	93	40	1	0
American Indian	226	81	20	0	0
Grade 8:					
Asian	271	96	71	23	1
Hispanic	241	87	42	5	0
Black	231	80	31	3	0
White	273	97	74	23	1
American Indian	252	92	54	8	0
Grade 12:					
Asian	308	99	90	60	17
Hispanic	273	98	70	23	3
Black	256	94	57	12	1
White	303	100	91	53	12
American Indian	286	100	89	33	2

Note.   Proficiency levels are defined as follows:
         Less than 200—Knows everyday science facts.
         200—Understands simple scientific principles.
         250—Applies basic scientific information.
         300—Analyzes scientific procedures and data.
         350—Integrates specialized scientific information.
From *Women, Minorities, and Persons With Disabilities in Science and Engineering* by NSF, 1994.

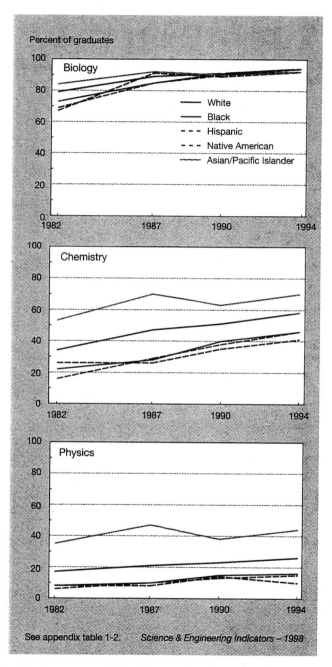

FIG. 2.5. Percentage of high school graduates earning credits in science courses, by race/ethnicity. From *Science and Engineering Indicators 1998* by National Science Board, 1998.

ation rate of 6%. Black Americans earned 5% of the bachelors' degrees in physical sciences, 8% in computer science, 4% in engineering, 5% in biological science, 7% in social science degrees, 6% in psychology, and 7% in health fields. Another clear equity goal is to double these numbers, which would at least make them proportional to the number of Blacks in the general population—12%. Gender differences among Black students exist, with Black women increasingly choosing science fields, but Black men moving away in greater numbers than any other group (see Fig. 2.6). For instance, among Black college graduates, Black women earned 53% of the science and engineering degrees in 1981 and 58% in 1991 (NSF, 1994). Over roughly the same period, U.S. colleges and universities steadily increased the proportion of foreign students who received degrees in science and engineering (NSF, 1996a), a steady source of tuition money compared with U.S. citizens who often need subsidized financial support or student loans. If colleges and universities were less financially strapped, would they turn their attention more to improving the science education for U.S. students rather than relying on the tuition of foreign students?

Hispanics

The term *Hispanic* includes people from across the Americas (see Fig. 2.7), ranging from Mexican Americans, who have lived in the United States for generations and who speak only English, to refugees recently arrived from war-torn areas such as El Salvador who speak no English and have had little exposure to formal schooling. It includes people who speak Spanish or Portuguese, including people of African, European, and Central and South American Indian ancestry. Hispanics make up about 9% of the current population. According to current projections, they are the fastest growing group in the United States, with the highest concentrations of population in the southwestern United States as well as New York, Florida, New Jersey, and Illinois (NSF, 1994). The median age of Hispanics is lower than that of the total population, 26.2 years versus 33.0 years, and this accounts, in part, for the high birth rate and population growth (Vetter, 1995). There is a large increase in the Hispanic population due to recent immigration, both legal and illegal, from Central and South America. These young Hispanics work. They are present in the labor force at the same rate as that of the total population—about 66%—but they are underrepresented in professional fields and overrepresented in janitorial and household cleaning occupations (Vetter, 1995). Hispanics received about 4.5% of the bachelors' degrees in 1991, with about the same proportion of degrees in science and engineering—4.5%.

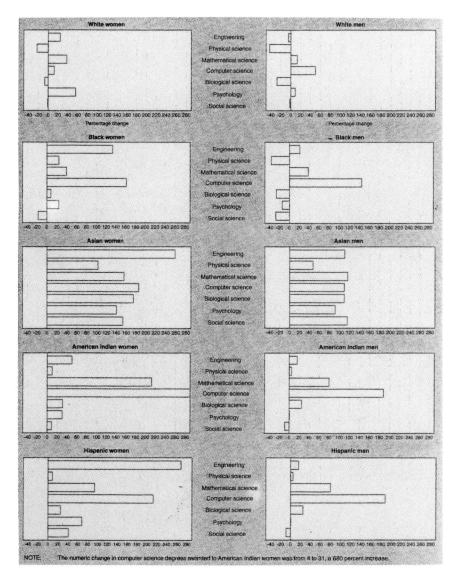

FIG. 2.6. Percentage change in science and engineering bachelors' degrees, by race/ethnicity and sex: 1981–1991. From *Women, Minorities, and Persons With Disabilities in Science and Engineering* by NSF, 1994.

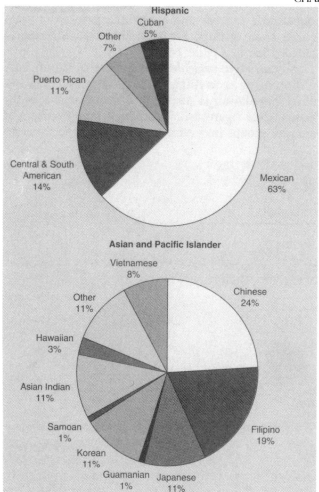

SOURCE: U.S. Department of Commerce, Bureau of the Census.
1990. Census Questionnaire Content, CQC-4,7

FIG. 2.7. Composition of Hispanic and Asian populations in the United States: 1990. From *Women, Minorities, and Persons With Disabilities in Science and Engineering* by NSF, 1994.

For Hispanic children, equity in K–12 education, particularly science education, is a serious issue. The achievement pattern in science and mathematics can be seen in the display of NAEP scores, showing the high rates of improvement. However, there are serious achievement gaps that are of national concern (see Fig. 2.4) and are, in part, the result of low levels of participation in high school science courses (see Fig. 2.5). Although there has been some growth in the total number of undergraduate degrees awarded to Hispanics in science, mathematics, and engineering since the 1980s, the proportion relative to other groups has remained unchanged. Hispanics are seriously underrepresented in these areas (see Table 2.4). This may be primarily due to the relatively high proportion of Hispanics who are not making it into postsecondary education. On average, only 57% of Hispanics received a high school diploma since the 1980s, trailing behind other groups in graduation rates. A large proportion of Hispanics are foreign-born and have not received much schooling in their native countries (Sanchez, 1996). Explanations for the achievement gap are complicated by the large proportions of Hispanic students who are poor and learning English as a second language.

Such generalizations are always dangerous, however. I am reminded of the irate Cuban American school principal whom I encountered at a meeting about school–university partnerships. He just discovered that his bright 9-year-old daughter, born in Miami and speaking flawless English, had automatically been placed in remedial English and ESL classes in her new school, simply based on her Spanish-sounding last name alone.

Hispanic young people who finish high school and go on to college, however, enter science, mathematics, and technology in numbers roughly proportional to their graduation rate of 4.5%. The percentage of bachelors' degrees received by Hispanics in science and related fields are: 4% engineering, 3% physical sciences, 5% computer science, 5% biological sciences, 4% social sciences, 4% health sciences, and 5% psychology (NSF, 1994). In order to achieve proportionate representation in the sciences, these rates should be doubled.

Figure 2.6 shows that Hispanic women are increasingly choosing science majors. Although there has been a steady increase in science and engineering doctorates awarded to Hispanic men and women over a 10-year period (NSF, 1994), overall among doctoral degree recipients, Hispanics received less than 2% of the degrees in every natural science and engineering field. Not surprisingly, their presence among science and engineering faculty is very small indeed (Vetter, 1995). These numbers would have to be increased fivefold in order to achieve representation proportional to Hispanics' membership in the population.

American Indians/Alaskan Natives

American Indians and Alaskan Natives account for only 1% of the population, but represent 50% of the diversity in the United States—a very small and diverse group has been lumped together under the title *Indian* since the time of Columbus. Although knowledge and tradition vary among Indian nations and people, there is a common worldview and collective experience that sustains them as the unique indigenous people

TABLE 2.4

Selected Characteristics by Race/Ethnicity: 1990, 1991, and 1992

Characteristic	Total U.S. citizens & perm. res.	Percentage distribution				
		White, non-Hispanic	Black, non-Hispanic	American Indian/Alaskan Native	Asian/ Pacific Is.	Hispanic
Total population, 1990 census	100.0	80.3	12.1	0.8	2.9	9.0
Persons 5–18 years old, October 1992	100.0	79.6	15.6	NA	NA	11.5
Persons 5–18 years old enrolled in school October 1992[a]	100.0	79.6	15.5	NA	NA	11.6
Undergraduate enrollment, fall 1991	100.0	76.9	10.0	0.9	4.6	7.7
Bachelors' degrees, 1991	100.0	82.7	6.0	0.4	3.9	4.5
Science	100.0	81.2	6.5	0.5	4.7	4.5
Engineering	100.0	78.4	3.9	0.3	10.8	4.4
Other	100.0	83.9	5.9	0.4	2.8	4.6
Graduate enrollment, fall 1992	100.0	81.8	5.2	0.3	8.3	4.4
Science	100.0	80.0	5.3	0.4	5.5	4.0
Engineering	100.0	74.6	3.1	0.2	11.2	3.2
Other	100.0	82.6	5.3	0.3	8.7	4.5

Masters' degrees, 1991	100.0	82.3	5.3	0.4	3.7	3.2
Science	100.0	81.0	5.9	0.4	4.5	3.5
Engineering	100.0	76.6	2.4	0.2	12.2	2.8
Other	100.0	83.1	5.3	0.4	2.8	3.2
Doctoral Degrees, 1992	100.0	84.5	3.9	0.5	6.2	3.2
Science	100.0	85.4	2.6	0.4	6.6	3.2
Engineering	100.0	74.7	1.9	0.4	17.8	2.9
Other	100.0	85.6	5.9	0.7	3.4	3.2
Civilian labor force, 1990	100.0	77.9	10.4	0.6	2.8	8.1
Scientists	100.0	85.5	5.6	0.3	5.3	3.2
Natural scientists	100.0	85.6	4.2	0.4	6.7	3.0
Math & computer scientists	100.0	83.9	6.2	0.3	6.0	3.2
Social Scientists	100.0	88.4	5.7	0.4	2.3	3.3
Engineers	100.0	86.0	3.5	0.3	7.0	3.2
Professional occupations	100.0	84.5	7.3	0.4	3.7	3.9
Other	100.0	76.6	11.1	0.7	2.6	8.9

Note. Because of nonresponse and rounding, percentages may not add to 100. *NA* = not available. From *Women, Minorities, and Persons With Disabilities in Science and Engineering*, by NSF, 1994.

[a]In the Bureau of the Census statistics, Hispanics are double-counted, both as Hispanic and under the applicable racial/ethnic category. Other data sources include Hispanic persons in only that category, regardless of their racial identification.

of U.S. society (Educational Equity Project, 1989). American Indians/Alaskan Natives speak more than 100 different languages. Although there are more than 300 tribes in existence, about one half of the American Indian population are members of 10 tribes—see Fig. 2.8 (Hodgkinson, 1990; NSF, 1994; Willetto, 1995)—and their numbers are concentrated in 10 states (see Table 2.5). More than one half of the Indian community lives in multitribal, multicultural urban situations (Hampton, 1991). Most American Indian and Alaskan Native students—85%—attend public schools, 10% go to Bureau of Indian Affairs schools, and 5% go to private schools. Some of these students (8.6%) can be categorized as having limited English, a high proportion (40%) are bilingual, but the majority speak only English (Hodgkinson, 1990).

The high school dropout rate for American Indians/Alaskan Natives is high—35% in 1988—and they are more likely than any other group to attend disadvantaged schools. Most of the teachers of Indian children are non-Indians, and poor student–teacher relations were found as a major cause of dropouts (Hampton, 1991). The incidence of poverty and severe health problems (e.g., alcoholism, suicide, and accidents) are among the highest in the country (see Table 2.6). Despite this, American Indians/Alaskan Natives' NAEP scores in science and mathematics fall

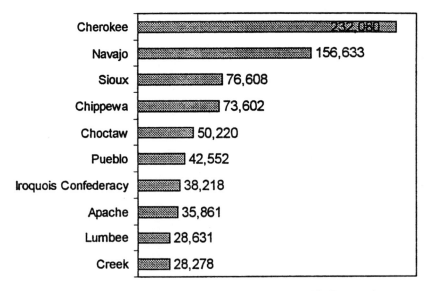

FIG. 2.8.   Ten largest American Indian tribes, 1980. From *The Demographics of American Indians: One Percent of the People, Fifty Percent of the Diversity* by H. L. Hodgkinson, 1990, Washington, DC: Institute for Educational Leadership Publications. Reprinted with permission of the author.

TABLE 2.5
Profile of American Indians in the Top 10 States: 1980

State	American Indian Population[a]	Median Age	Percent Female Headed Household[b]	Fertility[c]	Percent High School Grads[d]	Percent College Grads	Median Household Income	Percent of Persons Living in Poverty
California	227,757	25.8	22.5	1,510	65.5	9.6	$14,803	18.0
Oklahoma	171,092	24.0	18.5	1,604	56.2	8.8	11,369	23.9
Arizona	154,175	19.9	24.8	1,844	42.4	4.3	9,578	44.0
New Mexico	106,585	20.3	24.3	1,751	47.4	5.1	9,908	40.2
North Carolina	65,808	23.3	21.0	1,713	38.5	5.8	10,742	27.9
Washington	61,233	23.0	25.5	1,693	63.2	7.4	13,291	25.0
Texas	50,296	27.2	12.6	1,593	63.2	12.4	15,420	17.5
South Dakota	45,525	18.6	38.1	2,138	46.1	4.7	8,507	47.5
Michigan	44,712	22.8	24.6	1,718	56.0	6.2	14,580	22.1
New York	43,508	26.3	31.0	1,628	55.7	8.1	11,976	24.6
U.S.	1,478,523	23.5	22.7	1,688	55.8	7.7	12,227	27.5

Note. From The Demographics of American Indians: One Percent of the People, Fifty Percent of the Diversity by H. L. Hodgkinson, 1990, Washington, DC: Institute for Educational Leadership Publications. Reprinted with permission.

[a]Includes Alaska natives; does not include Eskimos and Aleuts.
[b]As a percent of all families.
[c]Children born per 1,000 women age 15–44 years.
[d]As a percent of persons age 25 years and over.

TABLE 2.6
Profile of American Indians, non-Whites and the United States

	Total Indians	Total Nonwhite	Total United States
1988 Population[a]	1,699,000	8,581,000	246,329,000
Percent Increase 1980–1988	+18.9%	+19.9%	+8.1%
Median Age, 1980	23.5 years	24.9 years[b]	30.0 years
Birth Rate, 1986 (per 1,000 population)	27.5	21.4	15.7
Births to Unmarried Women, 1987	45%	53%	24%
Infant Mortality, 1987 (per 1,000 live births)	9.8	15.4	10.4
Mortality Rate, 1987 (per 100,000 population)	571.1	688.0	535.5
Suicide Rate, 1988 (per 100,000 population)	15.0	6.9	11.7
Poverty Rate, 1980 (as a percent of all families)	23.7%	28.9%[c]	10.3%

Note.   From *The Demographics of American Indians: One Percent of the People, Fifty Percent of the Diversity* by H. L. Hodgkinson, 1990, Washington, DC: Institute for Educational Leadership Publications. Reprinted with permission.
[a]Indian estimates are for "Resident Population," which excludes armed services personnel abroad.
[b]African American only. (The median age for total non-Whites was not available.) The median age for Asian/Pacific islander was 28.7 and Hispanic was 23.2.
[c]African American only. The 1980 poverty rate for Hispanics was 23.2%.

between those of Blacks and Hispanics, and Whites and Asian Americans (see Table 2.4). Like Black American and Hispanic students, American Indians take chemistry and physics less frequently than other ethnic groups, which may be the result of a lack of access to such courses.

Few American Indians/Alaskan Natives attend 4-year colleges. Although they make up about 1% of the population, they received only .4% of the science and engineering bachelors' degrees awarded in 1991, about evenly divided between men and women. Figure 2.6 shows that these numbers are increasing, but this certainly remains a major area of concern. The 1990s could be an ideal time for American Indians and Alaskan Natives to join the education mainstream, but educational and occupational opportunities may further fray the fragile connection between being an Indian and being an American (Hodgkinson, 1990). This dilemma is discussed throughout this volume—how to teach students from various ethnic groups so that they can participate fully in the world of science, while respecting cultures that may not align closely with Western values and views. Indian people want their children to value culture and tradition because "it is not important to preserve our traditions—it is important to allow our traditions to preserve us" (Gail High Pine, cited in Hampton, 1991). Yet, Indian people also want their children to have the competencies and subject matter knowledge to enhance employment opportunities, to gain access to high-paying jobs, as well as to allow each young person to contribute to the community (Educational Equality Project, 1989; Hampton, 1991).

Asian Americans and Pacific Islanders

Okhee Lee, a member of the Project 2061 Equity Blueprint Committee, remembers an episode of the cartoon television program *The Simpsons*, where Principal Skinner was showing a visitor to the school the students' projects at a science fair and remarked: "Pretty good science projects for a school with no Asian students, wouldn't you say?" The remark is telling. Asian Americans have been described as a "model minority" for their academic performance in general, and as "math or science whizzes" in particular. Yet, as is the case with many groups, the use of an encompassing term, such as *Asian Americans*, masks the fact that the group is comprised of many substantially different subgroups. The successes of some may mask the failures of others, as well as the struggles of many to learn science in American classrooms that are mostly English-speaking and characterized by Western values and teaching styles. In addition, many of the Southeast Asian refugees suffer from emotional traumas of wars in their homelands. Some children from these families experience repeated academic and social difficulties at school; others succeed academically against all odds (Lee, 1995, 1997).

The 1990 U.S. Census invented the category *Asian/Pacific Islander* and federal statistics reflect this grouping. The term includes an extremely diverse group of peoples with distinctly different ethnic backgrounds. Figure 2.7 shows the distribution of Asian American/Pacific Islanders according to the last census, Chinese (24%), Filipino, (19%) Korean (11%), Japanese (11%), Asian Indian (11%), Vietnamese (8%), Hawaiian (3%), Samoan, (1%), Guamanian (1%), and others (11%). Rather than having a common cultural bond, each of these groups has a unique historical, social, religious, and linguistic background, and the category covers an enormous geographic swath of the planet. For example, another group, *American Indians/Alaskan Natives*, has descended from Asian ancestors and is probably more closely related to Asian Mongols, than are Mongols and Pakistanis who are both included in the *Asian/Pacific Islander* category.

Asian/Pacific Islanders make up about 3% of the total U.S. population, obtain about 4% of the bachelors' degrees, and about 6% of the doctoral degrees. (See Table 2.4 for a more complete overview.) About 10% of the scientists and engineers in the U.S. labor force are of Asian descent and the majority of these are foreign-born (89%), although 54% of these are naturalized U.S. citizens (NSF, 1994).

Asian American students consistently score high on the science NAEP (see Table 2.3). This is generally true at the fourth-grade level, with the gap widening with age. Similarly, they take high level science and mathematics classes at the highest rates (see Fig. 2.5). Of course, this pattern of achievement has been a hot topic with education policymakers and widely reported in the popular press. It has spurred a large number of comparative international and crosscultural studies in science and mathematics.

What should a text on equity and science education reform make of the superior performance of Asians and Asian Americans in science and mathematics? First, it should be pointed out that it is easy to fall into the trap of using White American students as a baseline from which to judge other groups, making Asian American students seem like overachievers. If science literacy for all is the goal, then this mind-set is not helpful. Many researchers in crossnational comparisons have concluded that it is the U.S. education as a whole that underachieves in science and mathematics. We should be proud that at least one group is doing well, in spite of the conditions that have led to less-than-stellar science achievement in general. This brings us to the second point—an examination of the factors that lead Asian or Asian Americans to successes can help us to understand how we might tweak, massage, or pummel the system for other ethnic groups in order to increase U.S. science literacy. In addition, we should not lose sight of the fact that there are significant differences among groups of Asian Americans and Pacific Islanders in mathematics and science performance, with some groups doing very well, whereas others are experiencing learning difficulties (Lee, 1995, 1997). Language alone can present a formidable barrier to recent arrivals from East Asian countries, especially for children displaced by war and who have had only sporadic schooling. English and East Asian languages have very different structures and few common roots. The United States has a dearth of teachers who can speak Asian languages and few teachers of Asian ancestry, so bilingual education programs are rare.

Although Asians/Pacific Islanders make up 3% of the population, they earned about 6% of bachelors' degrees in science and engineering in 1991 (NSF, 1994). They received bachelors' degrees at these rates in the following fields: 10% in engineering, 6% in physical science, 8% in computer science, 9% in biology, 4% in social sciences, and 3% in health fields. These statistics include U.S. citizens and permanent residents.

Caution is recommended when making generalizations about participation rates of Asian Americans/Pacific Islanders in science (Lee, 1995,
1997). It is difficult to obtain information about participation rates within
various subgroups, and some studies do not make the distinction between
U.S. citizens and noncitizens. According to Chipman and Thomas
(1987), Asian American females participate in science areas more often
than any other group of males or females except Whites. Yet, this varies
depending on the area of science, with engineering and physical sciences
having the fewest Asian American women scientists, and the social sciences the most (NSF, 1994).

SUMMARY

In this chapter, I attempted to briefly outline a gross picture of achievement and participation in science for male and female students, as well as
for various ethnic groups. The primary indicator for judging achievement
in the K–12 system is the NAEP, chosen because it is taken by the largest
number and range of students, not just those who are college-bound.
Grades also might have been used, but they vary greatly and provide a
very relative standard. The sources used to report these achievement
statistics—recent NSF documents—also provide SAT scores, SAT science achievement scores, ACT scores, and Advanced Placement (AP)
test scores. All of these tests, of course, are taken by older high school
students intending to go to 4-year colleges and universities and consequently, do not provide a view of the broad-range performance of U.S.
youth in science. However, the pattern of performance on these other
tests, in general, repeats the pattern of the NAEP, with female students
closing the gap with males, and the greatest improvements in recent years
made among Blacks, Hispanics, and American Indians/Alaska Natives.
Participation rates on these tests reflect the rate of participation in upper
level science courses among groups. Yet, the disparities in achievement
and participation between groups should be a national concern and a
major plank in an equity agenda. These variations in test scores and
upper level coursework rates may reveal important differences in readi-
ness to do college-level work in the sciences and in turn can account for
the pattern of students who graduate from college with majors in science
and related fields. Or they may reflect something more complex—attitude
toward, interest in, confidence in one's ability to do science—all more
elusive themes that are investigated in this volume.

When someone mentions equity in science education, the common
response seems to be to immediately identify gender and ethnic group

with issues of fairness. Categorizing individuals by gender or ethnicity is easy, especially in an era of identity politics. However, facile identifiers may not be the most salient ones in terms of an individual child's chances of achieving science literacy or subsequent greater successes in science-related areas. Other factors that cut across all ethnic groups, such as SES, presence of a disability or being identified as gifted and talented, geographic location, or mastery of English, may play a far more important role than ethnicity or gender in determining the quality of science education the child receives. These are the issues explored in chapter 3.

3

Diversity Defies Generalization: Don't Fence Me In

As a black lesbian feminist comfortable with the many different ingredients of my identity, and as a woman committed to racial and sexual freedom from oppression, I find I am constantly being encouraged to pluck out some one aspect of myself and present this as a meaningful whole, eclipsing or denying the other parts of self. But this is a destructive and fragmenting way to live. My fullest concentration of energy is available to me only when I integrate all the parts of who I am, openly, allowing power from particular sources of my living to flow back and forth freely through all my different selves, without the restrictions of externally imposed definition. Only then can I bring myself and my energies as a whole to the service of those struggles that I embrace as part of my living.

—Audrey Lorde (1996, pp. 63–64)

If you live near a major U.S. metropolitan area and read the newspaper regularly, it is easy to associate the urban poor with Black and Hispanic Americans whose numbers are concentrated in the inner cities. This is misleading. About 40% of Black households in the United States are in the middle income range and 25% of Black households have higher incomes than average White households (Hodgkinson, 1995). In terms of poverty, in raw numbers, the largest segment of the population that is poor is White. A reasonable question to ask in a discussion of equity and science education is, therefore, which is more important in determining chances for success in K–12 science—socioeconomic status (SES) or ethnicity? Research on large samples of students and U.S. Census figures show quite clearly that poverty has replaced ethnicity/race as the most pervasive index of social disadvantage and school failure (Burbridge, 1991; Hodgkinson, 1995).

The last chapter explored the achievement gaps of groups that have historically been underrepresented in science—women, Blacks, Hispanics, and American Indians/Alaska Natives. However, these obvious categories—gender or ethnic group—reflect only one aspect of the individuality that each young person brings to the science classroom. SES, geographic location, immigrant status, presence of a disability, proficiency in English, religious affiliation, and sexual orientation all interact and can have an impact on both the student's performance in science and on the school's expectations of that student.

CLASS NOT ETHNICITY/RACE

Social class or SES is a powerful factor in determining who succeeds in U.S. schools. It may be the single, most powerful factor. The United States has the highest rate of poverty among industrialized nations. The poverty rate for children is about 21%. Of all Americans below the poverty line, about 40% are children, although children make up only 27% of the total U.S. population. Since the 1980s, with the shrinking of the middle class, more children were plummeted into deprivation. Although there was a slight positive blip (but not statistically significant) in 1995 reflecting an increase of incomes at the lower and middle-class levels (Vobejda & Pearlstein, 1996), many economists predict a worsening trend. The growing number of poor children will not be balanced by the lucky few whose parents join the ranks of the rich. Moreover, the slight increase in median household income was due in part to more family members working more hours, a situation that can mean that more children are left alone to fend for themselves. The effects of these trends on our society will be profound, and the schools will bear much of the brunt. Exclusive private schools will increase their enrollments somewhat, and overburdened public schools will scramble to make room for even more poor and needy children. Although no one can predict the consequences of the recision of the federal welfare act, with few established job programs in the states compensating for reduced aid for poor children, most experts agree that the immediate situation for the children of parents who were on welfare is bound to get much worse before it gets better (Wilson, 1996). Yet, one thing is sure: Children will suffer and schools and teachers of poor children, already stretched to the breaking point in some places, will be asked to do even more.

Poverty is not evenly distributed in the population, nor is great wealth (see Fig. 2.3). The Black, Hispanic, and American Indian/Alaskan Native ethnic groups have the highest percentage of children living at the poverty level. In 1995, for the first time, the poverty rate for Hispanics (30.3%) rose above that of Blacks (29.2%); compare this to 11.2% for Whites. In contrast, Asian Americans have the highest median incomes, followed by Whites (Vobejda & Pearlstein, 1996).

It is not easy to unravel the influences of social class from those associated with ethnic group membership in measuring science achievement. However, it appears that social class has trumped ethnicity/race, when it comes to determining who succeeds in U.S. schools (Kahlenberg, 1995a, 1995b). Thus, a middle-class Black student in a good school has a greater chance of success than any poor child in a poor school. With recent challenges to race-based affirmative action, it has been suggested that SES replace ethnicity/race as the basis for affirmative action (Hodgkinson, 1995; Kahlenberg, 1995a).

The priority given to race over class has inevitably exacerbated white racism. . . . Every year when SAT scores are released, the breakdown by race shows enormous gaps between blacks on one hand and whites and Asians on the other. The NAACP cites these figures as evidence we need to do more. Charles Murray cites the same statistics as evidence of intractable racial differences. We rarely see a breakdown of scores by class which would show enormous gaps between rich and poor, gaps that would help explain the difference in scores by race. (Kahlenberg, 1995a, p. 24)

The NSF *Indicators* (1996a) report did such an analysis for the 1988 NAEP mathematics scores. A glance at Fig. 3.1 shows two things rather clearly: First, for each ethnic group, there is a clear relation between mathematics achievement scores and SES—the higher the SES, the higher the achievement. Second, SES alone does not account for all of the differences among ethnic groups. High SES Asian students have higher scores than high SES White students, who have higher scores than high SES Hispanic students and so on.

Figure 3.1 can be misread, however: The illustrated differences between groups on the graphs do not reflect differences in test scores directly, but rather show the percentage of students who reach each level of proficiency on the NAEP. The statistics in Table 3.1 provide a slightly different view of the situation. In the column labeled *Low SES*, note the performance of poor children of each ethnic group who score at the lowest level—about 26% of White children, 33% of Black children, 33%

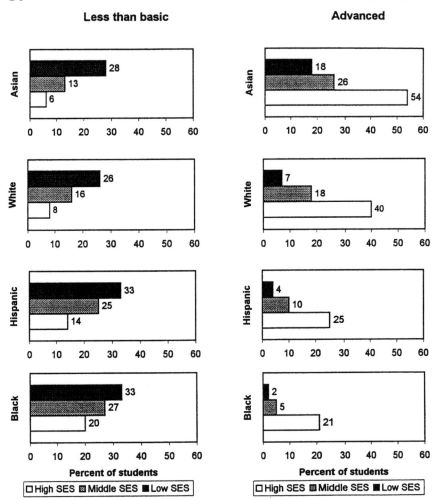

FIG. 3.1. NELS mathematics proficiency levels in eighth grade, by race of ethnic origin and SES: 1988. *Note.* From *Indicators of Science and Mathematics Education, 1995* by NSF, 1996a.

of Hispanic children, and 28% of Asian children. Although the large percentages of students who function below the basic level are distressing, the point should not be lost—these numbers are not very disparate for the various ethnic groups. Poor children of any ethnic group are clearly disadvantaged when it comes to mathematics achievement, which is closely related to science achievement (Arnold & Kaufman, 1992; Burbridge, 1991). This trend holds for low SES students of each ethnicity up to the advanced level, where there is a bubble of high achievement for Asian American youngsters relative to other groups.

TABLE 3.1
Percent of Eighth Grade Mathematics Students Performing at Each
Proficiency Level, by Race of Ethnic Origin and Socioeconomic Status: 1988

Proficiency level and race or ethnic origin	Total		Socioeconomic Status					
			Low		Middle		High	
Percent performing below basic level								
White	15.5	(0.7)	25.8	(2.0)	16.1	(0.9)	8.2	(0.8)
Black	28.9	(1.9)	33.4	(3.1)	26.6	(2.7)	20.1	(4.8)
Hispanic	27.6	(1.8)	32.8	(2.8)	24.8	(2.8)	14.0	(4.3)
Asian	13.4	(2.0)	27.6	(6.0)	13.0	(3.0)	6.4	(2.3)
Percent performing at basic level								
White	37.9	(0.9)	48.1	(2.2)	41.3	(1.3)	25.8	(1.3)
Black	49.4	(2.1)	51.3	(3.3)	50.9	(3.1)	34.7	(5.6)
Hispanic	46.8	(2.0)	49.3	(2.9)	46.6	(3.2)	36.5	(5.9)
Asian	30.7	(2.7)	38.3	(6.5)	39.5	(4.3)	15.9	(3.4)
Percent performing at intermediate level								
White	24.3	(0.8)	19.4	(1.8)	24.8	(1.1)	26.3	(1.3)
Black	16.5	(1.6)	13.0	(2.2)	18.0	(2.4)	24.2	(5.1)
Hispanic	16.9	(1.5)	13.5	(2.0)	18.9	(2.5)	24.2	(5.3)
Asian	21.2	(2.4)	15.7	(4.9)	21.4	(3.6)	23.8	(4.0)
Percent performing at advanced level								
White	22.4	(0.7)	6.8	(1.1)	17.9	(1.0)	39.8	(1.5)
Black	5.3	(0.9)	2.3	(1.0)	4.6	(1.3)	21.0	(4.8)
Hispanic	8.7	(1.2)	4.3	(1.2)	9.7	(1.9)	25.4	(5.3)
Asian	34.7	(2.8)	18.5	(5.2)	26.0	(3.9)	53.9	(4.7)

Note. Persons of Hispanic origin may be of any race. Standard errors appear in parentheses. From *Indicators of Science and Mathematics Education 1995* by NSF, 1996a.

The stereotyping of Asian Americans as a model minority with few problems can obscure the special needs of some Asian American children, especially new immigrants who are not so fortunately situated in this country (Lee, 1997). Although the median income of Asian Americans as a whole exceeds that of Whites, other groups have a low socioeconomic level and high level of unemployment. For instance, for some Southeast Asian immigrants, 20% are below the poverty line and 65% are unemployed (Bach, 1984; National Center for Educational Statistics, 1992a, p. 16; United States Commission on Civil Rights, 1992, p. 15).

Why is school success in science affected by SES (determined by annual income, type of job, and level of parents' education)? A national study of eighth-grade students in 1988 showed that the top three variables associated with science achievement were: parents' expectations about educational attainment, learning materials made available by parents, and the level of parents' education (NSF, 1994). The last factor, educational attainment of the parents, is a component of SES. The better educated the parents, the higher the income, and in turn, the higher the offspring's NAEP scores. Both the amount of money available to the family and the parents' education affect the next two factors—expectations for the child's future schooling and learning materials available at home. These statistics increase understanding of how family income influences science achievement.

There are reasons for a less than completely pessimistic view of the chances of science reform working in a society where, since the 1980s, families were getting poorer. First, there was a slight national upturn in income and lowering of poverty rates in 1995 (Vobejda & Pearlstein, 1996). Second, in addition to family income influencing education outcomes for children, the affluence and resources of the school are also critical. Poor children tend to go to *disadvantaged schools*—defined as schools where at least 50% of the students are participating in free or reduced price lunch programs. This may seem tautological, but there are other factors that characterize schools meeting this definition, such as low teacher morale, fewer certified teachers especially for science, deteriorating school buildings, fewer resources, less laboratory work, and more unmotivated students. A study using a large national data set showed that school characteristics, advantaged versus disadvantaged, better explained differences in science and mathematics achievement differences than did gender, ethnicity, or SES. Some of the negative factors associated with disadvantaged schools, such as quality of the facilities and preparation of the teachers, could be changed by an increase in funding, and we might be able to improve science education for the children who attend them. We could take the advice of demographer Harold Hodgkinson (1995) and eliminate "race-based integration" in exchange for SES-based integration and affirmative action, a proposal bound to be about as popular as Jencks' (1972, 1979) solution to educational inequities—the redistribution of wealth.

Figure 3.2 shows that children from ethnic groups underrepresented in science are more likely to attend these demoralized and demoralizing disadvantaged schools than do White and Asian American children (NSF, 1994). So, although it is possible, and even logical on a certain level, to talk about social class replacing ethnicity/race as the primary focus for an equity agenda in science education, ethnicity/race remains a salient factor. Economic disadvantage and its correlates are not evenly distributed across ethnic groups. Robert Kennedy (quoted in Kahlenberg, 1995a) said that it was pointless to talk about the real problem in America as being Black or White, it was really rich versus poor, a more complex subject. Yet, one must recognize the persistently pernicious effects of

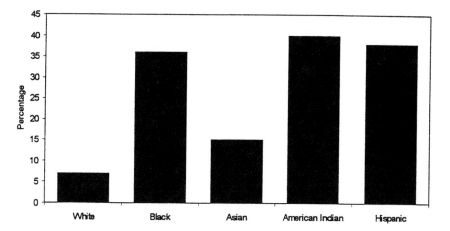

FIG. 3.2. Percentage of 1988 eighth grade students attending disadvantaged school by race and/or ethnicity. *Note.* Disadvantaged schools are schools with 50 percent or more of students participating in a free or reduced-price lunch program. Hispanics may be of any race. From *Women, Minorities, and Persons with Disabilities in Science and Engineering* by NSF, 1994.

racism both historically and currently (Kahlenberg, 1995a). Although it is not the goal of this volume to suggest that classism replace racism—both are repugnant—it is important to take into account how myriad factors interact to produce science achievement as well as the interest and motivation to do science. Research suggests that a middle-class student who attends a low SES school is at a greater disadvantage than a poor student who attends a middle-class school, and Black students are more disadvantaged at low SES schools than are White students (Kahlenberg; 1995a; Kohr, Masters, Coldiron, Blust, & Skiffington, 1991; NSF, 1994; Reyes & Stanic, 1988).

When considering group differences in achievement in science, three points are central:

1. It is important to avoid confounding ethnicity/race with class. A disproportionate number of Black, Hispanic, and American Indian/Alaskan Native students are from low SES backgrounds, but it is poverty, not ethnicity, that most inhibits school success.

2. A distinction must be made between the student's home background and the character of the school itself because resources are not distributed equally across schools of different types. Some suggest that, currently, integration based on social class may be more helpful in raising achievement than integration based upon ethnicity.

3. Achievement levels of students are circumscribed by the level and types of courses available, that is, students cannot learn what is not taught. Poor schools often have poor educational resources, low expectations, and a constricted range of course offerings.

STUDENTS WITH DISABILITIES

A September 1996 cover of the *New Yorker* magazine featured a slightly cartoonish drawing of a wide-eyed teacher (White) with a garish green-haired bun and prim pink blouse (the artist has spared her spectacles), posed in front of an obviously diverse group of students. On the blackboard behind her is written "Readin, Ritin, Ritalin." The title of the picture is "The Three Rs." Thus, by the reference to Ritalin—the new disability—attention deficit disorder (ADD) has become a sign of the times.

About 12% of all students (4,900,000 individuals) were reported to have a disabling condition and received special services in schools and related programs in 1992 to 1993 (NSF, 1994). In some schools, the proportion of students with disabilities is even higher.

National statistics show that learning disabilities constitute the largest proportion (45%) of identified disabilities, followed by speech and language impairments (20%), mental retardation (about 10%), serious emotional impairment (nearly 10%), and orthopedic, hearing, and other impairments (about 1% each, including ADD, disabilities related to parental drug abuse, disabilities acquired through trauma or illness, or multiple disabilities). As educational psychology and medicine find methods to identify more disabling conditions and learning anomalies, the number of children in special education will grow. This 12% of the school population must be addressed in a reform effort whose slogan is "Science for all."

Because of the vast differences in types of disabilities and the combinations of disabilities that may occur within one child, the implications for the science classroom are as unique as each student. Yet, inclusion, access, and adaptations for school science are common issues for all students with disabilities (be they physical, cognitive, or emotional) as they travel the road to science literacy along with those who have no identified disability. Therefore, this volume frequently uses the encompassing term *students with disabilities*, as well as refers to a specific type of disabling condition, where appropriate.

For children with disabilities who are under age 15, there are about two males to every one female. For the same group, the percentage of Whites with a disability is 5.4%, Blacks is 4.8%, and Hispanics is 3.1%, with statistics for other ethnic groups not reported (NSF, 1994). Of course, within schools and school districts, these numbers may vary widely, depending on the services available, and the attitudes of teachers and parents toward special education. In general, Black and Hispanic children appear to be identified in inordinately high proportions (Davidson, 1990; Heller, 1982)—although in some settings disproportionate numbers of affluent White children are diagnosed as having learning disabilities and ADD. Cawley (1994) commented that students with disabilities are frequently divided into two large categories that can overlap, when considering options and potential for science. One group consists of individuals with physical impairments (e.g., orthopedic, visual, or hearing disabilities); they have the same range of cognitive, social, and intellectual performance capabilities as that of the general population. About 1% of the 4,900,000 students with disabilities would fall into this category. Advances in technology, coupled with increased public awareness and willingness to provide the physical accommodations have enabled persons with physical impairments to enter careers in science in numbers that are beginning to approximate those of the general population.

The remaining 4,800,000 (99%) students with disabilities are those who manifest cognitive or social–personal disabilities that affect their ability to perform up to expectations in regular science classrooms. However, many members of this group still have the potential for the highest levels of science achievement. Einstein, Bohr, and DaVinci are three famous examples of persons said to have had learning disabilities and who overcame them or who used their unique intelligence in ways that earned them eminence. Yet, the successes of these famous individuals should not obscure their struggles, aided both by exceptional intelligence and their privileged families. Imagine the challenges before the child with disabilities who has average intelligence or lower and ordinary or poor families. Many of these students need accommodations in the science classroom in order to learn science, or prepare for a career in science, mathematics, or technology. The goal of science literacy is certainly valid for these students although, as with any other group of Americans, most students with disabilities will not become career scientists. The intent of science education reform holds a great deal of promise for these students.

A major obstacle for students with disabilities (be the impairment physical, social–personal–emotional, or cognitive) is the tendency of educators and the general public to make inferences about their intellectual capabilities predicated on their fluency in speaking (Stefanich, personal communication, December 8, 1995). It is all too easy to assume that people who are not able to express themselves easily (i.e., those with communicative disorders, physical disabilities, etc.) are unable to understand and do science. Gardner's (1983) Theory of Multiple Intelligences offers a reason that this supposition is flawed: Verbal and science abilities are separate and discreet intelligences and their occurrence in a single individual may or may not coincide. We can all probably think of examples of people that we know with one, the other, both, or neither. However, certainly the lack of ability to speak clearly does not mean that a person cannot think clearly or even brilliantly, as in the case of physicist Stephen Hawking. Stefanich (1994) hypothesized that as advances in technology provide vehicles for expressive communication, the percentage of people defined as having disabilities will decrease.

It is difficult to find national statistics that reflect the state of science achievement for K − 12 students with disabilities. About 86% of students with learning disabilities have access to science instruction similar to that of their classmates (NSF, 1994). See Fig. 3.3 for a more detailed breakdown by type of disability. Yet, it is unclear how many of these students are exposed to any sort of systematic assessment of their progress. *The 1990 Science Report Card* (National Center for Educational Statistics, 1992b) and the Goals 2000 reports do not disaggregate the NAEP scores of students with disabilities from other groups. This is unfortunate, and the situation will be remedied for future NAEP reports

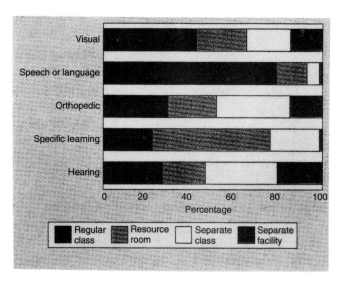

FIG. 3.3.   Percentage distribution of students 3 to 21 years old with disabilities receiving special education services, by type of disability and educational environment: 1990–1991. From *Women, Minorities, and Persons With Disabilities in Science and Engineering* by NSF, 1994.

(National Center for Educational Statistics, 1996). If the goal is science for all, then schools cannot continue to turn their backs in evaluating the effectiveness of the science program for students with disabilities. We must turn to measures other than NAEP to understand status of students with disabilities in science.

In terms of grades in general, students with disabilities make lower grades and have higher failure rates than their nondisabled peers. For instance, in one study of school grading patterns for over 500 students with disabilities in Grades 9 through 12, 50% to 60% of the grades were Ds or Fs (Cawley, Kahn, & Tedesco, 1989). The relative performance of students with disabilities is lower for science and math than it is for reading, vocabulary, and writing at the secondary school level (Gregory, Shanahan, & Walberg, 1985; Harnisch & Wilkinson, 1989). On average, students with disabilities attain about 1 year's worth of science achievement for every 2 years that they are in school, so at ages 16 through 18, students with disabilities, on average, function at the fifth- through seventh-grade levels of achievement (Jack Cawley, personal communication July 29, 1996). Of course, some students with disabilities will be performing at grade level or above, and there are cognitively gifted students with disabilities who may be achieving far above grade level in science.

Even though high school seniors with disabling conditions tended to score about 50 points lower on the SAT Math than those reporting no disabilities, the percentage of students with disabilities entering college increased from 7% in 1985 to 9% in 1991, with most of the increase coming from students with learning disabilities. Many of these students profit from special tutoring services that are increasingly available at colleges and universities. About 8% of all undergraduates report having disabilities, 9% males and 7% females (NSF, 1994). Because students with disabilities make up 12% of the population, this is an encouraging trend. The sciences and related areas draw a substantial number of students with disabilities (see Fig. 3.4), but the number of doctorates awarded to persons with disabilities is very small, for example, barely more than 1% of the degrees awarded in 1992.

It is difficult to isolate specific cause-and-effect relations among ethnicity, SES, and enrollment in special education programs. It is possible to attribute the overrepresentation of some groups of students in special education to teachers' lack of understanding of cultural differences among students, to poverty and health issues, and to problems related to drugs, crime, and violence in some communities (Cawley, 1994). Yet, this does not explain why the percentage of special education referrals widely varies across places with similar demographics or why schools, where the teach-

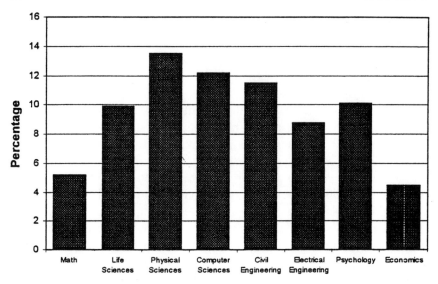

FIG. 3.4. Percentage of undergraduate students reporting disability by selected field: 1989–1990. *Note.* From *Women, Minorities, and Persons with Disabilities in Science and Engineering* by NSF, 1994.

ers' ethnicity is the same as the students', disproportionately identify students of color for special education (Wright & Santa-Cruz, 1983). For instance, a study by Brosnan (1983) showed that low SES school districts placed twice as many students in learning disability classes as high SES districts; school districts with large populations of students of color or low SES have overrepresentations of Black students in programs for students with mental retardation and learning disabilities.

Because of their mobility, migrant students with disabilities are difficult to reach through special education programs. For example, whereas California reports that students with disabilities make up approximately 8% of the school population, only 1.4% of migrant children are served by special education programs. How will science education reform respond to these poor, transient students with disabilities?

At the local school level, students with disabilities are often the last to be considered when issues of equity and science literacy are discussed. This is probably because of the persistent and erroneous stereotype of science as the province of the smartest few, combined with the lowered expectations a child entering special education frequently encounters. Moreover, the communities of special education and science education rarely seem to talk to one another, a gulf that becomes a chasm for students with disabilities in the schools.

Counterexamples to this lack of communication at the national level include the NSF Division of Science Resources Study and American

Association for the Advancement of Science (AAAS) Directorate of Education and Human Resources Programs, both of which have monitored and encouraged persons with disabilities to pursue science. The record of these organizations has been especially good for persons with physical disabilities and the increased attention to the largest portion of the population—persons with learning disabilities—is heartening.

RURAL STUDENTS

In the minds of many city dwellers, rural schools are frequently associated with farming communities, a sort of golden-tinged, hazy morning-in-America ideal representing a time past when things were simpler and better. Yet, a clear-cut definition of rural schools is elusive, noted Doreen Rojas-Medlin (1994), a science supervisor for schools in rural Georgia. The U.S. Census (as cited in Horn, 1995) defines *rural* in more prosaic terms: a residual category of places outside urban areas in open country, communities with less than 2,500 inhabitants or where the population density is less than 1,000 inhabitants per square mile. This definition encompasses areas as distinct from one another as farmland in Kansas, Florida, Washington, and Texas; mountain communities in Appalachia, Montana, and New Mexico; heavily forested areas in Michigan, New Hampshire, and Idaho; to say nothing of most of Alaska, which includes all of these types of habitats plus the arctic tundra.

About 28% of the nation's public schools are rural, with one in six students attending such a school (Baird, 1995). Every state has some rural schools, although the proportion varies from Rhode Island's 4% to South Dakota's 76% (Batey & Hart-Landsberg, 1993). The student population may be widely dispersed, geographically isolated, or simply small in number, as in the northwestern states. It is not unusual to have less than 200 students in an entire rural school district. Students may travel 30 or 40 miles to get to school (Rojas-Medlin, 1994).

Ethnically diverse students—Asian, Black, Hispanic, and American Indian/Alaskan Natives—make up about 31% of the total school population and about 18% live in rural, small town areas and attend rural schools. These students, as well as large numbers of White children living in rural areas, must struggle with the problems of poverty, isolation, and inadequate health care, all of which impinge on school learning. In addition to these problems, ethnically diverse rural students have special issues associated with achievement in science. Wilson and James (1995) identified three main science education concerns for these children: the need for validation and inclusion ("My ancestors or people like me engage in scientific endeavors"), limited English proficiency (LEP), and the need to include parents and community in the science classroom in order to help reconcile approaches to teaching Western science and traditional cultural practices. This last issue also applies to some predominantly White rural communities, particularly those communities deeply rooted in fundamentalist religious traditions that are at odds with modern science (Matthew, 1995).

Because rural schools are frequently very small and may lack curriculum support services, students may experience a very different sort of science education than in large schools. Large school districts usually offer a variety of course choices. Rural schools may have difficulty providing 4 years of high school science, especially chemistry and physics courses, and electives. The quality of the science education varies widely in rural schools (Rojas-Medlin, 1994). One of four U.S. teachers works in a rural school and is younger, on average, than the rest of the teacher population. About 24% of such teachers are assigned to teach science subjects in which they are not certified (Baird, 1995); one in three teaches courses in two science disciplines and one in eight must teach three or more different courses (NSF, 1996a).

Despite this, rural students seem to be holding their own in science achievement. The 1990 NAEP results show that rural students' science proficiency, although lower than advantaged urban students, is higher than that of disadvantaged urban students (see Table 3.2). This is an improved standing from NAEP results in the 1970s. How is this possible? The small school setting and greater personal attention may enhance science achievement, overcoming the influence of lower SES (Baird, 1995). There is a lesson here. In contrast to large schools that segregate students by SES (the result of tracking), the small numbers of students in rural schools make ability grouping impractical. Instead, rural teachers are more likely to rely on multiage grouping practices and the teaching of science disciplines in a more integrated way, sometimes around themes. This encourages students to make connections to life that increases their chance of nonsuperficial understanding of science concepts. Both practices dissolve the boundaries between traditional science disciplines. These teachers have a more personal approach to their students due to the closeness of community ties and the continuity of relationships with students and their families over years (Rojas-Medlin, 1994). These practices are very similar to innovations recommended in the education reform literature, an insight not at all lost on rural educators.

Rural schools successfully prepare students for colleges and universities, although statistics on the percent of rural students majoring in science

TABLE 3.2
Distribution of Students and Average Science
Proficiency by Type of Community

Proficiency level and race or ethnic origin	Percent of Students		Average Proficiency	
Grade 4				
Advantaged Urban	11	(1.7)	252	(2.4)
Disadvantaged Urban	9	(1.1)	209	(2.6)
Extreme Rural	11	(1.8)	235	(2.6)
Other	69	(2.8)	233	(1.0)
Grade 8				
Advantaged Urban	10	(2.1)[a]	283	(4.1)[a]
Disadvantaged Urban	9	(1.7)	242	(4.2)
Extreme Rural	11	(2.1)	257	(3.2)
Other	69	(2.8)	264	(1.5)
Grade 12				
Advantaged Urban	10	(2.4)[a]	304	(4.4)[a]
Disadvantaged Urban	12	(2.5)	273	(5.3)
Extreme Rural	11	(2.7)[a]	291	(3.9)[a]
Other	67	(3.5)	296	(1.6)

Note. The standard errors of the estimated percentages and proficiencies appear in parentheses. It can be said with 95 percent certainty that for each population of interest, the value for the whole population is within plus or minus two standard errors of the estimate for the sample. From *The 1990 science Report Card: NAEP's Assessment of Fourth, Eighth, and Twelfth Graders*, National Center for Education Statistics, U.S. Department of Education, 1992b.

[a]Interpret with caution—the nature of the sample does not allow accurate determination of the variability of these estimated statistics.

are hard to find. Anecdotal accounts of graduate students in science education classes indicate that some rural students may experience a shock when matriculating from the intimate and nurturing environment of the small country school to the large impersonal university. They may no longer be the top students in the class and may find that their high school science experiences fall short of those of students from advantaged urban–suburban environments.

One thing is certain, however: Rural students who go on to higher education seldom return to their communities (Horn, 1995). For this reason, education is viewed as a mixed blessing in many rural settings.

ENGLISH LANGUAGE LEARNERS

Another category that cuts across gender, ethnicity, and other groupings is proficiency in English. It is interesting to note that U.S. schools, in contrast to systems in other countries, label a child learning to speak

English as a second language as *limited English proficient*, rather than some other euphemism that would more positively connote the incipient accomplishment of facility in two languages. This volume uses the term *English language learners* to describe such students (Lacelle-Peterson & Rivera, 1993). Nonetheless, such children are at a disadvantage when they make the transition from the ESL or bilingual classroom into the mainstream, where they must rely exclusively on their developing English skills to cope with the heavy demands of academic English. Science courses, especially those loaded with vocabulary as well as abstract concepts, are especially daunting (Lee, Fradd, & Sutman, 1995). The near-record immigration rates of recent years make this an issue for about 75% of our Hispanic and Asian youth. In 1989, about 12% of the U.S. population reported speaking a language other than English at home. Between 1985 and 1992, there was a 70% increase in the number of English language learners enrolled in public schools, about 2.5 million students. This constitutes about 6% of the total school population (Spurlin, 1995).

Language can play a crucial role in maintaining a positive ethnic identity. It is especially important to the survival of American Indians/Alaskan Natives. Hodgkinson (1990) wrote, "In that culture plays so much of itself out through language in American society, the pervasive pattern of not allowing Indian children to use their own languages is at the heart of previous failures in Indian education" (p. 21). Although 40% of American Indians/Alaskan Natives are bilingual and the number of languages spoken by these children is greater than any other group, the number of science teachers able to teach in these native languages is the lowest.

English language learners, of course, are not evenly distributed across the schools. There is one high school in metropolitan Washington, DC where 80% of the students were born outside the United States and more than 100 different languages are spoken. In other parts of the United States, there are no such students—yet. However, consider the case of a graduate student in a science teacher preparation program who seemed less than enthusiastic about the program's emphasis on meeting the needs of diverse learners. Why should he have to learn about English language learners? He was moving to a small town in Wisconsin to teach physics as soon as he graduated and assumed that its homogeneous community would provide few opportunities to exercise his knowledge and skill in multicultural education. In fact, he did get his job teaching physics in Wisconsin, along with two sections of physical science for Southeast Asian children who spoke only Hmong. Now, he wishes he had taken ESL/bilingual education methods courses as well as science ones.

This story illustrates a pervasive problem—science education publications tend to conflate the issues of ethnic diversity and proficiency in English. "*Language* as an obstacle to achievement is peripherally referred to, if at all" (Bernhardt, 1995, pp. 5–6). Too often, the discussion on the education of immigrants focuses only on low SES, health problems, differences in background knowledge and experience, or bias in classroom practice. For educators, being aware of and respecting cultural differences may be necessary, but not sufficient, to bring English language learners into mainstream education. In addition, we need to understand the linguistic aspects of the science classroom, what is known and not known about second language acquisition and how to use this knowledge to better teach science to English language learners. English language learners who have made the transition into mainstream science classrooms may be ignored or asked to do busy work by teachers who do not know how to work with them (Bernhardt, 1995). About 35% of these students are placed in classes below grade level and are more likely to drop out than native speakers of English (Spurlin, 1995).

Interestingly, this trend is not always true for Asian American students, despite substantial obstacles. As a small case in point, in an analysis of honors class enrollments by gender and ethnicity at an extremely diverse Washington, DC metropolitan high school with 2,200 students, the data show that Asian American females took more honors classes at 9.4 per graduate than any other ethnic group, whereas Black males had the fewest at 1.8 (J. Hawkins, personal communication, September 25, 1996). National data show that Asian American students are more likely than any other group to enroll in crucial gateway courses for science and mathematics, such as geometry, chemistry, and physics. About 40% of Asian American students tend to concentrate their high school studies in science and mathematics areas, as opposed to 19% for Whites, 10% for Hispanics, and 6% for Blacks (NSF, 1994).

Language problems are particularly acute for Asian Americans in the United States because Asian languages bear little similarity to English. Asian Americans speak a variety of languages and dialects, including Cambodian, Cantonese, Mandarin, Hmong, Japanese, Korean, Lao, Tagalog, Samoan, and Vietnamese. The number of Asian languages makes it extremely difficult to find bilingual teachers for each of these languages. Asian Americans' positive performance in mathematics, science, and engineering, despite their limited English language skills, may be an attempt to compensate for a relative weakness in more verbally dependent subjects by excelling in the areas of natural sciences (Lee, 1997). Mathematics is a subject area that is least dependent on language, having its own symbol system (Lynch, 1991). The performance of Asian American students versus other English language learners demonstrates how difficult it is to separate the factors of culture, language acquisition, SES, and bias and their relation to science achievement.

As in the situation of students with disabilities, it is difficult to find large national samples of achievement data for English Language Learners. NAEP scores are not available for students in ESL or bilingual education programs, although the scores of many such students may be included under ethnic group categories. For future NAEP reports, this situation is to be remedied (National Center for Educational Statistics, 1996).

SUMMARY

The last two chapters described participation in science for various groups using NAEP data when available, as well as statistics on college participation rates and advanced degrees earned. For anyone who regularly follows equity issues in science education for any one particular group—women, Black Americans, or students with disabilities—none of this will come as any surprise. Indeed, the thumbnail sketches given here may seem superficial, and can be improved on in the articles and books on equity in science education focused on a particular group, but the goal of this volume is to provide a wide-angle view of the total landscape of equity issues in science education. The picture is anything but crisp and clear. Rather, it is clouded by ambiguities and merging components. For example, issues of ethnicity/race cannot be separated from those of social class, and social class seems, in turn, to affect placement in special education. There is a strong correlation between SES and achievement in science. Poverty is not equitably distributed according to ethnicity, and a disproportionate number of the poor are children of color.

Female students are underrepresented in science and anyone visiting secondary school science classrooms can see marked differences in the classroom environment for boys and girls. However, in some poor urban communities, girls of color (whose skin may be lighter than that of many Whites) may be better situated for school science achievement—and survival—than boys.

Hispanics are often treated as if they were a single ethnic group, but this is, in many ways, an artificial category. No doubt the school achievement of Hispanics in science is affected by the fact that the majority of

Hispanic schoolchildren are learning English as well as the fact that they have the highest rate of poverty in the country. Large proportions of American Indians/Alaskan Natives, who are underrepresented in science, are also bilingual, poor, and go to rural schools, many of which are also disadvantaged schools. Yet, many rural schools show strong achievement in science.

As if all of this were not complicated enough, there are the Asian American students, who, as a group, perform better than any other in science and mathematics, despite the fact that many of these students are not native speakers of English and are new to the United States. It is almost as if Asian Americans and their high achievement present a way of defying suppositions that are all too facilely made. Yet, Asian Americans, as a group, also have the highest median incomes and tend not to go to disadvantaged schools.

What is to be made of all of this? It seems that the key to equity in science for underrepresented groups primarily boils down to two factors: First is the obvious relation between science achievement and SES—this includes both the SES of individual students as well as the advantaged or disadvantaged character of their school. This should be apparent from the statistics cited in the last two chapters, with some room for hope emerging from the fact that it is possible to change negative characteristics of disadvantaged schools. Much of the next seven chapters focus on how this can be done.

The second major impediment to equity in science education is the persistent stereotyping of science as the province of the privileged few—a subject too hard, too uninteresting, too irrelevant, and beyond the reach of most students. Given the way that science is frequently taught in schools, it is a small wonder that so many students feel this way. Consequently, another tough challenge is to replace this view with one of a science literacy that is as accessible to students as it is relevant to every citizen, and interesting and enjoyable as it is crucial for success in a variety of careers. How to dismantle this stereotype is also a major theme of this volume.

Finally, all of this splitting and parsing into groups—a national pastime in these days of identity politics—may be necessary to understand the issues before us in education reform leading to science literacy for all. Yet, no individual creates an identity solely according to his or her group membership and all of this categorization may be offensive. Lorde (1996), a self-described "Black Lesbian Feminist Warrior Poet," commented on this fragmenting of self in response to identity politics in the excerpt that began this chapter. Lorde (who died in 1992) managed to pack in memberships to several groups not advantageously situated in society. She found unity and fulfillment as an artist. A goal of science for all is to help young people build identities that include competent science student and scientifically literate citizen, in addition to the other facets of their individuality.

4

Culture, Worldview, and Prejudice

According to current reservation lore, being an Indian requires meeting two dozen anthropologists before you are twenty-one.
—Lincoln and Slagle (as cited in Hampton, 1991)

It is not important to preserve our traditions—it is important to allow our traditions to preserve us.
—Gail High Pine (as quoted in Hampton, 1991)

WORLDVIEW AND SCIENCE

Mr. N, a warm and engaging teacher in a culturally diverse high school, told the story of a young man in his earth science class, a recent arrival to the United States from war-torn Afghanistan. Although Mr. N. could not quite put his finger on why, this student seemed very different from his other students. One day, Mr. N, examining him closely, confidentially asked his age. After some hesitation, the young man replied that he was 25, but because he appeared much younger, he was able to fake his way through the U.S. high school as a student. "What did you do in Afghanistan?" Mr. N inquired. The young man answered that he had been a soldier in the Russian–Afghan war. "Did you ever have to kill someone?" He responded that he had aimed his rifle and fired and that Russian soldiers had fallen. "What on earth do you want from me and from this science class?" Mr. N asked. "I want to learn how to think like an

American," he replied. Mr. N took this to mean that the student saw scientific reasoning as the key to assimilation and success in his new life in the United States.

In this story, the Afghan student seemed aware of the dissimilarity between his worldview—influenced by his culture, age, and experiences as a soldier—and what he saw as an American one. From the teacher's standpoint, worldview accounted for the elusive something that separated the Afghan from the other students. Moreover, the teacher's worldview is also apparent, attributing Horatio Alger-like intentions to the young man's stated desire to think like an American, although other interpretations are possible. The teacher is a middle-aged, second-generation Italian American whose worldview was formed by an era when assimilation was possible, expected, and desirable for his family, and this probably influences his teaching practice.

Worldview is a concept with a great deal of intuitive appeal and is frequently found both in scholarly literature and the vernacular of our increasingly diverse U.S. society. In education, differences in students' worldviews may be called on to explain variations in science education achievement, participation, and motivation among diverse ethnic groups, social classes, and genders (Allen, 1995; Cobern, 1993a, 1993b; Lee, 1997; Rogers & Kaiser, 1985; Waldrip & Taylor, 1994).

Worldview is a construct that has its origins in the 18th-century philosophy of Kant and later in the work of Hegel and Goethe. Historically, its meaning has included both a philosophical view that is articulated, conscious, and coherent, as well as a life view that is an involuntary, socioculturally mediated view of the world. The two meanings have merged. *Worldview* is the fundamental organization of the mind that allows one to think and feel in a predictable fashion. It undergirds rationality, influences norms and values, and helps us to make sense of our experiences. It is a resilient and often conservative force, reconciling differences between beliefs (Cobern, 1991).

> A worldview is not merely a philosophical by-product of each culture, like a shadow, but the very skeleton of concrete cognitive assumptions on which the flesh of customary behavior is hung. Worldview, accordingly, may be expressed . . . in cosmology, philosophy, ethics, religious ritual, scientific belief, and so on, but it is implicit in almost every single act. (Wallace as quoted in Cobern, 1988, p. 16)

Within a culture, the worldviews of individuals may differ. For instance, in the United States, one's worldview can vary depending on how

one is situated—rural or urban dwellers, women or men, or retirees living
in Florida or Alaska Natives living on a frozen island in the Arctic.
Moreover, even within a given subculture, individuals develop different
worldviews—some, no doubt, are more compatible with contemporary
views of science than others (Cobern, 1988). There are important ramifications of worldview for constructivist science educators. If a student
has a worldview of science that conflicts with the notions of modern
science as they might be presented in the science classroom, then this
could explain why the student seems to regard science classes with dis-
taste or has difficulty learning science concepts or scientific habits of
mind. Or conversely, worldview may favorably predispose students to
science—for instance, I remember an Asian American seventh grader I
once taught whose father was a physicist. At breakfast each day, the
father proposed a physics problem for the family to consider, which he
posted on the refrigerator door. At the evening meal, the entire family
discussed various solutions, considering their merits. Imagine the sophistication of my seventh-grade student's worldview of science, compared to
that of other children's whose families never manage to even eat together,
much less solve physics problems as a form of entertainment at meals.

In school, students are exposed to a variety of different science worldviews reflected in science curricula or texts, in the science education
reform efforts, such as Project 2061, the National Science Education
Standards (NSES), or in an individual teacher's worldview. For instance,
I recently watched an eighth-grade physical science teacher give a lesson
(clearly well prepared and thoroughly planned) on the structure of the
atom where she compared the balance of charges within an atom to the
balance of forces of good and evil in the world (positive and good protons,
evil and negative electrons, neutrons like the Swiss in World War II). I
taught this same lesson many times, and it would have never occurred
to me to use this analogy, and I could not do it now. Yet, as the lesson
continued and the teacher's religious worldview became increasingly apparent, I wondered how the students were responding. No doubt that the
use of this metaphor was more helpful to some students than others, and
for all I know, her approach may have been consistent with the worldview
of many in this particular community.

It is possible to look at formal science worldviews, usually discussed in
the literature as the *nature of science*, in a number of different ways.
Perhaps the most prevalent articulated view of science is that of logical
positivism. This scientific worldview is uniquely Western and is characterized by a mechanistic, reductionist view of the world where machine-
type analogies are used to explain natural phenomena. This perspective

tends to represent the natural world hierarchically, with *man* (rather than *humans* or *women*) at the top of the heap. The scientist is thought of as a dispassionate, wholly objective, and rational explorer of a world that is knowable through observation and logic. This empiricism has its roots in 16th to 18th century Europe. Cobern (1988) argued that "although modern physics is modifying this classical scientific worldview, it remains a thoroughly empirical view that stresses the importance of testable hypotheses concerning natural causes" (p. 8). This seems to be the worldview of science to which lipservice is most extravagantly paid in American science education. It is hard to find a textbook that does not begin with "The Scientific Method," although it appears that most American students have the opportunity to do empirical explorations only infrequently. In 1990, only 41% of eighth grade students and 62% of their teachers reported that they did science experiments once a week or more (National Education Goals Panel, 1994). In a more personal and informal survey of classroom practice, in my last 30 hours of science classroom observations focusing on science classrooms characterized by high concentrations of diverse learners, I observed only one laboratory activity and never saw a computer in use. The emphasis more often than not was on the written or spoken word—*science* as vocabulary—rather than on direct experience with physical phenomena.

A strictly empirical view of science has been replaced for many by a postpositivist program, perhaps most clearly articulated by Kuhn (1962) in *The Structure of Scientific Revolutions*. In this view, *science* is seen to be the constructed knowledge of a community of knowers working together to solve problems using the scientific paradigm that, in actual practice, is less linear and more creative and intuitive than implied by traditional logical positivism. The observer and what is being observed are part of the same system and the cherished objectivity of the scientist crumbles. The scientist is no longer the disinterested observer, and theory-free and value-free investigation is impossible (Cleminson, 1990). Important advances in scientific theory, called *paradigm shifts*, occur in a revolutionary way when there is a collective breakdown around a set of commonly held theories, values, and beliefs, rather than through a slow accretion of facts as the mirrored knowledge of a positivist reality (Allen, 1995; Cleminson, 1990; Feyerabend, 1976; Kuhn, 1962).

The worldview of science articulated in important science education reform documents embraces both empiricist and postpositivist philosophies. For instance, in the NSES (1996) it was stated, "Science distinguishes itself from other ways of knowing and from other bodies of knowledge through the use of empirical standards, logical arguments, and skepticism, as scientists strive for the best possible explanations of the natural world" (p. 201). Yet, on the same page, we read that, "Scientists are influenced by societal, cultural, and personal beliefs and ways of viewing the world. Science is not separate from society but rather science is a part of society" (p. 201). NSES pointed out that explanations about the natural world based on religion, myths, superstitions, and beliefs may be personally useful and socially relevant, but they are not science. Certainly, the line is not so clear, for in the past, chemistry has arisen from alchemy and astronomy and astrology had common roots. No doubt, some of what is regarded as *science* today will be viewed as little more than superstition tomorrow—cf. the regular proclamations of the medical community on what constitutes a healthy diet (Proulx, 1997).

The postpositivist view of science is consistent with the feminist critique of science where the very objectivity said to be characteristic of scientific knowledge and the dichotomy between subject and object (scientist and the natural world) may be seen as a male way of relating to the world that specifically excludes women (Rosser, 1989). Feminist science questions the extent to which science is value-laden and biased toward men's perspectives both in the selection and definition of research problems and in the design and interpretation of research. One well-known example is the history of flawed medical research done at the National Institute of Health (NIH) for years that eventually prompted the hiring of a woman director, Dr. Bernadine Healy. Female subjects had been systematically excluded from drug studies for years because their hormonal cycles introduced variables difficult to control. The result was millions of dollars spent on medical research that tested treatments that worked effectively for males, but not for females with the same illnesses. This example leads to the question of whether there is a feminist science that is different from that currently practiced and most often by men, or whether "science is science"—gender neutral—and in the aforementioned example, the NIH research was simply bad science (Rosser, 1989).

Is there a feminist science? If there is, what about an Afrocentric science, an American Indian science, and so on? Are these sciences separate and different from modern science or is the methodology essentially the same—science is science—and the difference lies in who the practitioners are, and all that that implies politically, psychologically, and socially? If the methodology is the same, then the crucial differences in feminist, Afrocentric, American Indian, or other versions of science practiced by groups with particular sensibilities may reside in the research questions asked, the methods that are chosen, and nature of the explanatory models used (Rosser, 1989). This means that the only way to change science, viewed by some as Western, Eurocentric, Androcentric, and so on, is to change the composition of those who are doing science. The field must be increasingly accessible and desirable to those of various diverse groups. Consider, for example, the view of science provided by Martinez (1996), an American Indian/Hispanic environmentalist:

> But the systems analysis and chaos theory today show us . . . that the ability to predict trends in matter or living organisms is severely limited. That is a humbling thought. And we need humbling thoughts. We are fascinated with our intellectual abilities and capacities to predict and analyze, when what we need is to listen and observe over time and in one place, something indigenous peoples—indeed the ancestors of everyone here—once did. And they survived a long time. Survival is the acid test of cultural adaptability. That part of the indigenous past that is still retrievable is a better guide for the future than limited computer modeling although computers are useful up to a point. (p. 50)

Martinez (1996) seems able to straddle both worlds—that of indigenous peoples and that of modern science and technology—and not only to reconcile them for himself, but to provide the broader, historical perspective to the environmental science community.

This volume argues that science education, as it is experienced in the public schools, should exemplify the best of modern science and should allow students to understand what it is, how it is practiced, and its advantages, disadvantages, and abuses. It should permit students to experience the methods of modern science firsthand, practice using them, and explore real problems of concern to the community in order to best appreciate its value and limitations. This constructivist view of science teaching holds that humans learn by building on past experiences and ideas about a concept in order to restructure the concept in ways that are more powerful. For this to occur, the teaching–learning environment must be based on thoughtful, meaningful activities that allow students to make these conceptual changes—resulting in intellectual growth. As an example, if a science teacher wished to teach students the essential features of a coastal environment, the teacher might take the students on a field trip, show a film (pausing to discuss various features), or ask them to build a model. Memorizing definitions of words like *bay*, *cape*, *canal* may result in some students passing a multiple choice exam, but is less likely to help all students come to a real, meaningful, owned understanding of these terms.

These views of science education seem entirely consistent with those expressed in Project 2061 literature and the NSES. In addition, an enhanced appreciation of the role of worldview in constructivist science teaching would not only allow, but also seek linkages with the science, science-like activities, or perhaps even the pseudoscience of the students' cultures and communities. For instance, suppose rural students were to systematically explore and account for the success rates of *water-witchers*, diviners who use witching sticks to find the best places to drill for water, and who are regularly consulted in some rural communities, even by the scientifically literate and newcomers from the city. This would seem to be exactly the type of messy problem that would hold students' interest, as they insidiously learned about water tables, aquifers, and soil types, as well as developed an understanding of probability and the habits of mind associated with a rigorous examination of data and the nature of evidence.

However, the current situation in science education across the United States suggests that most of what passes for science education is not inquiry, in either the empiricist or postpositivist sense. Students seem to experience science as a rote regurgitation of science facts acquired in an innervating, authoritarian fashion that runs counter to everything known about the way that science is actually done. This is a major reason that science education reform is underway. This chapter examines the useful construct of worldview and explores its ramifications for science education reform and equity in three different ways:

1. Worldview as a partial explanation for variations in achievement, participation, and motivation in science.
2. The problem of incompatibilities between teachers' and students' worldviews and the consequences in the science classroom in terms of cultural continuity and learning–teaching style.
3. The dark side of worldview—dealing with prejudice, bias, and insensitivity in the science classroom.

WORLDVIEW AND STUDENTS' VARIED RESPONSES TO SCIENCE

William Cobern, a science educator at Western Michigan University, whose research program since the 1980s has focused on worldview and science, said that in ethnically diverse classrooms a *prima facie* case can be made for worldview as a factor in the educational process: "In modern America, a primary goal in science education is the development of a scientific worldview, especially with regard to scientific ways of thinking" (Cobern, 1988, p. 4). Differences in worldview may create avenues for variation in science achievement, participation, and attitudes that were discussed in chapters 2 and 3 of this volume.

Culture and worldview at odds with modern science are not limited to students who recently arrived in the United States. In a study of fourth- and fifth-grade students' beliefs about the causes of Hurricane Andrew, a cataclysmic event dramatically affecting their lives, Lee (in press) found that children in south Florida held very different explanations for the hurricane and the destruction it caused. Although students vividly remembered the event, few could provide clear explanations of the hurricane's causes. Scientific knowledge, however, seemed to vary according to SES. Low SES students (those on free and reduced-lunch programs) had less knowledge of and less accurate explanations for the hurricane than did their middle-class peers. The low SES students tended to talk about their personal experiences, even when queried about their science knowledge and explanations about the hurricane.

The differences in worldviews were evident among the three ethnic groups in the study. White students were likely to interpret the hurricane as the result of natural phenomena—"A lot of cold air and warm air hit each other . . . it started a tropical depression . . . and forms hurricanes"— or pollution—"Mother Nature is wanting to get back at us for all the pollution and cutting down trees." They usually expressed tentative beliefs in supernatural forces, such as God or the devil, although Mother Nature seemed to assume the role of a real entity rather than that of a metaphoric one.

In contrast, Black American students expressed worldviews in which people, nature, and supernatural forces interacted to cause the hurricane: "I think God is teaching us a lesson. He just sends out a hurricane to make people get straightened out, teach them a lesson, make them cooperate with people, and stop littering and violence." Some Black American students, despite their ability to provide scientific explanations for the hurricane, also believed that the hurricane came to the area either because White people were not treating Black people fairly or as a warning for Black people to become more spiritual: "I don't know if the Lord would do that, but He said that He was going to . . . the earth was destroyed by fire, so maybe that's a warning." Hispanic students had similar spiritual explanations, but unlike the White students, they did not identify environmental pollution as a cause, and unlike the Black students, they did not emphasize social problems—"The devil is the one who performs bad things, and God wants to stop it." The results are especially interesting because all of these students had been exposed to scientific explanations by teachers and the media for the causes for hurricanes and tornadoes. Still, many students held on to alternative views explaining these natural phenomena.

The ability to simultaneously hold two very different worldviews occurs among children and adults. For instance, U.S. geologists described what they saw as the incompatible worldviews of a scientist colleague in a developing country:

> While working in a developing country, a professor of geology from the local university once informed me that he believed both in evolution and special creation as viable explanations of origins. When I suggested that there was a disparity between these two explanations, he explained that he believed in evolution when he was at work, and special creation when at church. . . . We believe that this example typifies the assertion that many learners hold simultaneously . . . disparate explanations of naturally occurring phenomena: a "worldview" and a "school view." (Waldrip & Taylor, 1994, p. 1)

Cobern (personal communication, February 5, 1997) speculated that when a person allegedly holds two very different worldviews, in reality, the person has probably integrated both somewhat, shaving off the sharpest edges of disagreement. Such reconciliations increase with age or until one view is subsumed by another.

The lack of cultural continuity between the science taught in the schools and the beliefs that guide the lives of people is also apparent among American Indians. American Indians/Alaska Natives have a close relationship with nature, one that does not posit human superiority over the nature, but rather a spiritual connection (Lee, in press). Willetto (1995) pointed out that modern Western science is often viewed in schools as the only science. However, there are many ways of looking at the world and learning to use its resources. Often, the Native view is overlooked or seen as ancient, quaint, and mythological, when it fits readily in many areas of modern science teaching. Many of the important discoveries of American Indian/Alaskan Natives are ignored.

Allen (1995) conducted an insightful study comparing the science worldviews of Kickapoo Indians, the most culturally conservative Native American group in the United States, and those of the Anglo teachers and of the standard textbooks used in a Texas middle school. Allen found that the worldviews expressed by the textbooks were dominant as opposed to harmonistic, reductionist as opposed to holistic, positivist as opposed to relativistic, and linear in terms of time–space orientation rather than cyclic—in other words, the opposite of the worldview characteristic of the Kickapoo culture. However, it should be noted that the worldviews of the textbooks were also opposite those of the more contemporary understanding of science, insofar as science is seen as the product of a community of knowers working with a changing body of knowledge. In this, the Kickapoo and the contemporary view of science are more closely aligned.

In contrast, the science teachers of these children tended to have worldviews that were dominant, reductionist, linear, and authoritarian. So teachers' views were like those expressed in the texts. Allen found that differences in worldviews, language and communication patterns, learning and motivational styles created frustrations for both Indian students and teachers. Interestingly, there was a great deal of overlap between American Indian students and teachers in one area—epistemology. In this area, students, teachers, and texts were congruent: All three reflected a 17th century rationalist philosophy reflected by Newtonian physics. Teachers and students tended to have mixed epistemologies, with the students tending a bit more toward empiricism and the teachers more toward authority, but to all, facts were facts. The students, however, did not thrive in the school environment and seemed to dislike school science, in contrast to the interest they displayed with Allen when she visited the reservation. If the school's approach to science were updated to align with contemporary views of the nature of science and constructivist science teaching, the result would be more cultural continuity between Kickapoo worldview and school science.

The implications of this line of inquiry may explain the reasons why some students have difficulty learning science—a mismatch of worldviews. Yet, this explanation is too facile and is not supported by the current evidence. In fact, it appears that deep understanding of scientific worldview may be elusive in all cultures. It is more individual than cultural. To date, no one has identified a particular culture with a particular worldview that leads to science success or failure (W. W. Cobern, personal communication, February 4, 1997).

What about the success of Asians abroad in school science or the achievement test results of Asian Americans in the United States? Can this be accounted for by an Asian worldview that is culturally compatible with science or something else? Lee (1995, 1997) speculated that Asian achievement in science is more a matter of science and learning style rather than culturally compatible worldviews. Regardless of social class or language background, most Asian American students must cope with cultural differences between home and school. Asian cultures expect students to obey authority, including teachers, and not assert opinions in public. The Asian American cultures also expect students to be hard working, well behaved, and academically successful even in severe hardships. A consequence of this pressure is that many Asian American students become high achievers with good grades, but passive learners who avoid risk-taking or the creative process—attributes that are important for advancement in scientific and technological fields. The stereotype of Asian American students attaining academic excellence in mathematics and science hides the social and psychological problems associated with continuous stress related to high achievement. It may also mask learning difficulties in other subject areas (Lee, 1995, 1997). Worldview, as it aligns with the nature of science, is interesting, but the matter of worldview, as it is exhibited in learning style, may better explain differences in science performance.

CULTURE, WORLDVIEW, AND STYLE: CONFLICT OR COMPATIBILITY IN THE SCIENCE CLASSROOM

The Kickapoo study just discussed shows not only differences in worldview between the culture of school science and that of the traditional Kickapoo, but also dramatically documents differences in values, communication, and patterns in interaction arising from worldview (Allen, 1995). These differences can result in frustrating experiences for teachers and students in the science classroom. Allen pointed out that science classrooms in particular may be susceptible to value conflicts. For the Kickapoo and other American Indian/Alaska Native groups, certain materials, such as mammal or bird skins, may not be touched, dissections are repellent, and blood, saliva, or urine collection can cause offense that goes far beyond squeamishness. In the classroom, the Kickapoo students seldom participated in discussions unless in one group voice, did not seem to value grades, preferred cooperative work to competitive and individual activities, and often missed school for long periods of time (for travel to religious events). The teachers interpreted this as being disinterested in school or believed that the lack of communication signaled learning disabilities. On the reservation where the children acted freely as Kickapoos, Allen found them to be talkative, interested in science, and cooperative, engaging her in long hours of conversation on the nature of science and school. They enjoyed particularly using the 800 number she set up as part of data collection in her study. The teachers, on the other hand, never visited the reservation, did not understand the culture, responded insensitively to the children, and often negatively interpreted their Kickapoo students' responses to their teaching. Students and teachers both agreed that the nearby community responded with antipathy to the Kickapoo.

Differences in interactional styles between a White middle-class culture, typically characteristic of the school ethos, and that of other ethnic groups are often quite striking. Consider the following excerpt from an article by Eber Hampton (1991), an American Indian scholar and educator who directed a teacher education project for American Indian/Alaska Native preservice teachers at Harvard:

> In the homes of my white friends at Harvard, I was shocked to find that common child rearing practices involved such pseudo-dialogues such as: "Put your coat on. It is cold out today; you can see that the sun has gone behind the clouds. That is why it is cold. And when it is cold you will need to wear your coat. Put one arm here. Put the other arm here. Now I will zip it for you. Now you will be warm even though it is cold out. Are you going to be warm now?" . . . What wonderful training for multiple choice tests that teach there is one right answer and the authority figure knows it. . . .
>
> In Barrow, Alaska, my friend's children will not do well on multiple-choice tests. Riding in a truck in companionable silence, all I could see was the flat snow to the horizon when suddenly my friend's five-year-old pointed. His father stopped the truck and got the binoculars out. He used them to look in the direction his son had pointed and nodded as he handed them to me. After some searching I found five little dots in the snow. One moved. "What are they?" I asked. "Tutu" (caribou). "Are you going to shoot them?" his son asked. "No son, we have enough." And to me, "He has good eyes." (pp. 302–303)

Similar observations have been made about the learning style, interaction, and communication of Black Americans and the differences in the schools' expectations. Wade Boykin (1986), a Howard University psychologist who is a codirector of Center for Research on the Education of Students Placed At Risk (CRESPAR), a large project designed to improve education for "students placed at risk by the system," maintained that the cultural styles and patterns of West Africa still can be found in the culture of Black Americans today, despite the debilitating effects of 300 years of racism and oppression. Like the situation of American Indians/Alaska Natives, some aspects of the West African legacy may be culturally at odds with mainstream strivings. Boykin did not believe that the West African culture survived intact among Black Americans in the United States. Belief systems and worldviews have been transformed and now include mainstream values. Yet, behavioral practices, values, and outcomes consistent with West African traditions abound in the lives of Black Americans today. This may be true even if Black Americans are not overtly aware of the origins of such behaviors and beliefs. However, in addition to West African and mainstream cultures, Black Americans also must cope with minority status in the United States that has been linked to pejorative conceptions of race. Thus, Boykin saw a *Triple Quandary* for Black Americans: first, a worldview simultaneously influenced by coping responses to historical, pervasive racism; second, the mainstream ethic of rugged individualism—you can make it if you try hard enough—both of which are simmered in the broth of an old West African culture that may be the root of identity, behavior, and values, the third aspect of the quandary. Boykin (1986) stated, "The African Americans' psychological repertoire is not merely expedient or defensive and it does not just represent inadequate imitation of White people. It is a culturally indigenous basis from which Afro-Americans interpret and negotiate reality" (p. 66).

Boykin (1994) identified 9 elements of this Black American cultural style: spirituality, harmony, movement, verve, affect, communalism, expressive individualism, orality, and social time perspective. These cultural characteristics may not always align well with the mainstream culture that students encounter in the school. These differences create misunderstandings between teachers and students that are too easily interpreted as Black students' lack of ability or motivation, or as White teachers' lack of regard for their students when they try to correct behavior that may be culturally appropriate. If, for instance, free movement is part of a cultural fabric, and if school children are required to stay in their seats all day long, dissension may result if some children seem either unwilling or unable to sit for long periods of time and furthermore cannot see why they should.

There is also a danger of stereotyping and overgeneralization when schools clumsily attempt to respond to cultural differences. A small local scandal that occurred a couple of years ago when all of the Black American children in a socioeconomically and ethnically diverse middle school were invited to attend afterschool grammar classes designed, in part, to correct Black English and to raise verbal test scores. Middle-class Black parents were especially incensed and the situation was not improved by the number of errors in the letter of invitation from the principal.

Verve, defined by Boykin (1986) as a propensity for high levels of stimulation and action that is energetic and lively, is another attribute that may have different value in White and Black cultures. I recently saw an example of verve at work in the middle school science classroom: Dr. T, a Black American woman, invited me to visit science classes in an ethnically and socioeconomically diverse middle school. The school also had special programs for students with disabilities and a substantial number of ESL students. Dr. T was the science department chair, a highly experienced teacher who was also at home in the world of education theory. She was clearly an architect of a science program that attended to equity issues. This translated into an approach in which every student was seen as a valuable learner of science. Dr. T could report, without referring to records, how many children of color were included in the gifted and talented science sections and the types of certifications held by teachers working with students with disabilities (almost all were taught by certified science teachers). She saw to it that a Russian ESL student, recently mainstreamed into science, was paired with another Russian girl whose English was farther along. There was no ban on speaking one's first language in these science classrooms if it helped students to understand science concepts. (Elena, the Salvadoran child from chap. 1 would have a good chance at success in this school, a school that seems more the exception than the rule.)

After a cordial, lengthy conversation—highly professional and academic—about the structure of the program, Dr. T invited me to observe her teach a sixth grade science class. There, I witnessed her change into another person altogether. As she began to teach, her oral and body language segued into the Black vernacular. Her speaking voice got loud, her expressions more animated, and she peppered her speech with rhetorical flourishes and dramatic pauses. She became a sort of supercharged teacher. The students responded in kind. When the volume of the lesson increased to a point where I would have sought to settle the students down, she added fuel to the fire by making a joke that the students thought was outrageous. The children responded as if they were being entertained as much as taught. Sixth graders, like puppies straining at their leashes, actually begged to be called on. Moreover, there was something about the interactive nature of the discussion that required the students to listen to one another (rare in teacher-directed classrooms like this one), even though Dr. T was clearly seen as the ultimate arbiter of what was correct or not in their responses. Most important, this lesson was not educational fluff. It was on identifying independent variables that might affect a variety of real-life situations, and one of the few I have seen that seemed even vaguely in line with my conception of the new science standards. She derived it from resource material designed for gifted and talented children, but this was a heterogeneous classroom.

Every child was involved. Every child answered questions, even those who were recently mainstreamed from the ESL. One Hispanic girl (our Elena?) softly gave the same perfectly uttered, one-word response "temperature" to several of the situations, but she was always correct and safe with her answer. Everyone, including Dr. T, seemed to have a wonderful time. A student sitting near me, a White girl, gave an unsolicited testimonial to Dr. T's skills—Dr. T was the best teacher because she understood middle school kids.

Indeed, walking down the school corridors with Dr. T you could see students' faces light up as they greeted her. This seemed especially true for the Black children—there was a special bond there—but certainly Dr. T's sunny ministrations rained on all, insisting that each student whom she came upon in the hallway or lunchroom acknowledge that there was a unique relationship between the two of them that both delighted in. Thus, Dr. T. seemed to be the perfect example of a teacher with verve. Is this an artifact perhaps of her West African roots? Certainly not all Black American teachers have this sort of flamboyant teaching style or exuberant warmth—there is obviously a huge range of styles, personalities, and skills among all teachers of any ethnicity. Yet, it seemed that Dr. T's manner, sensibilities, and position in the school as a person in authority helped to make the school an exciting place where all students could learn thoughtful, inquiry based science.

It is reasonable to wonder about how the cultural style and worldview of the teacher affects students in his or her classroom. Are there some matches that create both better interpersonal understanding and a more effective learning environment? Lee and Fradd (1996a, 1998) are two researchers at the University of Miami who began to systematically explore the effects of cultural congruence and the active engagement of students in the science classroom. In one study, they matched the language and ethnicity of teachers—White, Hispanic, or Haitian Creole—with that of pairs of students and recorded the patterns of interaction over a series of science activities. For White monolingual English speakers, verbal discourse dominated, with little nonverbal communication. There was relatively little body movement and greater physical distance between teacher and students than in any other group. Teachers seemed to convey the importance of individual effort rather than group participation, with emphasis on academic performance. Teachers and students focused on the task and there was little social interaction. Teachers tended to ask questions as opposed to telling. This is the mode of interaction encouraged in inquiry-based education, a style recommended by the new science education reforms. It should perhaps be noted that the majority of the authors of the reforms are White, so the stylistic similarity is predictable. On the other hand, many of the contributors are also practicing scientists, and seem well qualified to make observations about the centrality of inquiry to science.

In the second group, bilingual Spanish speakers, the Hispanic students and the teachers engaged in multiple simultaneous speech, unlike the other groups that used sequential speech patterns. When one person started a sentence, another might complete it, creating overlaps in discourse. At times, both teachers and students gave long, uninterrupted monologues. Students displayed little body movement, but used their hands extensively to supplement or enhance meaning. There was frequent physical contact between students and teacher. The teachers tended to teach directly rather than probing students for answers. There was an emphasis on social interaction as teachers and students playfully coconstructed stories and shared ideas.

In the third group, bilingual Haitian-Creole speakers, teacher talk dominated and the students appeared to be shy or reserved. The tempo of the discussion was at a slower pace and there were longer silences (i.e., wait time) than in other groups. Teachers often switched languages to make sure that they were being understood. Students used little body movement but extensive hand motions to replace or supplement speech. The exchanges seemed to be characterized by respect for the authority of the teacher. Teachers seldom praised students verbally, although they reinforced them through smiles and nods. When unsure of an answer, students looked down, and female students sometimes hid their faces in their hands if asked to perform individually.

It is not hard to imagine how cultural congruence, or a lack of it, might affect students in science classrooms. Students must cope with differences in culture and worldview, as well as with unfamiliar teaching styles. Moreover, science is often experienced as a new language for even native speakers of English, with more abstract, new vocabulary encountered each day than one would expect in a foreign language class.

How likely is a student to draw a science teacher of the same ethnicity? In other words, what are the chances of cultural continuity between home and school for a given student? If the student is White, the chances are excellent. The vast majority of science teachers are White, and White males predominate more as the grades in school ascend. According to 1990 NAEP information for mathematics, 93% of White students had White mathematics teachers in Grade 4 and 95% by Grade 8. In contrast, only 40% of Black students had Black teachers in Grade 4 and by Grade 8, the percentage was reduced to 21%. For Hispanic students, the percentages were 8% in Grade 4 and 13% by Grade 8 (NSF, 1992; see Table 4.1). The situation seems to be worsening rather than improving; the percentage of Black teachers in elementary schools decreased between 1986 and 1993 from 10% to 5% (NSF, 1996a). At the high school level, about 93% of Grade 12 science teachers were White, with the remaining 7% divided equally among ethnic groups. For American Indians/Alaska Native students, Hampton (1991) saw the fundamental educational need for the future as increasing the number of native persons as teachers and administrators. The situation for any underrepresented group is not likely to change in the foreseeable future—the proportion of science teachers of color is not increasing.

Now, if science is science, then *cultural continuity*—the ethnic match between teachers and students—ought not to make a jot of difference. Yet, in reviewing the tantalizing and intuitively sensible material on worldview, as well as the research on learning and interactional styles, and in visiting science classrooms taught by real teachers, it seems impossible to escape the conclusion that school science would be vastly improved if the population of science teachers more closely mirrored the population of students who were sitting in front of them. White teachers, especially, might stand to gain from working collegially in science departments that were more diverse in terms of language, ethnicity, and gender. However, there is the dearth of new science teachers of color coming through the teacher preparation system.

TABLE 4.1
Percent of Students With Mathematics Teachers of Different Races and Ethnicities, by Student Characteristics, Grades 4 and 8: 1990

| Grade and student characteristic | Percent of Total | Percent With | | | Teacher's race not reported |
		White teacher	Black teacher	Hispanic teacher	
Grade 4	100	85	11	2	2
Male	100	85	11	2	2
Female	100	85	11	2	2
White	100	93	5	1	1
Black	100	57	40	2	1
Hispanic	100	75	13	8	4
Grade 8	100	91	5	3	1
Male	100	91	5	3	1
Female	100	91	6	2	1
White	100	95	3	2	0
Black	100	77	21	2	0
Hispanic	100	80	5	13	2

Note.   From *Indicators of Science and Mathematics Education 1992* by NSF, 1992.

The average age of science teachers—mostly White, monolingual English speakers—is about 42 years (NSF, 1996a) and most have been in the system for years. One such teacher spoke wistfully of the times when his highly ethnically and socioeconomically diverse school was populated primarily by middle-class, orthodox Jewish children—"This was a good school before the minority kids arrived." If we can get past the obvious bias in his statement, it is possible to see a middle-aged man who finds himself less successful than he used to be. He has no frame of reference to analyze the situation without assigning blame to the new students who do not learn in the same way nor have the same motivations as his former students. His school system provided neither the training nor the incentive system to help him out—many of these students do not get the high achievement test scores so valued by his school system, nor are they easily drawn to science. Moreover, he is not likely to be assisted by some education literature that suggests that he, as a member of the dominant group, reinforce in his teaching practice a hegemonic system designed to deny power to his subjugated students. For the moment, let us leave aside the accuracy of this type of analysis and come back to this teacher. Unless he is an unmitigated bigot or totally burned out, he is probably working hard and long under stressful conditions. He finds that his old lessons, once successful, are simply not connecting with his new students.

His negative attitudes might be replaced by more positive ones if he could experience some success in his teaching practice, and accomplishment for him seems likely to mean success for his students. This human issue is crucial to effective science education reform for all. We are told that many White males who make up the majority of the secondary science teacher population value competition and individual recognition. If this is so, until we find ways to redefine student achievement in science—and standardized assessments are not fertile ground—and recognize teachers who are accomplished in getting substantial science performance from students in underrepresented groups, progress will be slow.

In the Project 2061 Equity Blueprint that was the impetus for this volume, Secada (1995) pointed out that within the discourse on virtually all student groups who are considered low achieving in the sciences, the belief that, somehow, the problems involving underachievement and underrepresentation can be traced to students' deficiencies. The sources of, and what to do about, such deficiencies may be open to debate; nonetheless, it is assumed that personal, psychological, and/or social deficiencies exist. For instance, often the assumption is made that Hispanics are less capable, are limited English proficient, are poor, do not have the right attitudes for persisting in science course taking, have beliefs about their abilities that do not match the beliefs of students who are good in science, are concrete thinkers, are field dependent (or field sensitive), live in high-crime areas, are crack babies, (choose all that apply). As lyrics in the *West Side Story's* Officer Krumpke go, "I'm depraved on account of I'm deprived."

The challenge, according to that literature, is to somehow overcome the deficiencies that Hispanic students bring with them to school. Indeed, Hispanic students, by virtue of their membership in a demographic group, are now considered educationally at-risk and a challenge to schools. One result is that people are often surprised to encounter a Hispanic who, in fact, is good in science. Hence, a pervasive barrier to Hispanics' making it in science-related careers is the belief that the lowering of standards through affirmative action—as opposed to personal knowledge, effort, and tenacity—is the root cause of an individual's having made it as far as he or she has.

Secada (1995) pointed out that it would seem difficult, if not impossible, to devise and promote a solution to Hispanic underachievement and underrepresentation as long as such beliefs are at the core of solutions to the equity issue. Rather, we must reorient the discussion: Assume that the basic premises of the reform movement in the sciences (AAAS, 1989; Mathematical Sciences Education Board, MSEB, 1990; NCTM, 1989, 1991; NRC, 1989) are correct—that the curriculum, as currently constituted, is full of disconnected facts, is organized in ways that interfere with how people learn, and is focused on out-of-date, essentially meaningless knowledge that has little relevance to participatory democracy and everyday life, including spheres of work. Assume that instruction repeatedly covers the same low level content and provides students with few (or no) opportunities to make sense of what they are encountering. In other words, assume that the reform movement is correct in its characterization of the current state of affairs.

Secada asked, what would a mature adult's reactions be? Most adults would resist such conditions. They might disengage from the activities that are so offensive—not read the materials, not participate in class activities, ignore the teacher, talk among themselves, and involve themselves in more meaningful activities. Not surprisingly, if tests were given, these individuals would perform poorly. What is more, they simply might stop taking such courses; indeed, in an extreme act of voting with their feet, they would simply drop out of the organization and activity that was treating them in such a manner.

If this constitutes a mature adult reaction to the inadequacies of school science, then the question is: Who, among students, behaves like a mature adult? The answer is precisely those populations who are under-achieving and underrepresented in science-related courses and careers (i.e., the poor, Hispanics, Black Americans, and some females). Instead of their being stereotyped as not possessing scientific knowledge or being deficient, maybe these students have reacted in an understandable man-ner to what the reform movement has recently realized. Their perform-ance and behaviors may, in fact, be the result of the social contexts in which they have encountered the sciences, and are the harbinger of what is increasingly the case for the majority of students who are less frequently choosing the sciences.

If this analysis is even partly correct, then, Secada (1995) suggested, it leads to three recommendations. First, the discourse surrounding un-derachievement and underrepresentation needs to be expanded, if not entirely changed. Like the canary brought into the coal mines to warn the miners of bad air because of its heightened sensitivity, underachieve-ment may have been an early warning of the sad state of school science in general. Second, additional research is needed on features in a par-ticular culture and the likely sociopsychological profiles of students in that culture and how this could explain why these young people sense and react as they do. This work would need to be based on sociopsychological notions of maturity and competent judgments. Third—and from the standpoint of science education reform, most importantly—the reform in the teaching of the sciences needs to begin with those populations who have resisted earlier school-based efforts to teach the sciences. These students are likely to be the best judges about whether the reform efforts have it right: Does the curriculum allow for sense making? Is the curricu-lum connected to the world in ways that are similar to the goals for scientific literacy? Does instruction really build on what students under-stand? Unless the reform efforts are tested with underachieving popula-tions, they cannot truly succeed in their mission.

THE DARK SIDE OF WORLDVIEW: PREJUDICE AND BIAS IN THE SCIENCE CLASSROOM

It's been a rough past few weeks for black America—from passage of an anti-affirmative action ballot initiative in California to the acquittal of two white police officers who had each killed a black motorist in Pittsburgh and Saint Petersburg. There have been revelations of widespread racial discrimination at Texaco, Inc. And allegations of it at Avis Rent-a-Car System, Inc. An FBI report released two weeks ago found that nearly two-thirds of all hate-crimes reported in the United States in 1995 were motivated by anti-black bias. So were most black church burnings. It all seems so bleak—especially given the American ideal of being a color-blind society. (Malloy, 1996, p. B1)

It seems that a chapter on worldview, a positive analytical interpretation of differing responses to science, must also sadly acknowledge the presence of bias, stereotyping, and prejudice that resides in the United States and must sometimes spill over into the schools and science classrooms. Especially troubling is the number of individuals whose worldview is driven by hate—manifest in the increase in the number of organized groups whose primary purpose is racism, anti-Semitism, sexism, and homophobia—skinheads, neo-Nazis, and militias (that are not always racist in intent, but frequently are), as well as the greater visibility of the Nation of Islam whose leaders sometimes sink to hate speech. In some parts of the country—rural, urban, and suburban—educators are organizing to teach students about human rights and how to understand differences, to counteract local symptoms of a worldview suffused with hate, distrust, and potential violence. Prejudice and bias are also outlooks inhospitable to the practice of critical thinking (weighing of evidence) and rationality and seem to be something with which science educators must concern themselves.

In schools, the discord may be more often based on ignorance rather than virulence. There is a simple lack of familiarity with the worldviews, cultural mores, and behaviors of some students that can result in misunderstanding, insensitivity, and worse, although most teachers do not do this consciously (Nieto, 1996). This is something that is not often documented in the quantitative research literature, although it sometimes creeps out. For instance, one fourth of non-Indian K–12 teachers reported that they did not want to teach Indian children, and at the same time, it was found that a major cause of dropout was poor student–teacher relationships (Hampton, 1991).

> Expectations are bound up with the biases we have learned to internalize. If we expect (poor) children . . . to be poor readers, then we reflect this in the modifications we make in the way we teach them. Similarly, if we expect girls to be passive and submissive, we may teach them as if they were. Perhaps our sensitivity to a deaf child's learning needs results in a belief that she cannot learn as quickly as a hearing child. Although our teaching approaches are either frequently unconscious or developed with the best of intentions, the results can be disastrous. (Nieto, 1996, p. 366)

The multicultural education literature is rich in typologies and recommendations for moving a school to a multicultural environment that goes beyond Black History Month and ethnic food days. The ultimate goal is to create a transformed school in which the educators and students have reflective and positive ethnic, national, and global identifications and the knowledge, skills, and commitment needed to function within cultures throughout the national or international world (Banks, 1994). A school such as this would draw from the various worldviews of its students, as well as its teachers, to build a lively and effective science program.

There is also the dilemma of what to do about affirmative action and the forms it should or should not take. Cora Marrett, a sociologist who is currently the Provost of the University of Massachusetts–Amherst and cochair of the original Equity Blueprint Committee pointed out that studies on intergroup relationships have illuminated what is called the *paradox of contemporary racial attitudes* (Bobo, 1988; Marrett & Zeige, 1995). This is the discrepancy between support for the principles of equality and the lack of support for policies designed to help bring it about. For example, research on attitudes toward affirmative action indicates that a majority of Americans believe that equal opportunity is no longer a problem for individuals or for groups and that in comparison to an average person, women, Blacks, and people from poor and working-class backgrounds have a better than average chance for getting ahead (Kluegel & Smith, 1986). They believe that structural inequality is a problem of the past, and thus, there is no need to address this in public policy. The recent recision of affirmative action initiatives in the State of California and decisions by the Supreme Court limiting affirmative action are indicative of this tendency (Kahlenberg, 1995a). On the other hand, in a 1991 study, economist David Zimmermann (in Kahlenberg, 1995b) reported that only 12% of the boys born into the bottom quartile of income rose to the top quartile, whereas 69% were in the lower half. This stubborn intransigence is echoed in other areas of achievement and progress—for instance, the persistent gaps among various groups in science achievement presented in chapters 2 and 3.

Adding to the complexity of this issue is the long-held, U.S. traditional commitment to the notion of *rugged individualism*—the ability for anyone, no matter how dire the circumstances, to bootstrap his or her way to success. Although group-level barriers are acknowledged, most Americans endorse the idea that such barriers can and should be overcome by individual efforts. For instance, Governor Pete Wilson, on the day that the California Regents Board voted to roll back affirmative action said, "We can't tolerate policies that trample on individual rights. What we want to do is celebrate the individual" (Booth, 1995).

Consequently, when members of groups do not appear to take opportunities, it may be seen as their fault, that they did not try hard enough, or that they do not have what it takes to succeed. This attitude plays itself out in science education. For instance, there is a well-documented tendency for Black, Hispanic, or American Indian students to take fewer courses in science and mathematics than Whites and Asian Americans (recent data show that females take only one semester less than males). Because admission to such courses is often not overtly denied or may be based on a school's definition of merit and past performance, the different participation rates of various ethnic groups has, until relatively recently, gone largely unremarked and uncontested (Oakes, 1985; Slavin, 1990). Why have such practices, even more prevalent in science than in other subjects, been allowed to occur unchallenged for decades? In part, because we expected science to be the province of the select few who could do it, as opposed to recognizing the need for science literacy for all (Lynch, 1994). Yet, we must discuss the unpleasant reality that social attitudes, stereotyping, and bias are also root causes of inequities in science.

Bias, stereotyping, and low expectations are also at work in areas other than ethnicity and gender. Cawley (1994) and Stefanich (1994), science educators who specialize in students with disabilities, pointed out that society tends to devalue persons with disabilities, leading many such individuals to come to devalue themselves as well. U.S. education's long-standing history of low expectations for students with disabilities influences: the amount of time students with disabilities spend learning science and being actively engaged in investigation in the science laboratory; the academic focus and quality of objectives; the sequence and depth of the learning opportunities afforded to these students; access to knowledge and resources; homework expectations; and curriculum alignment. The results of low expectations are often cumulative, forcing many students with disabilities to pursue careers that do not reflect scientific interests or talents.

Instruction for the majority of students with ample cognitive power but with physical or sensory disabilities also reflects low expectations. In a nationwide investigation of science opportunities for youth with physical disabilities, Redden (1978) reported that the majority of students receive science instruction that is inadequate to prepare them for a career in science or science education.

If it is true that bias, stereotyping, and restriction of opportunity covertly or overtly influence who takes science courses, who succeeds in these courses, and who goes on to careers in related areas, then educational situations designed to eliminate these negative forces ought to demonstrate very different results. Indeed, there is plenty of evidence that this is the case. In higher education, for instance, the extraordinary successes of women who graduate from all-female institutions (Tidball & Kistiakowsky, 1976) and of Black Americans who attended Historically Black Colleges and Universities are well documented. Treisman's (1990) work with Black American mathematics students at the University of California at Berkeley showed that Black students' success in introductory calculus classes could be bolstered if there was an emphasis on excellence and acceleration rather than remediation. Black students were helped to form social and study groups for math, as Asian students at that university often do. Other studies reported that students of color benefited from mentors (Gibbons, 1992) and that retention rates for engineering students of color were improved when students had close relationships with faculty, bonded with the institution, and felt a sense of community (Morning, 1988). A positive racial attitude on campus is associated with good academic performance and persistence. When students feel alienated from campus social and academic life, attrition rates increase (Clewell & Ficklen cited in Matyas & Malcom, 1991).

In order to encourage the participation of women in science in higher education, particularly in fields like physics and engineering, it may be necessary for women at a particular institution to achieve critical mass status. When enough women are present as students and faculty, classroom performance and retention rates for women become indistinguishable from those of their male counterparts (Dresselhous, Franz, & Clark, 1994). The physicists who conducted this study found the following:

> It is not enough for faculty members to give good lectures and conduct world-class research. As educators, faculty members must also be concerned about providing a welcoming environment for their colleagues and students. Constructive attitudes, a caring approach, open communication channels between faculty and students, and good will can go a long way for enhancing outcomes for students and faculty members. (p. 1393)

Do the lessons learned from higher education research on increasing participation and achievement for students of color apply to K–12 science classrooms? There is ample evidence that this is the case (cf. Hilton, Hsia, Solorzano & Benton, 1988; Matyas & Malcom, 1991). The same principles—conscious reduction of bias, creating a caring academic and social environment for students taking sciences, acceleration rather than remediation, and high expectations and open encouragement to pursue science—seem to apply to K–12 science programs as much as they do in higher education.

The work done by Casserly (1979), who focused on female participation in high school science, may be extrapolated for other groups. Casserly studied high schools that had high rates of female participation and achievement in the College Board AP science and mathematics examinations. The focus of her study was on gifted and talented girls. Casserly's formula for success, based on her analysis of school science programs that resulted in high achievement and participation rates for girls as well as boys, included recruiting promising female students by science teachers, negating the bias of guidance counselors' advice to young women, teachers explicitly encouraging girls in science class, forming critical mass, and nurturing social groups around academic science. In the 1990s, with science for all as the goal, Casserly's findings seemed applicable for all female students, students of color, and students with disabilities. Other examples of K–12 science programs displaying similar features can be found in a Ford Foundation publication documenting 163 precollege programs designed to encourage minority students' interest in the sciences in the middle school years (Clewell, Thorpe, & Anderson, 1987).

RECOMMENDATIONS FOR SCIENCE
EDUCATION REFORM

There is nothing magical, or in many cases, even financially costly about these recommendations to combat bias, stereotyping, and restriction of opportunity in K–12 science education. Within schools, it is possible to imagine a set of vectors, arrows, all pointed toward the goal of a more responsive science education for all students, one that is constructivist in practice, as opposed to giving lipservice to constructivism. Teachers need to understand their students' cultures, worldviews, interactional styles, and behavior patterns. In preservice teacher education, a required course in multicultural education or diversity often provides an opportunity for this exploration, but it is not enough. Courses that give new teachers opportunities to learn through fieldwork and research using methodologies borrowed from anthropology or psychology seem likely to capture the nuances and variations of a culture. Such courses may be more effective than those that generate laundry lists of cultural characteristics, perhaps leading to further stereotyping rather than a deep understanding of the culture and its subtleties and variations.

Veteran teachers need to understand their students as much as novices do. For example, an experienced elementary school teacher who taught in five states and abroad, accepted a teaching job in rural Florida. Before school started, her principal, a transplant from New York City, took all of the new teachers on a field trip to show them where and how their students lived. The teacher remarked about the importance of that outing in preparing her to teach rural, poor children, as she had never seen such conditions of poverty, nor children as removed from the mainstream.

Teachers who have been teaching at the same school for years may need a similar opportunity to get to know their students, particularly if they are working with new populations. Unfortunately, school organization often does not provide opportunities for teachers to do this, and the problem seems especially severe at the high school level where it is not unusual for teachers to see more than 150 students per day. The more personal nature of elementary schools and the middle school team organization makes these situations more promising.

In science education, the importance of knowing students well, is as important pedagogically as it is interpersonally. Virtually all current science education methods texts and the alternative conception literature (see chap. 5) point out the need for preassessment in some form, as new concepts are encountered. However, this seems to be one of those recommendations that is left behind in the school of education when teachers begin their practice.

It also seems wise that, within schools, there is a concerted effort to hire teachers whose ethnicity reflects the student population, who speak more than one language, or who have had extensive intercultural experiences. Given the huge numbers of science teachers slated to retire by 2010, this could be done without pushing any current teachers out of a job, if there was a will and funding to do so (read more about this in chap. 8). An excellent example of a principal who has done this is Maria Tukeva of Bell Multicultural High School in Washington, DC. Bell is a magnet school designed to serve ethnically diverse students, many of whom are new to the United States. Over the years, this principal has managed to recruit and hire a faculty, including science teachers, that mirrors the student population. Most faculty members speak at least two languages, represent ethnic groups, and all have as their explicit goal, teaching diverse learners in a setting in which multicultural educational is the warp and the instructional program is the weft of a vibrant school fabric.

Chapters 2 and 3 examined groupings of students according to various categories—gender, ethnicity, SES, presence of disabling conditions, and so on—in order to understand the parameters of an equity agenda for science education reform. However, these categories are crude—a more salient attribute in terms of school success is students' views of science in relation to the teacher's worldview and that of accompanying curricular materials. These heady, epistemological differences, however, may be of far less consequence than the cultural congruence of the students' learning styles and teaching style that prevails in the classroom. This unique concoction can lead to a rich and stimulating multicultural classroom, or one where the various parts never successfully blend and result in disappointments for all—teacher and students.

Those dysfunctional science classrooms exist. It can almost palpably be felt when the classroom is entered—students slumped over at their desk, not making eye contact with the teacher or even one another, only hoping not to be asked to do much. The teacher accommodating them with mundane assignments that spark the interest of no one, including the teacher. The results are that the students do not learn much science and like it even less, and the teacher blames the students for failing to learn. Over time, this can lead to prejudice and stereotyping that are reflected in school organization and inequitable distribution of resources and opportunity to learn.

On the other hand, science classrooms can be vital places in which teachers experiment with inventive methods to meet the needs of new populations of diverse learners. As with any experiment, many fail, but in talking to the teachers, you can hear them describe their students' differences in positive terms, like a puzzle to be solved. American teachers who have never traveled outside the United States are introduced to exotic places and hear of incredible hardships through their students, and many are inspired by their students' lives. (Mr. N, whose story began this chapter, liked his Afghan student and wanted to help him.)

It must be recognized that there is more to meaningful and substantive science education than simply creating a nurturing environment for students who have been bypassed by science education in the past. There are plenty of examples of school districts where measures of self-esteem related to science and mathematics are high, but performance measures are low. This sets students up for failure when the students make the transition to higher education and find that they do not have the academic background necessary to succeed. This often occurs in urban as well as rural schools and in high poverty schools everywhere.

The science education community has offered the teachers who are on the line and in the trenches little beyond broad recommendations (sometimes platitudes) on how to teach diverse learners. The research has not kept up with the demographic changes and new expectations for the inclusion of students with disabilities in U.S. schools. Commercial curricula are just beginning to respond to the intent of the new science standards and the diversity of U.S. students. The evaluation and reward system has not caught up with the teachers who are doing the most challenging and valuable work—bringing diverse learners to success in science.

The science education reform efforts have the potential for creating important changes in the way we educate students, beginning with better defined goals. The next chapter examines bedrock curricular issues, what students are expected to learn, and the tools that assist teachers in helping students to attain these outcomes.

5

Curricular Issues: Whose Science Is It? Whose Could It Be?

"Cheshire-Puss," she began rather timidly ... "Would you tell me, please, which way I ought to go from here?"
"That depends a good deal on where you want to get to," said the Cat.
"I don't much care where—" said Alice.
"Then it doesn't matter which way you go," said the Cat.
"—so long as I get somewhere," Alice added as an explanation.
"Oh, you're sure to do that," said the Cat, "if you only walk long enough."
—*Alice's Adventures in Wonderland*
(Lewis G. Carroll, 1946, pp. 71–72)

MISCONCEPTIONS

The film, *A Private Universe* (Harvard-Smithsonian Center for Astrophysics, 1993), provides a view of a world different from the one that Alice experiences in Lewis G. Carroll's classic, but one no less idiosyncratic or puzzling. The film begins with the solemn tolling of a bell, heralding new Harvard University graduates at their commencement ceremonies. The students are resplendent in their crimson and black caps and gowns and seem full of equal measures of hope and confidence. The voice of an unseen interviewer asks them an apparently simple, yet odd question, given the setting: Can you explain why we have the seasons?

The graduates, with the quick, cooperative instincts of good students everywhere, respond with explanations—thoughtful, articulate, and completely wrong. Most believe that the seasons are caused by the earth moving closer to or farther from the sun. They hold an exaggerated notion of the earth's elliptical orbit. Of the 23 Harvard graduates, alumni, and faculty interviewed, 21 cannot accurately explain the causes of the

95

seasons or for the phases of the moon. One graduate, secure in his erroneous explanation, even ticks off the related courses he had taken—physics, astronomy, and planetary motion. Yet, his answer is no better than that of another who points out how far she has gotten by avoiding science courses. All of those interviewed have common, tightly held misconceptions of the earth's orbit and the nature of light, despite the fact that each has received an education that most would regard as being among the best in the country.

The film proceeds to explore the phenomenon (misconceptions about the seasons) in ninth grade students who have had far less science. It focuses on one obviously bright and motivated girl, Heather, and illustrates the tenacity of her beliefs, even when timely and specific instruction is provided over weeks and months to help her reason and see a more accurate picture of the situation. Although Heather makes some progress in clearing up her misconceptions, even at the end of the film, it is clear that she still clings to some of her private views of the universe, giving rise to the title of the film and series.

Since the 1970s, cognitive psychologists and science educators have made a cottage industry of unearthing and documenting commonly held misconceptions, or alternative conceptions, in science (e.g., living vs. nonliving things, natural selection, the nature of matter, and forces acting on falling objects). The misconceptions are intuitive or apparently logical explanations of natural phenomena. Even children's animated cartoons may be a source of incorrect notions, such as the trajectory of falling objects—for example, Wile E. Coyote is shown dashing in a straight line off a cliff, pausing in midair to notice his unhappy circumstance, and then plunging straight down.

Teachers are often unaware of their students' private theories. Many misconceptions even originate in the classroom and are intuitively appealing. For example, the difficulty in understanding what causes the seasons may lie in the exaggerated diagrams of the elliptical orbit of the earth's motion found in many science textbooks or in the case of the phases of the moon, Heather explained that she had learned this in a previous course, but never saw how the sun's light falls on earth and moon in their various positions.

The Private Universe films are powerful. Another segment has MIT graduates awkwardly cradling a heavy maple log in their arms, while they examine a maple seed. The interviewer asks them to explain how the log attained its mass. Most students believe that the mass is mostly from minerals and water in the ground that the tree has absorbed through the roots. Carbon is never mentioned, and when the interviewer prompts one student along these lines, the student says, based on what he knows of carbon's properties, he thinks that it is not likely to be a building block for living things.

During a screening of this clip, I remarked to colleagues viewing the film with me that there is a bright side to all of this: There may indeed be room for hope for equity in science education reform. It seems that if the result of such a costly undergraduate education (a degree from Harvard or MIT must surely cost at least $100,000) is widely held misconceptions about so basic a concept—photosynthesis and the carbon cycle—then surely other young people, those who are high school dropouts or who attend community colleges, could not really be that far behind the Harvard or MIT graduates in their understandings of science.

This relatively recent acknowledgment of the misconceptions research by persons worried about the quality of American science education, coupled with the concerns rising from the business community regarding the lack of science, mathematics, and problem-solving skills of young people entering the workforce, has stimulated the call for science education reform. In response, ex-President Bush with the strong support of the Governors' Conference (led by Bill Clinton, who was governor at that time) and leaders in U.S. business and industry, initiated Goals 2000 (National Education Goals Panel, 1994). This was later endorsed by President Clinton, with substantial nonpartisan backing in Congress. All agreed that the United States must be able to compete in the global economic markets and must have workers who have command over science, mathematics, technology, and problem-solving skills.

The main focus of the reform has been on creating a set of education standards that are high and represent the best thinking of scientists and educators about the learning and skills that are core—crucial for all students. Once the standards were created at the national level, states voluntarily adopt them and develop curricula designed to meet them. Yet, merely announcing higher standards is insufficient for change. The focus of this chapter is on crucial curriculum issues—the standards, curriculum frameworks and materials—although some instructional matters (discussed more fully in chap. 8) ineluctably creep in.

INTERNATIONAL COMPARISONS
OF ACHIEVEMENT AND CURRICULA

Although the misconceptions of research shows why teaching science concepts at a deep level of understanding is so enigmatic, a second approach for both concern and enlightenment emerges from international comparisons of U.S. students' performance in science and mathematics. American students have not performed as well in science and mathematics as their counterparts in other countries. The Third International Mathematics and Science Study (TIMSS), released in 1996, not only documented achievement differences, but attempted to ferret out the causes for the variations in student performance among industrialized countries (U.S. Department of Education, National Center for Education Statistics, 1996b). TIMSS examined the educational systems of 50 countries on five continents, assessing curricular and instructional factors that influence student learning in science and mathematics. It assessed achievement for 9-year-old students, 13-year-olds, and students at the completion of secondary school. The analyses of curriculum and instruction components of the study were primarily aimed at the eighth-grade level. TIMSS provides a more detailed analysis on mathematics curriculum and instruction than science, but the patterns are clear for both areas. Four questions guided these aspects of TIMSS:

1. What have students learned?
2. What are students expected to learn?
3. How is instruction organized?
4. Who delivers instruction (discussed in chaps. 6, 7, and 8)?

What Have Students Learned?

The answer to this question can be seen in Table 5.1. For science, the U.S. students in Grade 8 had an average score of 534, which was slightly above the international average of 516. This result was not significantly different from those of countries such as Germany, England, Canada, or other countries that can be seen clustered around the United States in Table 5.1. (The U.S. performance in mathematics was lower than in science across the board, with scores somewhat below average.) These scores still fall far short of Goal 5 in Goals 2000 (National Education Goals Panel, 1994): By the year 2000, the United States will be first in the world in mathematics and science. The top-scoring countries in TIMSS included Asian countries as well as central European ones. An irony of the U.S. educational system is that although it is world renowned in higher education, especially at the graduate level in science, mathematics, and technology, our K–12 preparatory programs in these disciplines are only mediocre.

A breakdown of the TIMSS science scores by academic discipline shows that U.S. performance was stronger in earth, environmental, and

TABLE 5.1
Nation's Average Science Performance Compared to the U.S.

Nations with average scores significantly higher than the U.S.		Nations with average scores significantly lower than the U.S.	
Nation	Average	Nation	Average
Singapore	607	Spain	517
Czech Republic	574	France	498
Japan	571	(Greece)	497
Korea	565	Iceland	494
(Bulgaria)	565	(Romania)	486
(Netherlands)	560	Latvia (LSS)[b]	485
(Slovenia)	560	Portugal	480
(Austria)	558	(Denmark)	478
Hungary	554	Lithuania[a]	476

Nations with average scores not significantly different from the U.S.		Nations lower (continued)	
		(Belgium-French)	471
		Iran, Islamic Republic	470
		Cyprus	463
Nation	Average	(Kuwait)	430
England [a,b]	552	(Columbia)	411
Belgium-Flemish [b]	550	(South Africa	326
(Australia)	545		
Slovak Republic	544		
Russian Federation	538		
Ireland	538		
Sweden	535		
United States [b]	534		
(Germany) [a,b]	531		
Canada	531		
Norway	527		
New Zealand	525		
(Thailand)	525		
(Israel) [a]	524		
Hong Kong	522		
Switzerland[b]	522		
(Scotland)	517		

Note. Nations not meeting international study guidelines are shown in parentheses. The international average is the average of the national averages of the 41 nations. Latvia is designated LSS because only Latvian-speaking schools were tested, which represents less than 65 percent of the population. From *TIMSS: A Sourcebook of 8th-Grade Findings*, by Mid-Atlantic Eisenhower Consortium for Mathematics and Science Education, 1997.

[a]These are nations in which more than 10% of the population was excluded from testing.

[b]These are nations in which a participation rate of 75% of the schools and students combined was achieved only after replacements for refusals were substituted.

life sciences, than in chemistry and physics (see Table 5.2). Some good news was that there were no significant differences in the scores of U.S. male and female students on TIMSS, and the same was true for 11 other countries. TIMSS scores were not, however, disaggregated by SES or ethnicity. The study permitted some students and schools to be excused from the test, but no more than 10% of the students in a country could have been disallowed. In the United States, it is common to exclude students with disabilities (approximately 12% of the population) and English language learners (about 6%). Actually, more accurate renderings of the euphemism *excused from* are *asked not to take* and *not given access to* standardized tests. If the reported figure of only 2.1% of U.S. students excused from TIMSS is correct, then TIMSS scores represent both a comprehensive view of nearly all students' performance on this test, as well as positive values about the need to include all students in any analysis of our education programs.

Yet, why does the United States, one of the most prosperous, indus-trialized, and scientifically advanced countries in the world and one that expends substantial resources on K–12 education, fare no better than average in science and mathematics achievement? TIMSS provides some clues in its analyses of curriculum and instruction.

What Are Students Expected to Learn?

For science educators, probably the most interesting part of TIMSS is the analyses of data on curriculum, provided in A *Splintered Vision: An Inves-tigation of U.S. Science and Mathematics* (U.S. National Research Center for TIMSS, 1996). The authors of this segment of the TIMSS report begin by saying:

> There is no one at the helm of US science and mathematics education. In truth, there is no one helm. No single coherent vision of how to educate today's children dominates U.S. educational practice in either science or mathematics . . . this is seen in what is planned to be taught, what is in textbooks, and what teachers teach. (p. 1)

Most people would probably view the situation described in this quote as a deplorable state of affairs, but not all, because many people believe that state and local control of schools is preferable to national influence or oversight, no matter what the level of expertise available or degree of bias present at state and local levels. In the United States, because we

TABLE 5.2
National Averages in Science Content Areas

Earth Science		Life Science		Physics	
Nation	Percent Correct	Nation	Percent Correct	Nation	Percent Correct
Singapore	65	Singapore	72	Singapore	69
(Slovenia)	64	Japan	71	Japan	67
Czech Republic	63	Korea	70	Korea	65
Korea	63	Czech Republic	69	Czech Republic	64
Belgium-Flemish [b]	62	(Netherlands)	67	(Netherlands)	63
(Austria)	62	(Thailand)	66	(Austria)	62
Sweden	62	Hungary	65	England [a,b]	62
Norway	61	(Austria)	65	Slovak Republic	61
Ireland	61	(Slovenia)	65	(Slovenia)	61
(Netherlands)	61	(Bulgaria)	64	Belgium-Flemish [b]	61
Japan	61	England [a,b]	64	(Bulgaria)	60
Slovak Republic	60	Belgium-Flemish [b]	64	(Australia)	60
Hungary	60	(Australia)	63	Hungary	60
England [a,b]	59	(Germany) [a,b]	63	Canada	59
Russian Federation	58	UNITED STATES [b]	63	Hong Kong	58
(Bulgaria)	58	Sweden	63	New Zealand	58
UNITED STATES [b]	58	Russian Federation	62	Switzerland [b]	58
Switzerland [b]	58	Canada	62	Russian Federation	57
Canada	58	Hong Kong	61	(Germany) [a,b]	57
(Australia)	57	Norway	61	Sweden	57
(Germany) [a,b]	57	(Israel) [a]	61	(Israel) [a]	57
Spain	57	New Zealand	60	(Scotland)	57
(Thailand)	56	Slovak Republic	60	Norway	57
New Zealand	56	Ireland	60	Ireland	56
(Israel) [a]	55 (55)	Switzerland [b]	59 (59)	UNITED STATES [b]	56
France	55	Iceland	58	Spain	55 (55)
Hong Kong	54	Spain	58	France	54
(Scotland)	52	(Scotland)	57	(Thailand)	54
Portugal	50	France	56	Iceland	53
(Belgium-French)	50	(Denmark)	56	(Greece)	53
Iceland	50	(Romania)	55	(Denmark)	53
(Romania)	49	(Belgium-French)	55	(Belgium-French)	51
(Greece)	49	(Greece)	54	Latvia (LSS) [b]	51
(Denmark)	49	Portugal	53	Lithuania [a]	51
Latvia (LSS) [b]	48	Latvia (LSS) [b]	53	(Romania)	49
Lithuania [a]	46	Lithuania [a]	52	Portugal	48
Cyprus	46	Iran, Islamic Republic	49	Iran, Islamic Republic	48
Iran, Islamic Republic	45	Cyprus	49	Cyprus	46
(Kuwait)	43	(Kuwait)	45	(Kuwait)	43
(Colombia)	37	(Colombia)	44	(Colombia)	37
(South Africa)	26	(South Africa)	27	(South Africa)	27

TABLE 5.2
(Continued)

Chemistry			Environmental Issues & the Nature of Science		
Nation	Percent Correct		Nation	Percent Correct	
Singapore	69		Singapore	74	
(Bulgaria)	65		(Netherlands)	65	
Korea	63		England [a,b]	65	
Japan	61		Korea	64	
Czech Republic	60		(Australia)	62	
Hungary	60		(Thailand)	62	
(Austria)	58		UNITED STATES [b]	61	
Slovak Republic	57		Canada	61	
Russian Federation	57		Ireland	60	
(Slovenia)	56		Japan	60	
Sweden	56		(Bulgaria)	59	
England [a,b]	55		Czech Republic	59	
Hong Kong	55		New Zealand	59	
(Germany) [a,b]	54		(Slovenia)	59	
Ireland	54		Belgium-Flemish [b]	58	
(Australia)	54		(Scotland)	57	
(Israel) [a]	53		Norway	55	
UNITED STATES [b]	53		Hong Kong	55	
New Zealand	53		(Austria)	55	
(Netherlands)	52		Slovak Republic	53	
Iran, Islamic Republic	52		Hungary	53	(53)
Canada	52		France	53	
Spain	51		Spain	53	
(Greece)	51	(51)	(Israel) [a]	52	
Belgium-Flemish [b]	51		Sweden	52	
(Scotland)	51		(Germany) [a,b]	51	
Portugal	50		Switzerland [b]	51	
Switzerland [b]	50		(Greece)	51	
Norway	49		Russian Federation	50	
Latvia (LSS) [b]	48		Iceland	49	
Lithuania [a]	48		(Denmark)	47	
France	47		Latvia (LSS) [b]	47	
(Romania)	46		Cyprus	46	
Cyprus	45		(Belgium-French)	46	
(Thailand)	43		Portugal	45	
Iceland	42		(Romania)	42	
(Belgium-French)	41		(Colombia)	40	
(Denmark)	41		Lithuania [a]	40	
(Kuwait)	40		(Kuwait)	39	
(Colombia)	32		Iran, Islamic Republic	39	
(South Africa)	26		(South Africa)	26	

Note. Nations not meeting international study guidelines are shown in parentheses. The international average is the average of the national averages of the 41 nations and is shown as the circled number. Latvia is designated LSS because only Latvian-speaking schools were tested, which represents less than 65 percent of the population. From *TIMSS: A Sourcebook of 8th-Grade Findings*, by Mid-Atlantic Eisenhower Consortium for Mathematics and Science Education, 1997.

[a] These are nations in which more than 10% of the population was excluded from testing.

[b] These are nations in which a participation rate of 75 percent of the schools and students combined was achieved only after replacements for refusals were substituted.

have constitutional provisions that place the power for educational decisions in the hands of state and local authorities, science curricula are invented over and over again. It comes as little surprise that our science and mathematics curricula, viewed from a international comparative perspective, are seen as incoherent, idiosyncratic, repetitive, and *thin*—too many topics covered in a superficial fashion. Although the connection between the cohesiveness of curricula and student achievement is conjectural, it is reasonable to think that comparative analyses of curricular and instructional practices across the TIMSS countries would be useful in understanding our lackluster performance in K–12 science and mathematics.

TIMSS uses a view of curriculum that distinguishes between what was intended that students learn (the *intended curriculum*), what the teacher actually teaches (the *implemented curriculum*), and what the students experience and learn (the *attained curriculum*), all are diagramed in the lower half of Fig. 5.1. These distinctions are useful because the three curricula are not always the same, and in the case of U.S. science education, alignment or overlap may be more the exception than the rule. Teachers may or may not know about, adhere to, or even pay much attention to, national or state curriculum guidelines. We know from the dramatic examples in the misconceptions research that what students learn (the attained curriculum) is often not the same as what the teachers believed they taught (the implemented curriculum).

The *intended curriculum*, the focus of this chapter, consists of the stated aims, goals, objectives, and plans of an educational system. Because the intended curriculum has so many levels of input (especially in the United States, with its state and local control of education), it seems analogous to a children's game, sometimes called telephone or conversation. In this game, one child quickly whispers a phrase or saying to the next, who repeats it to the next, and so on. The last child in the sequence says aloud what he or she has heard—which is often met with uproarious laughter because the message has become so hilariously garbled after many transmissions. The multiple helms influencing science curricula of the United States result in a similarly distorted message or splintered vision (see Fig. 5.1).

As a result of the education reform movement, at the national level, we now have two important documents designed to give some coherence to science curricula by providing standards for what K–12 students should know and be able to do. They form the foundation of the intended curriculum. Both are quite new and there is a strong national consensus behind them. The NRC's NSES emerged in final form in 1996, and the AAAS Project 2061 *Science for All Americans* and *Benchmarks* were pub-

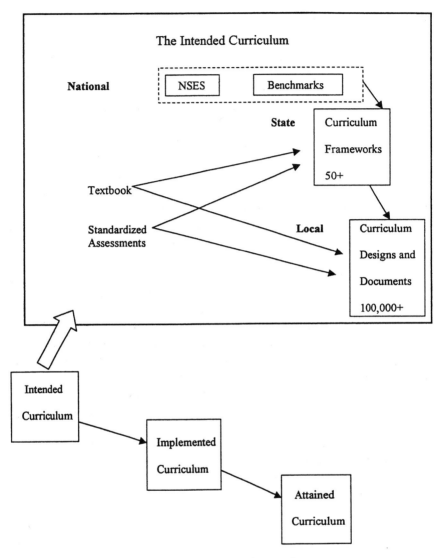

FIG. 5.1.   The intended curriculum.

lished in 1989 and 1992, respectively. These documents were available to educators in draft form long before those dates and have influenced state curricular frameworks that predate the actual publication of the national reform documents (Project 2061, 1996). Fortunately, there is a 90% overlap in the content standards of both documents (Project 2061, 1996), and both authoring organizations share similar philosophies and included some of the same committee members as drafters of the documents. "The overwhelming similarity between Benchmarks and the NSES means that curriculum materials that support students' learning benchmarks will likewise promote learning science standards" (Roseman, Kesidou, & Stern, 1996). The documents are well aligned but have different emphases, which add to their richness and utility when read in tandem (which is how I use them with my graduate students).

However, correspondence among the intended curriculum, Benchmarks, and NSES, does not do much to halt the national game of curriculum telephone. The first set of science curriculum transmissions of intention flow from national to state level, from state to local level, to individual schools within the local school districts, and finally to individual teachers within schools (see the upper half of Fig. 5.1). With 50 states, thousands of local school districts, and even more interpretations within school science departments and teachers, it is hardly surprising that curricular vision is splintered. The problem is exacerbated by the textbook industry, which also influences the intended curriculum in myriad ways—the concepts and skills taught, the labs provided, the types of performance expectations (e.g., what children are asked to do to demonstrate what they have learned; Schmidt et al., 1996). In a few states, the textbooks are closely aligned with the state curricular frameworks, but in most cases, they are commercial products designed to cover as much material as possible and written to offend the fewest people in order to sell to the widest possible market—good strategy for marketing, but a bad one for curriculum design. The intended curriculum may also be influenced at the level of the individual school science department, where teachers working together develop unique interpretations.

Given all of this, one can appreciate the predicament in which the makers of science assessments find themselves, especially if the assessment is to be used in more than one state. Needless to say, standardized assessments, if they are given at all, may or may not match the intended curriculum at any level—national, state, or local. Yet, teachers are very aware of the contents and demands of such assessments because they and their students' performance will be judged on this basis. So these assessments also play a big role in what students are taught and, in a sort of feedback loop, no doubt influence the intended curriculum, although in theory, the assessment should merely reflect it.

How Is Instruction Organized?

The 1996 TIMSS results elucidate the splintered vision problem because they allow comparison of the U.S. organization of science education with that of other countries. TIMSS shows that U.S. science and mathematics curricula are relatively unfocused and deal with far more topics than is typical, internationally. Because the amount of instructional time is roughly equivalent to that provided in other countries, the average amount of time spent on any one topic in the United States is less than in other countries (U.S. National Research Center for TIMSS, 1996). At the same time, focus on some topics seems to persist over years, unlike topic coverage in other countries where there is less repetition.

Although a major goal of mathematics and science reform in the United States has been to limit the number of topics covered (less is more), the opposite seems to have occurred. Textbook publishers have also added more topics to their traditional texts (U.S. National Research Center for TIMSS, 1996). The result is larger, more ponderous science textbooks attached to more secondary school students hunching from class to class, lugging these weighty tomes in their backpacks. Sometimes, topics remain, whereas explanatory text is shortened or removed, result-ing in telegraphic, incomprehensible explanations of complex, elegant ideas. A major problem in our reform effort is how to rid intended curriculum documents of unnecessary topics and emphasize fewer, more important ones in ways that promote conceptual change.

TIMSS also found that the level of performance expectations required of U.S. students, what they are actually being asked to do to demonstrate learning, is relatively low. U.S. science texts, in contrast to most other countries, do not ask students to understand the concepts presented. This comes as no surprise to anyone who has read the questions included at the end of the chapters of these textbooks, which typically ask the student to pick out answers embedded in the text or to solve formulaic problems. In addition, such textbooks do not require theorizing, investigating, or communicating. Science education is characterized by memorization of definitions and facts and emphasizes process skills.

SCIENCE CURRICULA IN THE UNITED STATES

Social Class and Curricula: Filling in the Blanks

In terms of equity, is the effect of an unfocused science curriculum with myriad topics covered in a cursory fashion the same for all students? Is the playing field level? Probably not. Students with more background in science, from home and from informal venues (e.g., visits to museums, summer camps, books, toys, television programs, and computer games), probably have more of a chance of making sense of this muddle than those who have not had such experiences. Social class, and to a lesser extent culture, probably have an important impact on these background experiences (Oakes, 1990a).

An example of art imitating life: In a television episode, Frasier, the snobbish but cultured psychologist of the eponymous show, does not receive the toys he purchased for his son through an upscale educational toy catalog in time for Christmas. All of the gifts are nerdy science toys that the boy's grandfather is certain the child will hate. Frasier is reduced to shopping with "the rabble" at a gauche, commercial toy store, where more typical parents buy a popular action figure doll for their sons. Frasier manages to replace the nerdy science toys (i.e., surgery toys, a model of the brain, and a microscope), then learns that all his son really wants is the action figure doll. Yet, the child is not worried because he is convinced that Santa will bring it. The day is saved by the grandfather who managed to buy the popular toy. He gives it to Frasier as an early Christmas present that Frasier, in turn, can give to his little boy. These experiences are replayed across the United States during the holiday season. (At our house, we have had similar struggles over Barbie dolls.)

The point is that children come to school with very different background experiences in science and the fractured, overloaded science curriculum does not have the same effect on every child. Some seem far more able to make sense of it, to fill in the blanks. This seems related to SES. It involves verbal facility with science terms (although not always deep understanding of them) that some students acquired from out-of-school experiences. Consequently, some children can learn from disjointed science lessons or poorly written texts because they have somehow acquired the background mortar. The teacher can wave in a general direction for learning and the students come along, often with support from their parents, if need be.

A lot of science knowledge, especially the type that is measured by standardized tests, is learned outside of school and is in place, or nearly in place, without formal classroom instruction. Evidence of the existence of this substantial background knowledge is the results of some previous research done with academically talented young adolescents who in this sample, were mostly upper middle class, White and Asian Americans, aged 12 to 15 years. In pretesting junior high students, before they took a course in high school science, we discovered that the average pretest scores for this group on high school biology or physics comprehensive standardized tests (College Entrance Examination Board subject area achievement tests) were, respectively, the 25th and 34th percentiles for college-bound high school seniors (Lynch, 1992). These younger students had not yet formally taken biology or physics in school. Such children are certainly at an advantage when faced with science courses that require learning mountains of abstract concepts at breakneck speed, the result of an overweight and undernourished curriculum.

Equity and Curriculum Materials

Less affluent children and children who have had less exposure to science would seem to have much to gain from a more focused, better structured intended curriculum. Yet, at a finer grain size, the individual teaching units within the curriculum should provide a thoughtfully sequenced series of engaging activities that help students learn a targeted concept, as opposed to memorizing vocabulary for a test. The units should build on students' current understandings of science phenomena. The teachers' guides should supply information on common misconceptions and suggestions that encourage students to explain their ideas. With this information in hand, teachers use connected activities designed to build students' understanding.

Instruction in U.S. classrooms is heavily dependent on textbooks; for instance, 54% of eighth grade science teachers reported that they rely primarily on the text (National Education Goals Panel, 1994). The recognized weaknesses of science texts predate the TIMSS study. Textbooks are often seen as conservative influences that constrain students' knowledge and inhibit teachers' creativity. As a result, may reform-oriented teachers disdainfully renounce them, creating original lessons and activities (Ball & Cohen, 1996). The science teachers most likely to do this are either experts in their disciplines, very experienced teachers, or both. These are the teachers least likely to be found in classrooms for diverse learners (Oakes, 1985; U.S. Department of Education, National Center for Education Statistics, 1996a), which are often occupied by the least qualified teachers.

For instance, a graduate student-teaching intern in ESL was drafted into teaching eighth grade earth science in her first teaching job. She had no background in science. She brought into our graduate classroom an example of a science lesson that she recently taught. There was a nicely wrought concept diagram on minerals and rocks that she created for ESL students, showing that the difference between rocks and minerals was that one was nonliving and the other living! Apparently she had meant inorganic and organic—still incorrect—but not as egregious as teaching about living rocks. Several classes of ESL students had already been taught this lesson. Although there is no excuse for schools placing either a teacher or students in this sort of position, it happens all the time. Better curriculum materials would have helped her.

Yet, curriculum materials cannot dictate instruction. Rather, they are interpreted by teachers (for better or for worse) in the science classroom. We need reform curricular materials that guide teachers to learn how to assess students' conceptions, support teachers' understanding of the science concepts, propose interconnections with other topics, or suggest alternative pedagogical approaches (Ball & Cohen, 1996).

NSF's Curriculum Evaluation. The NSF, the primary funder of instructional materials, has begun to examine the curricula it supported in light of their alignment with the NSES and the goals of science education reform (NSF Directorate for Education and Human Resources, 1996):

> Many states and districts have developed curriculum frameworks in mathematics and science that build on or adapt [the new national] standards efforts. The question now is, do we have the tools required to successfully transverse the new educational terrain? The national and state standards perhaps set the compass and provide a large scale map, but it falls on districts, schools, and teachers to identify the best materials and programs to make these reforms a reality. Without quality materials even the best teachers can make little headway. (p. 1)

NSF conducted a review of middle school science materials that it funded, analyzing them for content accuracy, how well the materials provided for conceptual growth in science, and how well they aligned with NSES. Because some materials predated the NSES by years, it was not likely that all would match the standards. However, the evaluation would allow suggestions for modifications in subsequent revisions, resulting in improved alignment. Nineteen projects were rated on an overall scale of 1 to 5, with 5 being the high point. None received a 5 or a 4. Thirteen got a 3, including comprehensive multiyear programs, such as Full Option Science System (FOSS), which was originally designed for children with disabilities, but has an inclusive range, and Improving Urban Elementary Science, which has an obviously urban focus.

There was an equity component to the evaluation. The reviewers found that the materials reflected approaches to equity that were "more likely to be sins of omission rather than commission." Many of the materials simply did not address equity in any explicit way, although there is no obvious bias in the materials. The panel members thought that almost all of the materials would be improved by explicit attention to equity issues. They praised materials that focused on societal issues as having an inclusionary effect, because such materials used events and materials familiar and relevant to students (NSF Directorate for Education and Human Resources, 1996).

Two things stand out in the NSF curriculum evaluation report. First, none of the projects received especially high evaluations—a 3 out of 5 might be read as a grade of C—and it represents a sign of how far we have to go in developing excellent materials based on the new science standards. Second, the reviewers' call for dealing with equity issues directly in curricula raises the following issue: The report specifically mentioned the need for information for teachers on how to obtain the supplies associated with the new curricula, recognized how difficult it could be for some schools to get access to the expensive technology that some curricula required, and raised pedagogical issues on how the curricula might address the challenges of teaching heterogeneous groups and students with diverse learning styles.

NSF is joined by other agencies and organizations that have also come to recognize the need to analyze curricular materials in light of science education reform requirements, as well as to realize the centrality of equity concerns in the process. In a series of case studies on science reform curricula, Stake and Raizen (1996) reached conclusions similar to those of the NSF: "Given the size of the equity problem, we found its role in the eight innovative programs to be underplayed, as revealed in the case studies" (p. 151). These researchers uncovered a number of equity issues. For instance, a new high school chemistry curriculum, ChemCom, was designed to appeal to high school students not attracted to traditional chemistry. It makes fewer mathematical demands on students and stresses applications. Although the ChemCom developers were interested in attracting more students to chemistry, what they found was that in many schools, the typical ChemCom student is in the bottom 40% of the class. They are the less able students. In tracked schools, students took the course to knock off a graduation requirement and ChemCom seemed to be the easiest science course available (Stake & Raizen, 1996). There is a message here: Science education reform could be seen as the return to basic skills for the less able, reifying the status of first and second class science citizens in the schools. The first class takes the traditional science course that stresses abstract concepts, memorization, and mathematics, whereas the second class students do the reform curricula that stress understanding and relevance. This seems roughly analogous to reform curricula in the 1960s, Physical Science Study Committee (PSSC) Physics versus Harvard Project Physics. Although both are available today, one is likely to find PSSC physics in use in honors high school physics courses, whereas Harvard Project (conceptual and requiring less mathematics) has faded from view, perhaps stigmatized and doomed as a course for weaker students. Moreover, high status science assessments that hold the keys to college admissions for the most elite colleges and universities (i.e., ETS, The College Board AP Examinations, and CEEB science achievement tests) are more likely to reward traditional knowledge and help reinforce the notion of science education reform as the province of the less able, rather than for all.

The Stake and Raizen study (1996) also found that other reform curricula, such as *Voyage of the Mimi* (1998) and *Kidsnet* (1998), required expensive resources, with the result that fewer urban and high poverty schools could participate. For curricula that heavily relied on the use of computers, the researchers noticed that boys tended to use the materials more than girls, and the working scientists depicted in some materials reinforced the notion of science as being the province of White males.

Project 2061's Curriculum Analysis.   Curriculum evaluators are beginning to recognize that equity issues are not a mere category to be tossed in as an afterthought or as a nod to political correctness, but something more integral and central if the curriculum is to be successful in schools with real teachers and students. Project 2061 has also launched a major effort to find curriculum materials that align with Benchmarks and the content standards of NSES. To do so, the Project 2061 staff developed a rigorous procedure to analyze both content and instructional aspects of units of study from selected curriculum materials. The central feature of this evaluation is how well the curricular materials are likely to contribute to the attainment of specific learning goals (Roseman et al., 1996). The instructional analysis consists of separate sets of questions for analyzing a unit of instruction. For instance, it inquires if the unit:

- starts from ideas that are familiar or interesting to children
- explicitly conveys a sense of purpose
- takes into account student ideas, specifies prerequisite knowledge and skills, and conveys suggestions for teachers to find out what their students think about the phenomena related to the benchmark
- provides for firsthand experiences with phenomena
- has students represent their own ideas about phenomena and practice using the acquired knowledge and skills in varied contexts.

These questions are only a small sample from the Project 2061 analysis, but they seem to be at the heart of effective instruction for diverse learners. Yet, what about equity issues? The instructional criteria are so comprehensive and sound that if an instructional unit met all of the criteria, it seems likely that all students would be well on the way to learning the particular targeted standard or benchmark. The criteria are consistent with equity concerns because they imply recognition of individual differences and the need to provide explicit goals, hands-on experiences, and teacher modeling, or scaffolding, of science reasoning. These curriculum attributes would seem to serve diverse learners well. One could hardly argue with the just-plain-good-teaching approach embodied by the Project 2061 curriculum analysis, which promotes equitable science achievement for all.

One criterion from the analysis deals with equity. It is: "Welcoming all students. Does the material help teachers to create a classroom community that encourages high expectations for all students, that enables all students to experience success, and that provides all different kinds of students with a feeling of belonging into the science classroom" (Roseman et al., 1996, p. 5). The indicators associated with this criterion include avoiding stereotypical language, illustrating the contributions of women and minorities to science, role models, alternative formats for students to express their ideas during instruction and assessment, and suggestions about modifications for students with special needs (Jo Ellen Roseman, personal communication, February 5, 1999).

In addition to these indicators, an analysis attuned to equity issues might include the following types of questions:

- What is the reading level of the student materials and is the syntax complicated or straightforward (important for poor readers, students with learning disabilities, and English language learners)?
- Do the materials alert teachers to activities (e.g., lab work or group projects) that are likely to exclude certain students unless provisions are made for them?
- Are the materials or technology required to teach the unit likely to be difficult to obtain for teachers in high poverty schools or schools experiencing financial rollbacks?
- Are the materials likely to be at odds with the worldviews of certain groups of students, such as those having to do with environmental protection or evolution (controversial topics for some)? If so, do they prepare the teacher to handle such topics?
- Do the assessments included in the materials have *context validity* as well as *content validity*—are students assessed using the skills that they are practicing in the classroom or does the assessment change the task to require high levels of reading and writing skills?

- Do the materials ask the student to behave in a fashion that is culturally incongruent with the practices of his or her community (e.g., constructing an "evidence-based argument" may be difficult for those whose community values consensus)? If so, how should the teacher deal with the student? (James Rutherford suggested that because science is, over the long haul, both a consensus- and evidence-based enterprise, it should be represented as such to students instead of sidestepping attributes that some groups may find unattractive; personal communication, February 27, 1997.)

Each of these criteria, singly or in combination, could be crucial for science learning for any given student. For instance, *readability*, although neither a new nor a terribly exciting criterion, could certainly be the critical factor in the success or failure of curriculum materials for English language learners, students with learning disabilities, as well as many from high poverty schools where the readings levels often are low. However, rather than reducing the reading level of all science texts to low levels, the ideal would be alternatives from which to choose.

Research on Curriculum and Diverse Learners: Not Colorblind

Cawley (1994) and Stefanich (1994) noted that science curricula of high quality for students with disabilities have not been a priority in schools. The available curricula and materials are not sufficiently geared to the populations who use them and do not suggest effective modifications or recommendations for adaptation provided for students with disabilities (Parmar & Cawley, 1993). A variety of learning materials, especially computers, should replace total dependence on textbooks in reformed classrooms (National Center for Science Teaching and Learning, 1994). However, as new materials are developed, it is crucial that they not rely on expert reading ability. Children who do not read well can learn science and can demonstrate their understanding of concepts only if they have choices to do so with media that are not totally dependent on reading and writing (Lee & Fradd, in press). This is not to say that reading proficiency is unimportant in K–12 education—it is a worthy goal—but it ought not to be the prerequisite for all intellectual development in science.

Project 2061's rigorous and ambitious effort to identify curricular materials that embody the best instructional practice for science reform goals should help schools to find effective curriculum materials aligned with science standards. As the results of the evaluation are made available, assuming school districts will respond by using such materials, the effect should be improved science education for all. Yet, the proof of the pudding will involve pilot testing the materials with diverse groups of students. For now, questions related to equity remain. One set of curriculum materials that fared among the best in Project 2061 analysis had, in fact, mixed results when used in Lee and Anderson's (1993) classroom study. The study indicated that not all students learned well from the materials that were premised on conceptual change theories. Moreover, students who benefited from the materials, versus those who did not, were divided along the lines of SES and ethnicity that we can all too easily predict: "Of the 12 target students in this study, the six most successful in understanding were all white. Of the six less successful students, two were white, two were African American, and two were Mexican American" (p. 606). One student, a Hispanic girl, actively resisted the materials, the teacher, and the science course. The researchers said that a limitation of the materials concerned their lack of attention to race, culture, and social class.

Why might there be a gap between the results of an analysis by experts based on best practices and results of implementation studies in a real classroom of diverse learners? One possibility is that various groups of children will respond differently to distinctive curricular approaches. This implies that schools should match curricular approaches to the students. This is easy to say, but potentially disastrous to implement because the task of matching curriculum to learning styles, be they group or individual, is daunting and could result in stereotyping and the type of battles that the Ebonics controversy inspired in language arts (Heilbrunn, 1997). This is something that science reformers would want to avoid. Moreover, many schools are so diverse in terms of ethnicity, language, and SES, and are increasingly including with disabilities in mainstream classrooms, that the notion of matching curriculum materials to a specific group is impractical, unless of course students are resegregated in some way. Again, this needs to be avoided. One must depend on the teacher as the translator of curriculum materials, modifying them for his or her students as need be or using a variety of approaches.

In addition to the work of Lee and Anderson (1993), there are few examples of the type of curriculum research that takes into account the differential responses of diverse student populations to educational reform interventions. Research on elementary mathematics education reform efforts raises some interesting questions and concerns that may well parallel problems in reform science curricula. Fennema, Carpenter, Jacob, Franke, and Levi (1998a) conducted a longitudinal study of gender differences in the mathematical thinking of a group of elementary school students as they progressed from first to third grades. The focus of the intervention was professional development activities for the teachers of these children. The project's goal was to instruct teachers on children's mathematical understanding and problem-solving strategies, which corresponded to NCTM recommendations. (Most of the children were White and middle class.) No specific curriculum materials or teaching techniques were recommended. Rather, the teachers were free to develop their own instructional responses based on their understanding of children's developing math concepts. At the end of 3 years, the researchers found that although there were no gender differences in achievement for number facts and routine addition and subtraction problems, there were consistent and strong gender differences in the strategies chosen to solve more complex problems. The boys tended to develop more abstract strategies that required conceptual understanding and would likely lead to higher level mathematical accomplishments. The girls chose concrete strategies and algorithms used by the teachers.

These results led the authors to the crucial equity question for education reform related to curriculum and instruction:

> Another major concern has to do with the idea that without explicit attention to traditionally underachieving groups, all children will learn mathematics equitably. This concern calls into question many of the unexamined assumptions of the reform movement. . . . These classrooms (in this study) emphasized complex mathematical tasks (problem solving), communication about mathematics, and learning with understanding—all of which are major tenets in the mathematics education reform. Many advocates of basing curriculum on understanding as well as most scholars who study teaching and learning believe that equity issues can be addressed by such an emphasis. . . . This study's results do indicate that equitable mathematics education, even in classrooms that promote understanding, may not happen without specific attention to underachieving groups, such as females. Saying that all should learn mathematics, while necessary, is insufficient. The entire education community . . . needs to continue to engage in discourse about and to explore ways to deepen our understanding of how equity can be achieved. (Fennema, Carpenter, Jacobs, Franke, & Levi, 1998b, pp. 20–21)

We need more discourse, it is true, but we more urgently need the type of research that Fennema et al. do—research that looks at group differences in response to reform-based curriculum and instruction interventions within classrooms.

A second example of research attentive to equity issues is Woodward and Baxter's (1997) study of the effects of a reform mathematics curriculum (e.g., *Everyday Mathematics*; Bell, Bell, & Hartfield, 1993). The subjects were third grade students with disabilities and other students at risk for failure, that is, those who scored below the 34th percentile on the Iowa Test of Basic Skills (ITBS). Most of the students were White and middle class. This study included intervention schools at which the new mathematics curriculum was being used, as well as a comparison school with a traditional mathematics approach (using *Heath Mathematics*, Rucker, Dilley, & Lowry, 1988). In addition to focusing on the progress of the low-achieving students, the study also examined the effects of the curriculum intervention on average ability students (i.e., 35th to 67th percentiles on the ITBS) and high-ability students (i.e., above the 67th percentile on the ITBS).

The total group results for all of the children in the study showed that the students in the intervention schools significantly outscored those in the comparison schools on the ITBS, and on a nontraditional measure of problem-solving ability and strategies, the Informal Mathematics Assessment (IMA). Results were especially strong for the IMA, which is expected because the IMA is more closely aligned with the intervention curriculum and the general goals of the reform.

Yet, the within group results are the most interesting part of the study. There were no significant differences between the scores of intervention and comparison low-achieving children at the end of the year on the ITBS. On the IMA, strategy analysis showed that when presented with complex problems, learning disabled and low-achieving children, under both conditions, continued only to guess, repeat numbers, and express bewilderment. Neither curricular approach seemed very effective. High-ability students at the intervention school performed better on the ITBS and IMA than did comparison school students. The average students at the intervention schools improved in one category in the ITBS compared with those at the comparison school, but showed huge gains in problem solving on the IMA. This was the most surprising and encouraging aspect of the study.

This study showed that the reform curriculum benefited the majority of students, especially average students, in the intervention schools, but there were only marginal improvements in students with disabilities and low-achieving students. The researchers concluded that although this curriculum is successful for most, it will be necessary to develop other interventions for students with disabilities. The researchers did not believe that current practices in mathematics special education are likely to hold the key to progress because these practices emphasized memorization of facts and rote mastery of algorithms instead of multiple solutions and problem-solving approaches that lead to understanding. Without systematic evaluation of this nature, the value of the current mathematics curriculum reform is likely to remain speculative or merely a policy debate.

Despite the fact that most of the students in these studies were White and middle class, these are two examples of what one might call research that is not *color blind*, if *color* is used as a metaphor for diverse learners. Both sets of researchers were interested in the effects of the reform on subgroups. They found that the common wisdom—that reform curricula are equitable—is not necessarily true and that the effects of the reform vary with the groups that are studied. We need similarly structured research to better understand the effects of the reform on students who are ethnically diverse, English language learners, and so on.

THEORY AND RESEARCH MODELS

Most of the research cited here appears to be based on theoretical assumptions that can be ascribed to *individual constructivism*—that each individual constructs knowledge for himself or herself. This includes both personal (conceptual change models) and social constructivism (which stresses the importance of communication in constructing knowledge; Atwater, 1996; Driver, Asoko, Leach, Mortimer, & Scott, 1994; Phillips, 1995). Although these are powerful theories that explain well how an individual learns, there may be other theories that can be tested to explain why some students do not learn, why some groups of students learn less well than others, or, most important, why some groups of students learn well in some situations but not in others.

For instance, Hmong children who are English language learners make up the largest proportion of the non-White population in the state of Wisconsin. The relatively low literacy rates among Hmong people in Southeast Asia could result in low performance for Hmong students in American schools. A state educator who monitors this group reported that Hmong children in very integrated schools showed many of the problems associated with low literacy—high rates of failure and dropping out. Yet, in a Milwaukee high school solely devoted to bilingual education for Hmong students, their performance is excellent, with more than 90% graduating from high school and many going on to college. Can this phenomenon be explained best by curriculum? Teaching methods? Group dynamics?

Theories that focus on group dynamics, motivation, the structural characteristics of schooling, the social organization of instruction, and on the tools of language may lead to productive research and powerful explanations of student achievement and attitudes toward science (Eisenhart, Finkel, & Marion, 1996; Greeno, 1997). Consequently, more research is needed not only on the effectiveness of curriculum materials for various groups of diverse learners, multiple research perspectives to guide this inquiry are also called for (Anderson, 1996).

Curriculum Issues: Whose Science Is It? Whose Could It Be?

So far, this chapter on curricular issues and equity has shown that many science concepts are resistant to instruction because of the persistence of the misconceptions that are held by individual students, and this phenomenon seems applicable to all students. Consequently, many students fail to learn in the current system with its structurally weak, bloated science curriculum. The advent of NSES and Benchmarks as the well-defined core of an intended curriculum is the important beginning of a solution. When fleshed out at the local school level through thoughtfully integrated curriculum materials, this should mean improved science for all. Diverse learners may have the most to gain by a more explicit and responsive curriculum because they may have had the weakest curricular support in the past if they were placed in low-level science classes. Yet, we have a long way to go before we are able to understand exactly how a given unit of study or curricular approach affects students with disabilities, girls, those who are poor, those who are Black American or Asian American, those who are just learning to speak English, and so on.

The curriculum section of the American Association of University Women report (1992), *How Schools Shortchange Girls*, pointed out that although Project 2061 describes equity as a central organizing principle (p. 44), the materials produced to date send contradictory messages. Although acknowledging the international nature of scientific discoveries, the Project 2061 materials primarily refer to European scientific history and the usual great men. "So far, women are no more visible in Project 2061 than in standard science-curriculum materials" (p. 64).

Rodriguez (1997) criticized NSES for being both colorblind and theoryblind. In fact, NSES makes more than 40 references to equity in the generic sense and prominently features pictures of students of both sexes, of color, or of those with disabilities—more than 58% of the people featured in NSES appear to be from ethnic groups underrepresented in science (Rodriguez, 1997). Yet, NSES has taken the colorblind tact, preferring to discuss equity in general, rather than delving into particular equity issues for various specific groups (as this volume attempts to do) or confronting the really difficult and divisive issues in education that are key to understanding and ameliorating equity concerns, such as unequal allocation of resources, ability grouping, and prejudice. On the other hand, if NSES provided such specificity, it would be a very long document and probably would not do justice to the concerns of any one group. (A result one may anticipate for this volume.)

Neither science nor science curricula are colorblind (culturally neutral) or theoryblind. An American Indian educator, Eber Hampton (1991), is well aware of this:

> The contemporary American school is a political, social, and cultural in-stitution that embodies and transmits the values, knowledge and behaviors of Anglo culture. The call for higher standards in education is invariably the call for the standards of the Anglo. It is never a call for more adequate presentation of the knowledge of devalued minorities, creative thinking about pressing social problems, higher standards of equity or respect, or recognition of institutional racism. The idea that different cultures and different races may have standards just as worthy seems never to have crossed the minds of the proponents of "higher standards". Rather, they assume that they possess the one true standard yardstick and that any consideration of Blacks, Indians, or Chicanos would simply lower stan-dards. (p. 301)

Yet, in the same article, Hampton also admitted that most Indian parents want their children to be taught the things necessary for success in both the White and Indian worlds; he recognized that American Indians/Alas-kan Natives are poorly represented in the sciences and mathematics. He saw the need for more Indian engineers, managers, business people, and natural resources specialists who can meet non-Indians on equal terms and understood how important it is that science, mathematics, and tech-nology be accessible to Indian students (p. 366).

This is, then, the central dilemma for curriculum reform and equity issues: Should science curricula be determined locally or nationally, and what are the equity implications? Can a curriculum be designed that is respectful of local conditions or a particular culture, while providing opportunities that allow the students to compete equitably and gain access to the community of science and the rewards of the dominant or mainstream culture? Equality of opportunity (inputs) would seem to de-mand that all students have the opportunity to learn high status knowledge. The reform documents (NSES and Benchmarks) have, in a sense, thrown wide open the gates to science knowledge, and the importance of this should not be underestimated. As the consensus documents of hundreds of scientists and educators under the sponsorships of the NRC and the AAAS respectively, the standards could be the keys for achieving equity in science education.

However, ignoring the reality of local conditions would doom any effort to improve science curricula to failure. The American Indian Science and Engineering Society (1995) described some of the problems encountered in curriculum development for American Indians/Alaskan Natives in the past. Many of these issues are applicable to other ethnic groups or geographic locations.

- Community needs and concerns are neither adequately identified nor integrated into the educational process, resulting in unnecessary and unresolved conflict between school and community.
- Current curricula are not inclusive of American Indian/Alaskan Native views. Research has shown that this constant neglect negatively affects minority students and how they view themselves as learners in the dominant society.
- Elders and other American Indian/Alaskan Native experts are not consulted to ensure that their knowledge is incorporated into the development process.
- Current curricula are not holistic in scope. The American Indian/Alaskan Native lifestyle of balance and holism is not supported in the hierarchical style of modern science and mathematics.
- Curriculum evaluation practices do not reflect cultural relevancy. Additional or adapted evaluation instruments are necessary to evaluate student progress, as current test-taking practices dot no accurately reflect American Indian/Native Alaskan students' understanding of science.
- Spirituality comprises an important aspect of American Indian/Alaskan Native learning and lifestyle, and current curricula do not foster the spiritual relationship among people and their environment. Ignoring this aspect devalues the important relationship that American Indians/Alaskan Natives have with the Earth.
- Financial support of programs is insufficient for sustainability. When such resources become available to help facilitate growth, they often disappear before a program is firmly established and integrated into the school and community.

- Good academic programs do not always get support from the school and community. Communication among school and community groups is not adequately in place, causing confusion, apathy, and mistrust. (p. 12)

There have been attempts to fashion science curricula responsive to a particular community or group, for instance, feminist (Rosser, 1993) or Afrocentric (Adenika-Morrow, 1996) curricula. Other approaches are to develop an inclusive or multicultural approach to science (Barba, 1995). Clearly, the intentions here are admirable: to create science curricula that are welcoming to and relevant for students who have been bypassed by science education in the past. Yet, some of these materials are politically volatile, and others focus on science topics that seem marginally important as science, but have great cultural significance. It is important that curriculum materials be accurate—present information that is data-based, verifiable, and able to withstand critical analysis, while acknowledging the worth of individuals and groups and weaving together the needs and experiences of males and females (Wilbur's study as cited in American Association of University Women, 1992). Perhaps more consequential is how well curriculum materials support the core—NSES and Benchmarks—in terms of content and pedagogy. A specialized, inclusive, or multicultural curriculum that does not lead to achievement of standards will not lead to equitable outcomes or opportunities to do science in the mainstream culture. (In fairness, however, the same can be said of standards-based curricular materials that are inaccessible, irrelevant, or unfriendly to some students.)

The current thinking among policymakers and funders is that the creation of effective science curricula should be left to teams of curriculum experts rather than developed at the school level. Consequently, NSF will fund only major projects that can demonstrate that they have this expertise, which includes collaboration with scientists, mathematicians, teachers, and educators (NSF Directorate for Education and Human Resources, 1996). On the other hand, there is support to train local school district level curriculum specialists and teachers to evaluate existing curricula (an effort underway at Project 2061), so that they can better choose materials that support the standards, as well as fit them to the needs of a particular school district.

Fleshing out the intended curriculum with specific materials and activities acceptable and accessible to all will be difficult because school communities seldom have uniformity of outlooks or purposes. There are some exceptions, such as specialized schools for the gifted and talented or for students placed at risk, or schools serving an identifiable group such as Navajo students or Hmong students recently immigrated to the United States, but a single school community is oftentimes far more diverse than these examples, especially large, comprehensive urban and suburban schools. It may be hard to get community consensus on science themes or simply to hear all of the disparate voices within the community—voices so often drowned out by those with the greatest numbers or the most power.

Consensus building and curriculum development require a great deal of time and resources. Schools with the fewest resources and schools stretched thinnest by attempts to respond to increasingly diverse and needy student populations may be least equipped to build from scratch a K–12 science curriculum reasonably faithful to new standards (Lynch, 1995). Consequently, there is promise in the development of commercial materials, especially if they have been evaluated in the field with students who have historically been underserved in science education.

Another problem that underscores the need for better standards-based curriculum materials is the fact that the weaker the teacher's preparation in science or experience in education, the more likely he or she is to rely on the textbook. Who are the teachers likely to have weaker backgrounds in science? They are the teachers of elementary school children (National Science Board, 1996), students with disabilities, and English language learners, as well as teachers in high poverty urban schools. Moreover, recent reports indicate that secondary science teachers generally depend on texts a great deal—for example 54% of eighth-grade science teachers (National Education Goals Panel, 1994). It is logical to suppose that the better the curriculum materials, the better the chance that students learn science, especially if their teachers are weak in science. This is not to encourage the creation of teacher-proof curricula—the results of such hubris are well known—but teachers and their students would greatly benefit from access to good materials based on standards. Currently, much of the special education and ESL science materials seem aimed at helping these students get through traditional, ill-structured science classes rather than emphasizing understanding. They send teachers in the wrong directions. TIMSS results, reviewed earlier in this chapter, indicated that the U.S. science texts are abysmally unsuited for the type of science education called for in the science reforms.

A Reformed Vision of Science Curricula

James Rutherford, former director of Project 2061, has a view of a science curriculum that is architectural (personal communication, December 18, 1996). The curriculum is analogous to a building and the benchmarks are its *specs* (specifications). Each local school district could design its own curriculum (or building). Some may look very much alike and others very different, but all intend the same learning outcomes because the specs are the same.

The building blocks of the structure are large-scale, planned learning experiences, similar to what we think of as quarter-, semester-, or year-long courses. The blocks, rather than being of uniform size or style, could vary greatly. For example, the style variations in the curriculum could include seminars in which the objective is for students to discuss and communicate their ideas about science, group project work during which the students would do real investigations, or independent study in which an individual would be allowed to explore an idea in depth, whether the idea is advanced or based on a concept that has been difficult for a given student. Other blocks might look like more traditional courses. These blocks could be discipline based (e.g., physics or earth science) or integrated (e.g., health of the environment). The size of these blocks, the amount of time a block would take, is approximately equivalent to a one-quarter or one-semester course, but the course would not necessarily meet 50 minutes per day, 5 days per week. Rather, the course's schedule would differ with need—a seminar might meet 90 minutes per week, but so might a course on the weather, which would require meeting 90 minutes per week over 2 years, long enough for students to see weather patterns repeat themselves. Courses focusing on group projects might meet daily for 4-hour periods for 1 month. The schedule would be used to enhance learning rather than frustrate it.

Local school districts would assemble an array of different sorts of courses, all aiming toward teaching a common core of understandings and skills (Benchmarks or NSES) that all students learn. Students who complete the core would go beyond it and take AP courses, applied courses directly related to jobs, or other more creative classes designed for students with interest in science beyond the comprehensive literacy called for in the Benchmarks and NSES. With the aid of technology or more curriculum designed to challenge students at different levels, it may be possible to do advanced work within blocks.

In the lower grades, almost all of the time in science would be devoted to achievement of the core, but as students move up in grades, more learning opportunities outside the core would be offered. This arrangement would also allow students who need more time to learn a particular benchmark, the opportunity to take it.

The core courses would be taught by the best teachers, the master teachers. In Rutherford's curriculum scenario, students who mastered the benchmarks could go on to take advanced topics (in the classroom, at a field site, or via new technologies such as distance education) with professionals who would not necessarily be certified science teachers, but experts in an area of science. This is, of course, contrary to the typical situation in schools today where the most skilled teachers often wind up teaching honors classes with students who are talented and motivated. Conversely, students who have the greatest needs are taught by the least prepared and least capable teachers (Oakes, 1990a; U.S. Department of Education, National Center for Education Statistics, 1996a).

Designing a science curriculum can be thought of as assembling these varied blocks of instruction into a structure that would fit the locality (i.e., the students in it, the resources available, the values of the community) the way that some well-designed buildings seem to have grown organically from a landscape. Some of these curricular blocks would rely on high-quality curriculum materials from commercial or publicly funded sources. School districts would not be expected to manufacture curriculum materials, but rather to obtain them from suppliers, although some of the curriculum blocks might be suited to local issues, for example, topics related to environmental study or community health. Curriculum blocks devoted to inquiry and problem solving would have special relevancy if based on real-world problems that the students experience themselves in their communities. All of the core blocks would be constructed to target specific benchmarks, so that eventually a student, in completing the core, would have achieved all of the benchmarks.

There are dangers inherent in this type of approach. Curriculum builders would need to be sure that there was no misinterpretation of the intent of a benchmark, leading to an inadvertent mismatch between it and the curriculum. They would have to resist the temptation to add topics unrelated to the benchmarks to core courses. In Rutherford's vision, there would be a high degree of agreement between the intended curriculum (i.e., Benchmarks, NSES, state and local curriculum documents), the implemented curriculum (i.e., what teachers teach and the materials that they use), and the attained curriculum (i.e., what the students learn and on what they are assessed).

In the context of equity, Rutherford's plan has two features:

1. It puts an ambitious core at the center of the curriculum and insists that school systems must find ways to insure that all students have the opportunity to attain the core's learning goals—high expectations for all students and the system.
2. Provisions for serving the special needs of all students, whether those needs are to deal with individual learning difficulties, to

develop special talent (in music, sports, science, language, or what-ever), to prepare for work or college, or to participate in school and community affairs (personal communication, February 26, 1997).

CONCLUSIONS

The research reviewed in this chapter confirms the need to rethink the structure of U.S. science curricula. The NSES and Benchmarks, as science standards, form the bedrock of the intended curriculum. They are potentially transformative—creating a substrate for change. This positive vision of standards is a marked contrast to a perspective that sees standards as leverage—or as a club used to beat students into better performance. There are many dangers associated with high standards viewed in this way, if one thinks that science education will be improved by merely announcing high standards and bullying the system into compliance without creating the conditions to achieve them. Moreover, in terms of equity, clearly some students have much more to win or lose than others.

It is neither overly optimistic nor unrealistic to think that, on the whole, equity issues could be well-served by science education reform that aims to create an explicit, focused, in-depth science curriculum intended for all students. The promise of curriculum reorganization may be the single most positive aspect of the reform for students who have histori-cally been excluded from access to high quality science education. The keys to the gates of science have been handed over, but there are con-comitant dangers to curriculum reform, especially if its success ultimately depends on financial resources (which are inequitably distributed) and school reorganization (which is highly resistant to change)—issues to be examined in the next chapter.

6

Resources and Opportunity to Learn: Pole-Vaulting Without the Pole

YOU CAN WATCH PEOPLE ALIGN THEMSELVES
WHEN TROUBLE IS IN THE AIR.
SOME PREFER TO BE CLOSE TO THOSE
AT THE TOP. OTHERS WANT TO BE
CLOSE TO THOSE AT THE BOTTOM.
IT'S A QUESTION OF WHO FRIGHTENS THEM
MORE AND WHOM THEY WANT TO BE LIKE.
—Jenny Holzer untitled (From The Living Series,
1989, Cincinnati Art Museum)

In 1991, Kozol published *Savage Inequalities*, a book that made dramatically public what most people who visit schools have always known: U.S. schoolchildren experience shockingly different conditions of schooling. Kozol not only contrasted the plush conditions of suburban schools to those of neighboring decrepit, demoralizing, and unsafe urban schools, but he also showed the vast disparity between schools within school systems. This chapter focuses on the differences between the education of rich and poor children and rich and poor schools. These contrasts show up in stark relief in science classrooms because science is a subject that can be so resource dependent. Science resources not only include obvious physical and material resources, such as decently functioning classrooms, adequate laboratory facilities, equipment, curriculum materials, and technology, but they also consist of human resources, such as well prepared science teachers and crucial professional development efforts that allow teachers to create an implemented curriculum consonant with science education reform goals.

126

The costs to the nation of implementing science education reform will be substantial, but perhaps far less than the costs of not producing a scientifically literate workforce. Science literacy for all means that there will be an increase in the sheer number of students served—all—as well as qualitative changes in instruction. Moreover, for the first time, science education is targeting those students who have been left behind in the past—Blacks, Hispanics, American Indians/Alaskan Natives, females, students with disabilities, and those who are learning English. These are the young people whom we are least sure how to reach and to teach science well. This implies the need for increased funding for research and development of innovative pedagogy and curriculum materials, supporting supplies for lab work, and technology. Yet, American education rushes toward implementation of systemic reform, despite the fact that it is an unproven theory (Bruckerhoff, 1997; Corcoran, 1997), and it is impossible to know its effect on underserved groups. Educational policy and evaluation expert, Thomas Corcoran (1997), raised some discomforting questions:

> The effects of systemic reform under varying conditions . . . need examination. Is fiscal equity a prerequisite condition for success? What are the educational and political effects of implementing standards and high stakes in situations with *inequitable resource distributions*? What are the consequences for schools with varying capacity to design and implement changes? What degree of fit is needed between teacher knowledge and skill and the standards? (p. 2; italics added)

These questions are the focus of this chapter. Although no one knows their answers, they should stand out in high relief, in order to draw the notice of the science education policy and research community, which seems to pay them scant notice beyond hand wringing or genuflecting to the equity theme. Yet, if logic has led us to believe that systemic reform can improve American science education and to pursue the reform vigorously, then application of similar logic compels us to conclude that equity input issues—unequal distribution of resources across schools—must be as crucial to the health of the system as proper nutrition is to the patient recovering from a serious illness.

The provision of adequate funding for science education reform is a particularly disquieting question because of its equity implications. Poor students attending dilapidated, inadequately functioning, underfunded schools are at a horrible disadvantage; these students are disproportionately children of color. This could mean that the extent to which the implementation of science reform is dependent on existing resources or the infusion of new ones, is the extent to which opportunity to learn will be further stratified, both along the lines of SES and ethnicity, unless something dramatic is done to create more equitable distribution of school resources. This is a frightening but real possibility—a science education reform that actually exacerbates the differences between the educational haves and have nots. Jesse Jackson, for instance, recently claimed that President Clinton's call for education reform is the greatest unfunded mandate of all time. Hyperbole? Perhaps. Yet, Jackson has realistic fears because he understands exactly which children stand to lose most as the educational bar is raised in the form of higher mathematics and science standards for all, when only some have access to the means to clear it (Raspberry, 1997). It is a little like providing some pole-vaulters with high-tech poles, others with old-fashioned wooden ones, and others with none at all, as the bar creeps up.

HOW CAN WE DETERMINE EQUITY IN K–12 SCIENCE?

In chapter 1, I introduced a general equity schema for science education reform (see Fig. 1.1). In chapters 2 and 3, by pointing out some of the achievement gaps that exist between various groups, the evidence revealed that we are a good deal away from equality of outcomes in reaching reform-based science education standards (Level 1 of Fig. 1.1). Although no assessments align perfectly with the NSES or Benchmarks (Bruckerhoff 1997; Corcoran, 1997; Lee, 1998), it is virtually a given that students cannot achieve the more demanding outcomes set forth in NSES or Benchmarks because of their relatively low performance on measures such as the NAEP and other existing standardized tests of science achievement and the dearth of students who score well at the higher levels of such tests. Moreover, state assessments that were better designed to align with the Standards and Benchmarks provide convincing evidence that their achievement is a distant goal (to be discussed in more detail in chap. 9). The equity schema might also be represented as a decision tree or a feedback mechanism where an educational setting is analyzed for imbalances and problems in systematic fashion (see Fig. 6.1).

The first test of educational equity in science education reform according to Fig. 6.1 is to view a particular population of students (e.g., at the level of the state, the school district, the school or individual classroom) and ask if the population has achieved the outcomes set forth in the national standards or a specific interpretation of the standards established

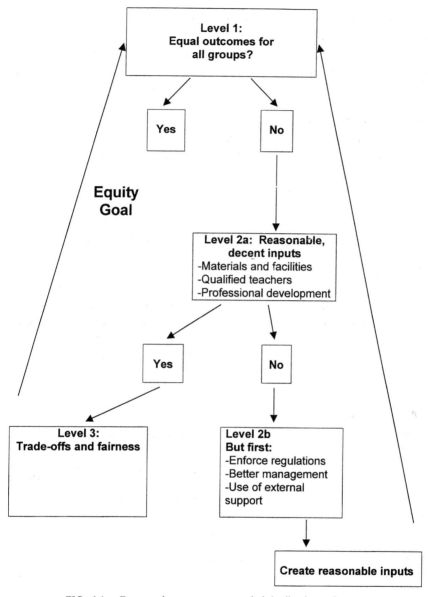

FIG. 6.1. Equity schema as an expanded feedback mechanism.

in the individual state (see Level 1 of Fig. 6.1). A concomitant question is whether various groups within this total population are meeting the standards according to assessment information. Aggregate data may disguise areas where the system fails to teach and reach some groups. The equity schema's focus on results or achievement outcomes is consistent with recommendations for shaping school finance policy for improved productivity (Odden & Clune, 1995).

If group differences in achievement are found, then it is reasonable to ask why, examining resources available, or inputs (see Level 2 of Fig. 6.1). This examination of inputs, within states, school districts, schools, or classrooms is major concern of this chapter. If it can be clearly established that within an educational unit students do not experience conditions of learning that are remotely equivalent to some reasonable norm, making achievement of the standards unlikely, then the situation must be remedied by creating a decent minimum floor of resources across the unit in question. This is not to say that all conditions must be the same or of country-clublike opulence. Rather, the point is that when achievement is down, educators must not shrink from a close and well-reasoned examination of conditions of schooling. The equity schema identifies three broad areas for concern, rather than proposing to indiscriminately blanket the system with materials or assistance that are unneeded or miss the mark.

Consequently, if we are reasonably persuaded that students in a given school district, school, or classroom within a school are not close to achieving the threshold outcomes set forth in the Standards documents (i.e., most have not risen to Level 1 of Fig. 6.1), we can begin to look for reasons why this might be so. Are differences in resources (Level 2) part of the problem?

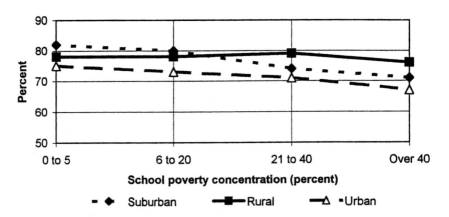

FIG. 6.2. Percentage of teachers who agreed that necessary materials are available in their schools by urbanicity and school poverty concentration: 1987–1988. *Note.* From *Urban Schools: The Challenge and Location of Poverty* by United States Department of Education, National Center for Education Statistics, 1996c.

Inequitable Resources: Savage Inequalities
in the Science Lab

Differences in the quantity and quality of physical resources in K–12 science education can be appalling and often create conditions that make even traditional science instruction virtually impossible, never mind the sort of education demanded by reform. Consider these examples reported by novice teachers. The first was written by a student-teaching intern who is a retired military officer, accustomed to better working conditions than his urban school provided:

> The facility at Jackson High (not its real name) does not provide an appropriate atmosphere to conduct routine Chemistry 1 lab activities. The science labs were built in 1939. When built, they must have been nice—all with fume hoods, granite topped lab tables, and a multi-voltage electrical system. Nothing has been done since. There is no operating gas for the Bunsen burners. The sinks do not drain. No one remembers any routine maintenance. Every time it rains, water comes in the skylight and drops rain onto one of the four lab tables in the room, reducing the usable surface area by 25%. Cleaning seems to be limited to emptying the trash. In the last eleven weeks the classroom hasn't been swept and certainly not mopped. Dirt is everywhere. Every morning, falling paint from the ceiling must be wiped from student desks. I have been told that because the roof is slate, it would cost one million dollars to repair it, although the rest of the building seems structurally sound. The laboratories have a large amount of old glassware, which could be used if cleaned. I have nosed around and found lots of kits and materials for physics. Unfortunately, there is no organization, no inventory, and no desire to catalog or classify. Most supplies are bought out of the teacher's pocket at the drug or grocery store, to be used the following day.

In contrast, another student teacher describes his science facilities located in a suburban school district about 15 miles away:

> The physics section at Lincoln High (not its real name) has two classrooms and a computer room with 12 Macs, a 27 inch monitor and a good-sized physics storeroom located between the two classrooms. The storeroom is estimated to contain $250,000 of equipment accumulated over the course of many years—filled with pulleys, weights, stopwatches, optics, mechanical toys, etc. It also has new physics software, a/d converter, sensors and devices for instrumenting labs. The new computer room should make the technology available on a routine basis. The per student expenditure last year was about $8.50 per student, for a total of $14,000 worth of supplies.

These examples are illustrative and typical of the enormous variations in resources that occur across the country as one compares rural, urban, and suburban schools. Moreover, we can distinguish between schools with high concentrations of children living below the poverty line, schools that are underfunded no matter what the SES of the students, and schools that are both underfunded and attended mainly by poor children. Given the tax revolts occurring throughout the United States, vast differences in funding patterns are also likely to occur across regions of the country, which will, in turn, affect what sorts of resources are made available to K–12 science students in these regions (see Fig. 6.2, page 130).

The response of many people to problems such as those encountered in Jackson High or other disadvantaged schools is to psychologically throw up their hands in defeat, protesting that schools cannot possibly solve all of the problems of society, and look for reform venues more amenable to change. Another frequent response is to repudiate such situations because of charges of historical mismanagement of funds. However, no matter the accuracy of such charges, the bottom line for the students attending such schools is that they may be receiving a third-class education that probably does not prepare them well for much of anything—neither college nor jobs (Lynch, 1994).

Students attending high poverty schools (i.e., disproportionately students of color) have fewer resources than students attending advantaged schools (see Fig. 6.3). The downward slopes in Fig. 6.3 show that the higher concentration of children of color, the fewer the resources. Over-

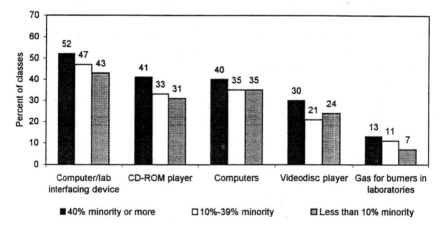

FIG. 6.3.   Percent of high school science classes for which teachers report various types of equipment are needed, but not available by percent minority in class: 1993. *Note.* High school includes grades 9–12. From *Indicators of Science and Mathematics Education 1995*, by NSF, 1996a.

all, urban teachers report more resource problems than rural or suburban teachers. These statistics reflect the views of all teachers in the schools across disciplines, not just science teachers. Science teachers' perceptions of need are likely to be more dire because science is the most resource-dependent academic subject. In 1996, only 65% of the nation's teachers of eighth graders reported that they had adequate facilities for laboratory science or that they had sufficient instructional materials and resources (O'Sullivan, Weiss, & Askew, 1998). The eighth grade students whose teachers reported adequate instructional materials in science scored significantly higher on the 1996 science NAEP than did the students of teachers who reported resource needs.

A *Washington Post* series on the District of Columbia public schools (where the vast majority of teachers and students are Black American) documented the abysmal conditions of the District's school buildings and the scarcity of essential materials and resources. Only 8% of the eighth-grade students had teachers who reported having adequate instructional materials for science (O'Sullivan et al., 1998). For instance, at Bell Multicultural High School, teachers have had to make do with makeshift science labs for years (Horwitz & Strauss, 1997), despite the efforts of a well-connected principal. Sometimes, the problems are more serious than a lack of lab tables and equipment—the school buildings themselves are falling apart or in such poor operating condition that students are forced to wear coats and gloves in class during the winter.

At another District of Columbia high school, where Angela, a doctoral student, teaches, there are not enough science textbooks to go around—students must rotate opportunities to take them home for study. In chemistry, she only has junior high school texts. She says she would kill for even one copy of *Chem-Com*, a reform-based chemistry series that she is convinced would work well for her students. Last summer, the school district provided her with an excellent professional development experience to prepare her to use the *Chem-Com* series, but funding for the actual books never materialized. Most of the materials she uses in her science classes come out of pocket—even reproducing materials must be done commercially because the copying machine at school hardly ever works or must be scheduled for use days in advance.

What resources are required to teach science as it is envisioned by the science reform? *Benchmarks for Science Literacy* (AAAS, 1992) is not explicit about this, save recommending that students use calculators and computers (p. 290) as well as have the opportunity to work with hammers, screwdrivers, clamps, rulers, scissors, hand lenses, cameras, tape recorders, and analog and digital meters (pp. 293–294). Yet, Benchmarks

certainly seems to assume access to textbooks or other curricular materials, as well as to the safety equipment and materials that certainly are
not always found in American schools. The NSES (NRC, 1996) are more
explicit. The actual standard is: "Conducting scientific inquiry requires
that students have easy, equitable and frequent opportunities to use a
wide range of equipment, materials, supplies and other resources for
experimentation and direct investigation of phenomena" (p. 220). The
standard describes general purpose equipment such as magnifiers or microscopes, measurement tools, tools for data analysis, and computers with
software to support investigations. More specific-purpose materials include a water table for first graders or a reduced resistance air table for
physics investigations. The standard recognizes the need for financial
support to annually replenish expendable materials. Moreover, examples
from the scenarios embedded within the Standards imply a fairly high
norm in material support—everything from earthworms, terraria, and
scales to density columns and star charts.

Because of the emphasis on student inquiry throughout the reform
documents (NSES and Project 2061 materials), it is implicit that not only
must school have such equipment and supplies, but they also must be
available in sufficient amounts to allow small groups of students to have
access to their own sets of materials to conduct their explorations. Thus,
one triple-beam balance, one voltmeter, or one computer would probably
be insufficient to engage in the kinds of inquiry required by science
education reform. There must be class sets available. Moreover, even an
activity as simple as boiling water requires functioning burners—work
stations with electricity or gas—as well as safety goggles, which, in turn,
require a means for cleansing them between uses. Fitting elementary
schools out for the kind of science activities envisioned by the reform will
be expensive. States that have increased the science requirements for
high school graduation have already found that their science facilities are
inadequate for the increasing numbers of students taking sciences.

Ironic good news–bad news results of education reform can be found
in a Baltimore City high school that has been *reconstituted* (taken over
by the State of Maryland because of a failure to adequately educate
students). The good news is that the focus on reducing the scandalously
high truancy rate has resulted in vast improvements is science class
attendance for the targeted ninth-grade class. The bad news is that class
sizes have increased dramatically to 36 to 45 students per class. Moreover,
as the reform measures are extended to other grades in subsequent years,
it is clear that the science facilities at the school will be woefully inadequate. School districts that take seriously the challenge of science for all

are likely to need additional laboratories and supplies, more creative scheduling of existing facilities, or both.

Technology Resources and the Culture of Power

Science education reform documents do not make particular recommendations about the use of technology in science classrooms, except to say that computer use should be widespread and computers should be used as tools to access, collect, store, display, and summarize data (NRC, 1996, pp. 145, 175). Students should have a sound understanding of the principles of technology and its relation to science literacy to encourage effective decision making as citizens (AAAS, 1992, p. 53). Yet, contrary to what some science educators seem to think, increased use of computer technology is not equivalent to science education reform. Indeed, some experts (Hofmeister, Carnine, & Clark, 1994) suggest that rather than rushing to use computers in the classroom, a more prudent and effective strategy is to use a systems approach to curriculum materials product research and development. The technological bells and whistles currently available to science teachers are less important than the systematic development of curriculum blocks aligned with standards and the accompanying technology to support them, using formative and summative evaluations to validate the materials. One could hardly argue with such sound recommendations, backed up by substantial research that says that the promise of technology to transform education has not yet been realized (Hofmeister et al., 1994).

However, one cannot help but notice all those affluent suburban schools—with the computer labs in constant demand, the PTA fundraisers to buy the latest equipment, and the use of sophisticated satellite data sharing, probeware, robotics, and simulations—and not wonder again about the culture of power as it is played out in the K–12 science classroom. Technology is not used in the same way in rich and poor schools:

> The research evidence consistently indicates that computers, as well as other technologies, are not distributed equally nor are they used equally by all students in our schools. Poor, minority, and female students have less access to computers at home and . . . school. (Rockman, 1995, p. 26)

Girls have not had the same interest in or access to computers as boys, and teachers have compounded the problem by viewing computers as a male technology with little meaning for the future careers of girls. Recently, strong gender differences in technology use are emerging as the new CD-ROM technologies are primarily marketed for boys and the preponderance of internet users are male (Rockman, 1995).

Access to computers and other technology is not an "ethnically neutral factor"—schools with higher proportions of students of color report greater shortages (see Fig. 6.3). Statistics show that Black and Hispanic students have not had as much access to computers in school as White students, although the 1993 figures for secondary education in Fig. 6.4 are encouraging. The use of computers at home reflects these trends, but is more uneven (see Fig. 6.4) with White students reporting about three times more access at home than Black or Hispanic students.

Social class, as well as ethnic differences, affect how computers are employed in schools. Students in poorer schools receive a different, qualitatively poorer kind of instruction, using different types of materials (than

Grades 1-6

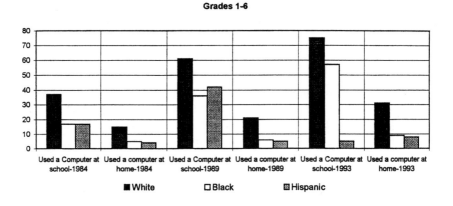

Grades 7-12

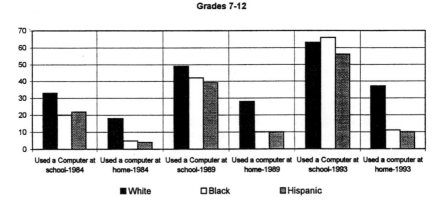

FIG. 6.4.   Percentage of students who used a computer at school or at home by race or ethnicity. *Note.* From *Indicators of Science and Mathematics Education 1996*, by NSF, 1996b.

wealthier areas) and resulting in inequitable outcomes. They receive fewer assignments that incorporate hands-on and higher-order thinking activities to engage young minds and help them to think critically, write better, and develop groupwork skills they will need in the workplace . . . Students at risk of failure . . . tend to receive instruction using the computer for isolated skill development and remediation . . . and never get beyond repetitive applications of basic skills . . . (Rockman, 1995, p. 26)

Consequently, even when poor students and students of color use computers regularly, differences in the quality of their experience may become an equity issue if they are engaged in drill-and-kill activities while their suburban counterparts use computers to track weather patterns or engage in inquiry on acid rain.

Although the differential use of technology seems to contribute to inequities in science education, technology's potential to improve science education for all is promising. Some of the newer curriculum materials are tremendously popular. Some students seem to connect to science through technology, whereas traditional teaching leaves them nonplussed.

At one public high school in Prince George's County, Maryland, the faculty made it their business to bring technology to a student population that is predominantly (90%) middle-class Black Americans. There were seven computer labs in the school in constant use. A teacher could sign his or her class up for 30-, 60-, or 90-minute blocks of computer time. In a 10th-grade world history class—called *multilevel* at this school because one third of the students had identified learning disabilities—the students eagerly headed for the computer lab to do an assignment on PC Globe software, where each student explored a different country in South America, locating specific demographic information. Not a single student required help getting into the system or accessing their data, nor was it possible to distinguish students with disabilities from other students, as all went about their work in a businesslike fashion, casually proficient and enthusiastic. Especially noteworthy was the fact that because there were sufficient numbers of computers and all students were comfortable with them, students each had their own workstation and were able to do individual exploration rather than having to work in groups. Apparently, this drive to create a technologically literate high school originated from a few faculty members who wrote successful grants for hardware and software. As the quantity of, and access to, good computing facilities increased, less techy faculty were drawn in and began to incorporate the technology regularly into their classrooms. This access and enthusiasm was buoyed by in-school organizational policies that encouraged teachers to experiment. As a result, this school was more technologically literate than any other school in the county, including the magnet schools, and the technology was accessible by every student.

Yet, merely dumping expensive technology into science classrooms is not equivalent to science education reform. The eighth grade test scores on the 1996 science NAEP showed no relationship to the prevalence of computers in the schools (O'Sullivan et al., 1998). Technology can be ill-used if unaccompanied by thoughtful planning and a clear vision of how it can advance reform goals. We have all heard the horror stories of boxes of computers stored untouched in school basements because no one knows how to install or use them, or of a donated shipment of computers that sits idle because the school's wiring is inadequate—and the difficulty in even getting phone lines installed for Internet access, or of buying expensive software that is ill-matched to student skills or curriculum goals. Clearly, an infusion of technological resources must be accompanied by teacher professional development so that teachers will understand how to use them and be preceded by well-defined curriculum goals that align with the technology. Equally crucial is a school organiza-tion system sufficiently flexible to support computer use.

Teacher Resources

Teacher Qualifications. The reprehensible differences in physical facilities and teaching materials for science between have and have-not schools are glaring. In addition, there is a relation between a school system's ability to attract the best science teachers and the adequacy of the facilities for teaching. Urban principals report the most difficulty hir-ing qualified teachers (Oakes, 1990b; U.S. Department of Education, 1996c). Still, there are many talented and highly qualified teachers in poor urban and rural schools, who, despite the options available to them, prefer to work with students whose needs are greatest and whose access to resources are the most inequitable.

The distribution of teachers with relevant preparation in science and teacher education is an important equity issue because schools with high numbers of students of color and low SES students are taught by less qualified teachers. For instance, eighth grade science students in *disad-vantaged schools* (defined as those with more than 50% student participa-tion in free-lunch programs) have a greater chance of having teachers with virtually no formal training in science, about 42%. In contrast, in schools where less than 5% of the students receive free lunches, the figure is about 28% (NSF, 1992). Also, the poorer the school, the higher the concentration of inexperienced teachers (U.S. Department of Education, 1996c). This is due to a high turnover rate.

When analyzing teacher resources by community type, teachers in rural schools have the fewest advanced degrees (i.e., 55% have bachelors' degrees and 44% have masters) compared with suburban and urban schools, where respectively, 62% and 58% have masters' degrees (NSF, 1996c). This trend may be a function of the difficulty that rural teachers have in accessing advanced degree programs from a rural location, a condition that seems to be rapidly changing for the better as more universities go online with degrees offered via distance education. Rural schools also tend to have the highest concentrations of inexperienced teachers (U.S. Department of Education, 1996c).

Yet, there are subtle differences in the quality of the science teaching staff across types of schools that these data do not reveal. This is because group data tend to lump together certain categories (i.e., coursework and degrees in education are not usually distinguishable from degrees in science disciplines). This creates an inaccurate picture of the distribution of teacher resources and may affect the quality of the science instruction. There is some accumulating evidence that when studies examine specific measures of teachers' educational backgrounds, such as the number of college courses that the teacher has taken in science, a significant positive effect on student learning is found (NSF, 1996b). It seems that school systems that hire teachers with strong backgrounds in science content and with more teaching experience provide better science instruction than school systems where teachers are less prepared. This may seem intuitively obvious, but the research data has been equivocal and there is less than clear agreement on the effect of these variables on student achievement (NSF, 1996b; O'Sullivan, Reese, & Mazzeo, 1997). Results for the 1996 science NAEP in Table 6.1 show the proportions of teachers having degrees in science, science education, education, or other fields. At the eighth grade level, there is a tendency for students having teachers with science backgrounds to score higher than those who do not. This is not true at the fourth grade level.

The real story behind teacher resources encountered in schools and school districts seems far more problematic than statistics suggest. For instance, in one urban school district, on paper, 94% of the teachers report that they are certified to teach in their main assignment area, but the majority were certified in general science 20 or 30 years ago and many had their science preparation at teachers' colleges that vary dramatically in the quality of the science instruction. Why is this a problem? In this urban school district, although most teachers are technically qualified to teach science, only one half of the high school science teachers hold teaching certificates in the specific subject that they teach—biology, chemistry, or physics. In

TABLE 6.1
Teacher's Reports on Their Undergraduate of Graduate
Fields of Study: Public and Nonpublic Schools Combined

	Grade 4		Grade 8	
Fields of study	Major	Major or Minor	Major	Major or Minor
Science				
Percentage of students	5	8	45	52
Average scale score	144	151	154	154
Percentage at or above *proficient*	29	35	33	33
Science Education but not Science				
Percentage of students	5	8	11	10
Average scale score	151	156	148	144
Percentage at or above *proficient*	26	34	27	25
Education but not Science or Science Education				
Percentage of students	74	69	20	18
Average scale score	152	151	149	149
Percentage at or above *proficient*	31	30	28	28
Other				
Percentage of students	6	5	8	3
Average scale score	140	139	150	149
Percentage at or above *proficient*	18	18	27	29
Missing/None Indicated				
Percentage of students	9	9	17	17
Average scale score	142	142	142	142
Percentage at or above *proficient*	20	20	21	21

Note. Numbers may not add up to 100 due to rounding. From NAEP, 1996 Science Assessment by National Center for Education Statistics, 1996.

terms of minimum undergraduate course requirements for teacher certification in this state, the differences in general science certification and, for instance, certification in high school physics, are considerable. This state requires at least 24 semester hours of physics and 9 hours of mathematics (calculus level and above) for teacher certification in physics. In contrast, for general science certification, the physics requirement is only 6 semester hours and no college-level mathematics is needed. Biology and chemistry teacher certifications have similarly rigorous standards. For this particular urban school district, this means that about one half of the high school students are receiving instruction from teachers who may have had only a couple of college courses in the science that they are teaching. If teachers have only a superficial understanding of their subject, this can have a profound effect on the quality of classroom instruction.

In another example of what group statistics on teacher qualifications fail to reveal, a large urban junior high school has a somewhat different situation—every science teacher in that building holds certification in biology. The school, of course, offers a full compliment of science subjects. Consequently, although, on paper, this school or the school district appears to have complied with state teacher certification requirements, in fact, the education students receive is quite different from that of the surrounding suburbs where most of the secondary school science teachers have majors or advanced graduate work in the subject matter that they teach.

One might argue that the situation described really is not so bad because teachers, as life-long learners, acquire content knowledge as they teach. Although this is certainly true, in a microcosmic counterexample, when five high school physics teachers in this urban district took an introductory refresher course in college physics at a local university, only three passed. Yet, all had been teaching high school physics for years. Moreover, because student science achievement scores in this district are consistently in the nether reaches of measurement, it seems reasonable to surmise that science instruction would be improved by having teachers with stronger backgrounds in science, although admittedly, there are myriad factors that contribute to poor student achievement. Urban principals report the great difficulties in hiring qualified teachers, and the suburbs frequently hire the best ones away, offering higher salaries and better facilities in safer environments (Geary, 1997).

Teachers working out-of-field is also common in rural environments, where a school may have only one or two science teachers who must teach all the science subjects and sometimes others as well. Although this presents a substantial challenge, there are advantages as well because rural teachers will come to know their students well as they teach them in successive years. This kind of environment provides the opportunity for teachers to integrate subject matter and draw connections (Medlin, 1995). There may be less repetition than in massive school systems where communication is a problem. Still, it must be recognized that these are very demanding situations and the teacher who is knowledgeable and competent across science fields and able to manage a number of different preparations each day is a tremendous asset to the school, but also should be protected from teacher burnout.

Professional Development. Teacher qualifications in terms of science-content knowledge, pedagogical skills, and experience may be necessary but not sufficient for science education reform. Teachers must also have sound understanding of the goals of the reform, and this is most likely to come from professional development experiences because only a small proportion of science teachers are so new to the profession that they would have been exposed to this in a preservice program. The most important opportunity to learn factor is how what is taught in school is aligned with curriculum standards (Porter, 1993). It is the science teacher who must be aware of the standards, interpret what they mean, and decide on pedagogical approaches that are effective for students. Although there is little information on how professional development resources are distributed across school districts, it appears that the affluent school districts have more up-to-date, focused, and coordinated professional development programs than poorer ones. Certainly, urban and rural teachers report that they are less sure about their preparedness to teach science than suburban teachers (Oakes, 1990b).

Responding to Inequitable Resources

Shared textbooks, makeshift labs, inadequate safety equipment, teachers with little background in the subject matter are hardly consistent with the intent of science education reform. It seems as if we have arrived at a sort of catch-22 in the science education reform policy. On one hand, we can say, with reasonable certainty, that most students have not reached the reform goals and the shortfall is particularly egregious in poor schools that disproportionately contain students who are of color and live below the poverty line. These schools tend to have the fewest resources (broadly defined) to teach science well. Some policymakers believe that the goal should be to build capacity within the most poorly functioning schools, with the understanding that the focus is on achieving the science standards. This means directing extra resources toward these schools as well as creating conditions for better management. This is commensurate with our third definition of equity, equity as fairness or trade-offs, Level 3 of our equity schema in Fig. 6.1. Yet, because such schools are generally not even close to minimum operating conditions in science, the argument to infuse extraordinary funds so that students may reach the desired outcomes obfuscates the current situation—paralyzing inequities of baseline minimal resources. Because Americans tend to be more accepting of equity defined as equality of inputs (Level 2) and less of affirmative action measures (Level 3; Marrett & Ziege, 1995), the case for extra funds for science in poor schools may result in wheel-spinning, political posturing, and hand-wringing indecision.

This suggests at least three strategies for funding for systemic reform:

1. School funding can be maintained at the current levels, funds can be shifted away from richer school districts to those that are more needy. This is currently being done in the state of Maryland where the state

legislature has just approved an infusion of $254 million for the City of Baltimore Schools, whereas the combined school funding for the rest of the state is $167 million ("Maryland schools," 1997).

2. School funding can be increased somewhat, and some experts agree that the prognosis for at least modest increases is favorable (Monk, 1994). Sources of income outside the public funding system may also be captured so that the have-not schools are able to come up to minimal decent standards for science education without decimating funding for those that are better equipped.

3. We can turn our heads from current inequities in resources and allow the science education reform effort to do the opposite of what many reformers intended, multiplying inequalities among our students.

There are, however, some remedies that cost more in terms of moral courage and political will than they do in monetary funds. Each has equity implications in the world of school policy, politics, and finance. Rather than beginning with an extravagant wish list for improved resources in science education that is likely to remain in the realm of fantasy, we explore some of these less costly measures, such as enforcing extant regulations, creating better conditions for management, and gathering extra resources.

Enforcing Existing Regulations. Many of the existing regulations designed to create or control reasonable resources go unheeded or violations are swept under the rug for one reason or another. In the District of Columbia public schools, for instance, the school buildings have been allowed to reach a state of disrepair that makes teaching and learning somewhere between a considerable challenge and nearly impossible. Monies set aside for school improvement were diverted into salaries, especially administrative salaries (Powell & Loeb, 1997a). A lawsuit initiated by a watchdog activist parents' group resulted in the closing of every school in the District schools by a courageous and tenacious judge in the fall of 1994 because of fire code violations (Powell & Loeb, 1997b). Although such action does not directly contribute to improved science education, the high profile of this case (thousands of outraged parents had to cope with closed schools for weeks and the *Washington Post* ran the story on its front pages) resulted in the exposure of other school resource issues. This, in turn, encouraged the takeover of District schools by a federal control board. Better, safer, more equitable conditions were created simply by enforcing existing statutes and regulations, although the judge's fortitude and political bravery should not be underestimated.

Teacher certification regulations set by individual states are also routinely ignored when the demand for teachers exceeds the supply, resulting in a legacy of inadequate, but tenured teachers. For instance, in 1994, 11% of the teachers in California were working with either a temporary or emergency license or no license at all. Under Governor Wilson's initiative to reduce class sizes in the early elementary years, this figure has since risen to 33% (Geary, 1997). In large urban school districts such as New York City, some rural areas, and some states, there is a chronic shortage of certified teachers. The shortages are especially severe in science. State accreditation agencies respond with emergency certification measures, allowing schools to get by with unqualified teachers, rather than reinforcing their own quality controls. Increasing the teaching salaries for hard-to-fill positions such as science is one solution, a market response to the problem. However, it is seldom implemented, perhaps because of ambivalence about teacher certification standards or perhaps because the students who are most likely to suffer because of unqualified teachers are those whose parents have the least power in the political system. Wealthier school districts can afford to lure experienced teachers from other parts of the country or from neighboring urban schools, forcing the poorer districts to rely on less experienced and qualified teachers, exacerbating the problem (Geary, 1997).

It takes considerable conviction and fortitude to close a school because of fire safety code violations, to point out that a school is in danger of losing its accreditation because of substandard laboratory facilities, or to insist on the removal of uncertified teachers who have worked there for years. Yet, somehow, someone must exercise this will and courage, along with good judgment. Increasingly, the forces outside of the school system are the impetus for higher standards and the creation of equitable conditions for teaching and learning (Henig, 1997; Portz, 1997). However, although outside interventions from the courts (e.g., New Jersey, Texas, and Kentucky), the state (e.g., Wisconsin, Ohio, and Illinois) or federal agencies (e.g., Massachusetts, Maryland, and the District of Columbia) can get reforms off the ground and propel them forward through mandates and the infusion of new resources, it is local politics and grass roots commitment at the school level that allows change to be elaborated and institutionalized in the classroom (Henig, 1997).

It is possible to find encouragement in the radical takeover of the entire state school system in Kentucky, where the courts intervened because conditions of schooling were so disparate and unequal across the state and funding and resource distribution across the state were so abysmally unfair. Among other things, as the result of a court order, the state had to draw up a plan to better distribute resources among its almost all White, but very poor, population of school children. This led to new school financing formulas that provided the resources to address some of the fundamental barriers to equity in science and mathematics education, such as the lack of qualified teachers, professional development, textbooks, lab equipment, computers, and other essentials. Finance reform efforts such as these may well be necessary to close the gap in science and mathematics attainment (Shields, Corcoran, & Zucker, 1994).

Creating Public Confidence and Better Management. There is a crisis of confidence in American education, especially urban education, that the public perceives as unsafe, unsound, and locked in permanent decline (Traub, 1995). Although urban schools make up only 5% of the school districts in the United States, about 25% of our children attend these schools that have the highest concentrations of poor children and children of color. Although both urban and rural schools can suffer from poor facilities and a dearth of resources, urban schools may be viewed less sympathetically by the public because per pupil spending may be relatively high. Yet, adequacy of material resources and support for science education cannot be gauged by per pupil expenditures. For instance, in the District of Columbia public schools, the annual per pupil expenditure is high—$7,389—but the school buildings are wrecks and there has been shortages of supplies as basic as paper, crayons, and textbooks, so say nothing of science equipment. The financial control board appointed by Congress declared that "In virtually every area, and for every grade level, the system has failed to provide our children with a quality education and a safe environment in which to learn . . . the fault of an educationally and managerially bankrupt school system" (Horwitz & Strauss, 1997, p. A1). Past expenditures for science supplies may have little relation to current realities—equipment can be missing, broken, idiosyncratic, or simply not inventoried, as stable, experienced teachers cadge away supplies that allow them to teach science, disregarding the ebb and flow of the new and transient teachers that characterize high poverty schools.

The NSES (NRC, 1996) acknowledged the need to build an infrastructure for maximizing the use of materials and supplies: "School systems need to develop mechanisms to identify exemplary materials, *store and maintain them,* and make them accessible to teachers in a timely fashion" (p. 220; italics added), and "every teacher of science needs an easily accessible budget for materials and equipment as well as unanticipated expenses that arise as students and teachers pursue their work" (p. 221).

Obtaining money for equitable level of resources (Level 2 on our equity schema) may have a substantial price tag in terms of power if the school is thought to be mismanaged. A state takeover of the school could result. Forcing change might require a lawsuit that creates painful divisions at the local level. Moreover, even if some funds are made available, it is hard to know which improvements will make the most differences in student achievement (Monk, 1994): Better curriculum materials? Teacher professional development? Laboratory materials? Some, no doubt, are more effective than others, but who is to decide? Moreover, principles of systemic reform tell us that all three should operate in concert, in order to optimize change. The NSES provide Program and Professional Development Standards that can help clarify the choices that must be made. Yet, schools will need to devise intelligent, well-monitored, management plans for restoration of basic minimal conditions of science education in order to create change and build public confidence. Funding must be tied to demonstrated gains in student services and learning (Clune, 1993).

Once basic conditions are satisfied—decent science facilities, certified teachers, and good curriculum materials—the school would be in a better position to analyze and prioritize actions within the program, designed to help students to achieve science standards. However, until this decent minimum is in place, there does not seem to be much point in speculating about the nature of the compensatory programs that may be required or to make judgments about reallocating resources or tradeoffs. Moreover, with decent basic resources in place, the school would be in better position to determine monies that must be raised for specific student-centered, program-based purposes.

Reforming science education in urban schools, even when money is available, may prove difficult because the structure of urban school systems allows them to swallow whole most reforms and the resources they bring, simply incorporating them into the ineffective status quo (Hofmeister et al., 1994). The restructuring of urban education has proven, thus far, almost totally resistant to remedy, with the exception of reforms like the Coalition for Essential Schools, James Comer's schools, and the Accelerated Schools program, which seem to produce positive changes on a school-by-school basis rather than by systemwide change. This is also referred to as bottom–up reform. These on-the-ground changes cost more than top–down reform, which targets a wider range of schools for generalized dissemination (Massell & Goertz, 1994). Yet, bottom–up reform seems to build support that, in the long run, is sustainable. In this model, the school principal plays an essential role as the instructional leader by engaging in the traditional tasks of hiring, budgeting, scheduling, grouping students, and establishing rules and policies, but keeps an eye toward how all of these activities will affect science curriculum and instruction (National Center for Science Teaching and Learning, 1994).

On the other hand, a study of 11 urban school districts showed that small, school-based efforts, although commendable, did not result in city-wide programmatic impact nor the creation of systemic capacity to sustain change (Henig, 1997). In other words, the reform efforts stayed local and when the conditions that allowed their establishment disappeared, there was a tendency for the programs to follow suit. The current wisdom in school reform policy is that a combination of both top–down and bottom–up efforts is desirable, with top-level policies in place to foster reform or at least not obstruct it, and bottom–up efforts that result in support networks for teacher learning (Massell & Goertz, 1994).

Because of the nature of the changes called for in the science education reform efforts, it seems crucial that the reform is supported at the level of the school district central office administration (National Center for Science Teaching and Learning, 1994). Nancy Mincemoyer, the director of the State Systemic Initiative for Science in Michigan, believed that the single-most important factor in determining the success of the reform in the many school districts across Michigan was the degree to which the school superintendent supported it (personal communication, April 9, 1997). This was true whether the district happened to be a well-funded one or a poor one, although Michigan had a radical reconstruction of its school funding base so that the minimum per pupil expenditure in every school district is around the national average of $5,000.

The NSF Urban Systemic Initiatives seem to hold some promise for the restructuring of science and mathematics education in city schools, if the improvements initiated in the District of Columbia public schools were any indication. Despite the fact that the District had its NSF funding pulled after the third year (due to a federal takeover of the schools and a general crisis of confidence in the system), the science education reform begun with NSF seed money resulted in a much clearer sense of purpose through the establishment of a curriculum framework that drove decision making within the science and mathematics leadership, even though funds have disappeared.

School-Centered Activism and External Support.   Because funding levels are often not commensurate with wants and needs, schools are increasingly turning for help from parent groups, the community, or from business and industry, be it a major company like IBM or the local hardware store. Sometimes the situations are as dire as they were in the District of Columbia, when a private plumbing firm and school parents pitched in to help repair student lavatories or when a university paid for repairs on a nearby high school's collapsed stairway that had forced students to attend classes in a gymnasium. In other cases, even schools with extravagant resources raise money for extras or find innovative ways to get work done, as when high school students in Maryland wired the local science mathematics and technology magnet school for a complicated computer network. Of course, the example of the technology-rich high school (described earlier in this chapter) shows how a school can, with effort and determination, muster private funds for a specific purpose, resulting in an improved teaching and learning environment.

This kind of community support and cooperation is at the heart of American education and its commitment to local control. Symbolically, it helps focus the indigenous political coalitions that are seen as crucial to the maintenance of systemic reform in the long run (Henig, 1997). Computers and equipment can be overt indicators of progress for communities that may have more difficulty seeing the necessity of spending on less tangible school improvements such as professional development. However, the ability to garner external support can be an equity issue because schools do not always have equal access to funding sources, nor do they always have the internal capacity to organize to raise funds.

This leads us into Level 3 of our equity schema, equity as fairness or trade-offs (see Figs. 1.1 & 6.1). For instance, we know that students of color attending disadvantaged schools have fewer opportunities to use computers at school and at home. Must these schools be forced to rely on outside help from business, the community, or other agencies for technology funding? How will they pay for additional annual costs for maintenance of technology and updating? What about schools that are located in areas where business and industry are scarce, such as many rural environments and some urban ones? For instance, there are often dire shortages of resources for science education in schools with high populations of Native Americans in rural environments. Opportunities to tap local business and companies for help are virtually nonexistent, especially in the more remote areas of the reservations (Willetto, 1995). Basic phone service is often lacking. In order to teach reform-based science, such schools need more resources. The NSF's Rural Systemic Initiative provides seed money to jump start reform, but clearly there needs to be some help at the state level to assure an equitable, decent floor (Level 2) and perhaps compensatory funding for big ticket items like technology (Level 3) in order to create an environment where all children can achieve science literacy.

As parent and community groups and business and industry get involved in science education reform on a voluntary basis, it may be important for state or local educational agencies to provide some guidance on how to spread resources equitably. Parent–Teacher Associations (PTAs), for all of their good work, can exacerbate or create substantial resource imbalances between schools. For instance, the principal of an elementary school in an upper middle-class Maryland community boasted of having more than 50 scientists from the NIH, the local TV weather station, and National Aeronautics and Space Administration (NASA) help with their science fair. Meanwhile, in another elementary school, a magnet school for science and mathematics located in a less affluent setting in the same district, few visiting scientists can be found. Many of these children have poor or working-class parents who have recently immigrated to the United States. For such parents, it is difficult to muster this type of support and the school's middle-class parents shoulder a large burden. In another example, a parent of a child in a New York City public school in Greenwich Village described how she and her husband, both struggling performing artists, spent the weekend slaving away baking pies for a sale that raised more than $1,000 for their daughter's public school. They really were proud of their efforts until they learned that, simultaneously, a public school on the Upper East Side raised tens of thousands of dollars at its annual art and antique auction. What about schools in the Bronx or Harlem, where community support can be harder to garner because of conditions of poverty and social disintegration? Students and schools in circumstances where such extra support is not forthcoming will be seriously disadvantaged because it is difficult for school systems to offset these inequalities (Monk, 1994).

This seems to be a delicate equity issue, not often discussed. Of course, it is desirable to have generous and committed community and business involvement in the schools. This is an excellent way of building understanding and a common sense of purpose. It provides children with opportunities to learn that they otherwise might not have had. Yet, it also is true that well-situated, affluent parents are able to supplement inadequate school funding or prop up dysfunctional school management systems (albeit unintentionally) to provide their children with decent facilities, whereas children in poorer or less organized parts of the system experience substandard education under appalling conditions.

There is a need to integrate and distribute education resources from these unconventional and unpredictable sources (Monk, 1994). Boston public schools provide a positive example of how resources in the community and business can be assembled and organized for equitable school reform. *Compact III* is a coalition of local leaders of business and industry, higher education, and the teachers' union whose purpose is to implement an aggressive reform agenda that includes the development of new standards for curricula and assessment, a professional development leadership committee, more computer technology, and improved school buildings. In addition, a related group, the Boston Plan for Excellence, provides substantial funds to support site-based management and school improvement plans over 5 years. The mayor believes that the planets are aligned for successful school reform, as the support seems to be coming from inside the schools as well as without, with funding to back it (Portz, 1997).

Establishing Equity Floors for Resources.   Where no standards exist for science education resources, it would be helpful to have some specific guidance on what constitutes a reasonable equity floor (Level 2 of Fig. 6.1) for science equipment, supplies, and technology, so that schools and school districts can make the case for improvements without having to grovel for every meterstick or test tube. If we had a national science curriculum, it would be a much easier task to determine reasonable levels of resources, but because we do not, such guidelines might best be set at the state level because the state contributes the lion's share of education funding. However, this is the opposite of a current trend in education. For instance, the state of South Dakota has just dropped input standards (Level 2) in science. Monitoring inputs resulted in bean-counting exercises that did not always link to improvements in science achievement. Rather, the state will try to focus on equitable outcomes for science (Level 1). Perhaps in South Dakota, which includes the very poorest county in the United States—part of an Indian reservation—the have-not schools are easily identified, so this strategy may make the most sense.

On the other hand, the National Science Teachers Association (1996) recently published *Pathways to the Science Standards: High School Level*, which includes an appendix with detailed specifications for safe and adequate science facilities. A similar work is in progress for elementary school science, and one is planned for the middle-school level. These books will not include specific equipment and supplies, but that is understandable given that such materials are dependent on curricula that vary from school district to school district.

This chapter should not leave the impression that the key to science education reform is the purchase of a few test tubes, balances or microscopes, or even the installation of a million-dollar computer lab. Although the case has been made for equitable teacher resources in the form of certified teachers with strong expertise in science content, it is probably possible to locate an uncertified science teacher who provides fine instruction in science congruent with reform goals. Certainly, an abundance of commercial curriculum materials in a classroom does not guarantee that the students will reach science standards. We can all think of examples of teachers and schools that do amazing things with virtually nothing. For instance, my office at the university is within 15 feet of an alternative public high school, the *School Without Walls*, where bright, motivated DC students use resources across Washington, DC as their science laboratory. The school building itself is very modest and the science labs are mostly nonfunctional, but the students have access to facilities at the Smithsonian Institutions and neighboring universities. The school provides an exciting science program.

In another example, a high school in Baltimore with a high population of students below the poverty line has a science career academy with a curriculum based on environmental health issues. The school has few resources and a tiny budget, so enterprising teachers have built a curriculum around the materials that they have in greatest supply—living organisms in their natural habitats, i.e., cockroaches (as well as ants and mice). The science in which the students are engaged has resulted in roach-lore that could only have been obtained through inquiry and authentic learning. Students and teachers have honed their roach acquisition skills, which requires dressing for success—long pants and substantial shoes, not the ideal time to wear a skirt, high heels or anything that impedes swift movement. The capture techniques involve placing a large square of white paper on a bathroom floor and waiting. The classes experimented with various baits and lures. When a sufficient number of roaches have assembled, two students, working in swift unison, sweep together the corners of the paper and deposit the subjects in aquariums prepared in advance for maximum roach ambience. The students study roach behavior, their responses to various environmental stimuli. They have learned that institutional roaches are bolder than their residential cousins because they are acclimated to light and that roaches are solitary and simple creatures compared to ants. The students have been encouraged to expand their studies to industrial applications—how commercial roachtraps work using pheromone lures, and how a local, old-fashioned wholesale food market in the neighborhood successfully controls the roach population in an environmentally friendly, nontoxic fashion. Each day, the wholesalers pour boiling water over the cement floors of the market, which destroys any roach eggs on the surface and washes into the cracks to kill anything that lurks below ground. This is effective, the students have learned, because the roaches do not burrow deeply.

The class even developed an activist community outreach effort. Each year, the students and teachers sponsor a Tupperware drive for plastic containers, which are collected and given to local families along with advice on healthy food storage methods that foil the local fauna. With few resources, a decrepit building, and a science teacher certified to teach English, these students engage in authentic learning. They literally create relevant knowledge about the habits of these creatures and apply it to real-life situations. This seems entirely consistent with ambitious science reform goals. Still, the question must be asked: In the United States, should the teachers of poor students have such limited resources that they have no choice other than to ask their students to study creatures that are often regarded as vermin? Although there is nothing inherently wrong with using cockroaches as the objects of study, and one could easily imagine a better equipped science facility that leaves the students intellectually impoverished and not nearly as entertained, should we not be able to provide these students with other options? For children of color or poor children no matter what their ethnicity, what implicit messages are they receiving about their value in American society?

Clearly, there are some extremely talented and dedicated teachers who are able to take all of the lemons that an inequitable funding system provides and make lemonade. A Black science educator whom I recently met explained to me with passionate conviction what she saw as the legacy of the slave shack—that Black Americans have learned out of dire necessity to persist and make do with whatever is at hand in order to survive and to prevail. She did not want to hear about excuses for not learning due to anything as trivial as a lack of science resources. Although I listened carefully to her message and understand its fundamental truth, I also believe that systemic reform cannot rely on teachers with the dedication of Mother Teresa or Harriet Tubman. It is wonderful when we find such individuals, but they are too rare and not all of us go to work each day with the dedication of a saint. Rather, we simply want to do our jobs well, backed by a decent system for support. If this is true, then systemic reform requires conditions and resources that are both ordinary and enabling, if we are to achieve science literacy for all.

WHAT IS EQUITY? WHAT IS FAIR?

Most of the discussion in this chapter has been centered on two aspects of our equity schema (Figs. 1.1 or 6.1)—Level 1 (equality of science literacy outcomes as a goal) and Level 2 (a reasonable floor of decent resources, equality of inputs). In order to create more equitable conditions in Level 2, better resources with intelligent coordination and management are required to achieve the standards. It seems logical to suppose that improved conditions of science education, linked closely to clearly defined standards and embedded in a management plan designed to monitor and assess progress, is bound to result in some improved achievement for underserved students. Yet, will this be enough or are compensatory programs necessary to achieve science literacy for all? Students who have not had the exposure to science from home and the community or who go to poor schools may need something more. However, these additional science experiences must be enriching or even accelerative in nature, rather than remedial, because programs aimed at remediation tend to restrict the range of instruction and actually slow down learning (Colvin, 1988). They may also have a stigma attached to them, to say nothing of simply being boring.

What might be done to develop students' interests, knowledge, and skills in science when their immediate surroundings do not usually include day-to-day exposure to science, scientists, or scientific habits of mind, and if they attend schools that are educationally impoverished in mathematics, science, and technology? When middle-class parents want to provide their children with a challenging experience or give them a leg up in sports, the arts, or school subjects, they frequently look to extracurricular activities such as afterschool and weekend programs, summer camps, tutors, or special teachers. These activities supplement and extend the child's routine experiences in an informal and personally engaging fashion. To nurture developing interest in science and mathematics, middle-class parents locate summer science camps, afterschool and Saturday enrichment programs, environmental education opportunities, museum programs, or even computer camps at Club Med. A summer program effect accrues when youngsters are taken out of their typical education and home environments and given the opportunity to immerse themselves in a subject, such as science, with other equally motivated children (Lynch, 1990).

Moreover, for children who are not as affluent, the effects of such programs seem just as potent, if not more so (Lynch & Mills, 1990, 1993). The summer program effect may stave off the summer setback that is especially detrimental to students whose summer environments do not reinforce school learning (Ceci, 1991; Entwisle & Alexander, 1992). Science education reform efforts—with the help of federal, state, or private funding groups, folded in with State, Urban, and Rural Systemic Initiatives—should encourage the development of summer programs aimed specifically at reformed science education for children from poor schools. Such programs could provide the opportunity for curriculum developers and science teacher educators to test promising curriculum materials and teaching methods, as well as to train teachers to use them. These programs could become the crucibles in which to test the effects of science education reform measures on students who have been bypassed by science in the past—the acid test of their worth.

For instance, the Mathematics, Engineering, Science Achievement (MESA) program at Lawrence Hall of Science (University of California at Berkeley) offers a broad range of activities intended to enrich and advance students of color in science-related careers, including scholarships, study groups, summer programs, field trips, and employment opportunities. The program also emphasizes parental support. It is an extensive program operating at more than 30 university centers and has an impressive track record. MESA participants perform above the level of nonparticipating peers and at levels similar to college-bound students, regardless of ethnicity (Oakes, 1990a).

Such programs would benefit students across the nation, but may be especially important to encourage the development of science talent and interest in urban and rural communities. If science education reform is to decrease the distance between haves and have nots in school science, it may be necessary either to insure all students are brought into the reform or target school districts that do not have the resources to launch such ambitious efforts. The NSF Urban and Rural Systemic Initiatives are steps in the right direction, although it is too soon to know the results of these efforts.

It is fair to say that no one knows exactly what the costs may be to prepare a school to create a science education program that leads to the attainment of the science standards for all. Yet, the expenses may certainly include: hiring of new staff with specific kinds of expertise, providing empowering professional development for the current staff, new curricular materials, lab equipment and supplies, and technology.

The argument has been made that in order to produce equitable outcomes in science across groups, it may mean that some students will require more resources than others. This may indeed be true. However, in the case of resource allocation, one could find a great deal of hope if, initially, all poor schools were simply provided with the same basic decent facilities and human resources that are commonly found in more affluent schools. Once this equity floor is established, educators could do a better job in understanding the needs of diverse learners and intelligently planning to create conditions for learning that respond to those needs.

7

School Organization

Life expands or contracts in proportion to one's courage.

—Anaïs Nin

"Vanity asks: Is it popular? Politics asks: Will it work? Morality asks: Is it right?" That was Martin Luther King Jr.'s suggested test for proposed solutions.

—Gilliam (1997)

A TRUE STORY

Harrison High is a school of about 1,200 students in Farmington Hills, Michigan, just outside of Detroit. When I last worked there in 1982, the football coach, John Herrington, had once again amazed everyone by putting together a great football team that went on to win the Class A state championship. How did he do it? The school was relatively small, just barely achieving Class A status, and the community, primarily upper middle class, was not thought of as a football hotbed. Coach Herrington had a strategy: Virtually every male student in the school, no matter how unlikely, was perceived as potential material for the football team. Honor roll scholars were recruited as avidly as the burnouts hanging in the parking lot. Herrington did not see stereotypes, he saw possibilities. The gawky, slight ninth grader who never had touched a football or played sports was viewed in the light of the strong running back he could become 2 or 3 years hence. Attendance at try-outs was huge. Everyone wanted to play for Coach Herrington, and as a result, his pool of potential football players numbered about 600—nearly every boy in the school.

What if educators viewed science talent in exactly the same way? Would the result be more students enthused about science, clearing a path for science literacy? Would a corollary effect be a science research community that did not need to rely on people born abroad to fill many of its strategic positions? Is this where the equity–excellence dichotomy unify into a single coherent goal?

A RECENT HISTORY OF ABILITY
GROUPING IN SCIENCE

Just as resources are an equity issue across school districts and states, so it is within individual schools where school organization practices, such as tracking, can result in substantial differences in the distribution of resources. *Tracking* is "the practice of dividing students into separate classes for high-, average-, and low-achievers; it lays out different curriculum paths for students headed for college and those bound directly for the workplace" (Oakes, 1986, p. 13). Because such grouping schemes result in substantially different instruction in terms of both quality and quantity, students' outcomes vary according to their position in the hierarchy. This is true even after individual differences are taken into account (Gamoran & Weinstein, 1995). This means that tracking is not only a reflection of initial individual differences in the student population, but it also plays a causal role in widening the gaps between various groups.

American schools have often separated students into groups or streams based on perceived abilities and potential for higher education or vocational training. This practice was strongly promoted in science education in the post-Sputnik era (c. 1957), when beating the Soviets was the United States' primary goal for the Cold War and the space program (Salinger, 1991). The science education reform initiated in the 1950s and 1960s was an ambitious national effort that encouraged hands-on, inquiry-based teaching methods, with the aim of preparing the best students for science careers. Tracking or ability grouping for science within schools became a norm that few questioned.

Later, in the aftermath of school desegregation and busing, as White families began to leave urban areas, magnet schools for the gifted and talented were created as enticements for White families or middle-class families to remain in more integrated settings. Science, mathematics, and technology were common themes for many of these magnet schools, and extra resources were provided to create programs that could attract students with special interests and abilities in science. In some cases, this practice (so acceptable in the 1970s when educators were desperate to stabilize neighborhood schools) has come under fire in the 1990s as a second-generation segregation issue (Lynch, 1994). This is because in ethnically diverse American schools that are supposedly integrated, the designated level of a particular science class (i.e., honors, regular, or basic skills) can often be determined with 100% accuracy simply by observing the proportion of students of color within them. Lower track classes are disproportionately populated by students of color, except Asian Americans (see Fig. 7.1), working-class and low-income students (Oakes, 1985), and, students with disabilities (NSF, 1996a; Oakes, 1985, 1990b). The upper level science classes are populated largely by White and Asian American students from the higher socioeconomic strata.

In many of the magnet schools or upper tracks, the extra resources and inspiring programs chiefly benefited the most affluent students, who often happen to be White or Asian American. On the other hand, for females and students of color who are admitted into advanced academic science classes, the effects are compensatory—these students do better than they would have in the absence of tracking (Gamoran, 1989). The problem is that these benefits accrue to only those students of color and girls who are admitted to the advanced classes and may work against the majority who are not. Still, decisions to detrack schools require a great deal of thought and planning because the compensatory effect could be lost, unless the new design can ensure high standards and the resources that may be required to maintain them.

Charges of elitism and unfairness were (and are) countered with the observation that poor children and children with disabilities within the

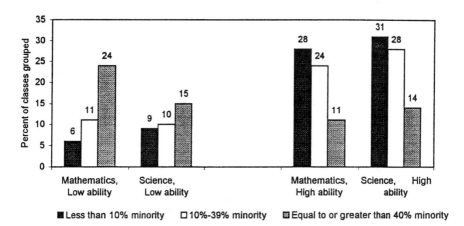

FIG. 7.1.   Percent of high school science and mathematics classes grouped by ability, according to percent minority in class: 1993. *Note.* High school includes grades 9–12. From *Indicators of Science and Mathematics: 1995*, in NSF (1996a).

same schools receive extra funding from federal programs such as Title 1 or Individuals with Disabilities Education Act (IDEA) and from state programs. In addition, it is often charged, with a great measure of fairness, that the students who get the least attention and fewest extra resources are those who are in the middle, the average students. They seldom have access to special programs. It is a major concern that they not be lost in the shuffle as educators focus on mandates and lobby for students who are better and worse off.

Tracking was accompanied by curriculum differentiation (e.g., varied content, texts, equipment, teaching approaches, and assignments for different groups of students) and a value system that seldom questioned the practice of giving superior resources to students who appeared to have the most promise for careers in science. Tracking in the United States contrasts with the type of grouping done in other countries where, after an extended period of common instruction (usually, until the age of 14 or so), students take tests and are assigned to different types of high schools with different goals, but with a common core curriculum. Of course, because the United States has no common curriculum, the danger of stratifying opportunity to learn science through a differentiated curriculum is ominously present.

Many things have changed in U.S. science education since the 1950s. Above all, Americans now recognize that it is in the national interest to prepare all students well in the areas of science and mathematics and that U.S. educators have a lot of ground to make up in order to do so. Still, ability grouping in science is a common practice, with 34% of U.S. high schools assigning incoming students to science courses by ability compared to only 11% of middle and junior high schools (NSF, 1996a). Furthermore, at least in the Washington metropolitan area, one seems more likely to find ability grouping in schools that are more ethnically and socioeconomically diverse than in those that are more homogeneous. Is this a pragmatic response to differences in achievement levels in such schools or racism and classism? This is one of the thorniest issues in U.S. education.

RESEARCH ON ABILITY GROUPING

The current science education reform with its goal of science literacy for all is a significant departure from old values and practices that are firmly entrenched in our schools. Attitudes toward tracking have changed dramatically since the 1950s, with many influential educational organizations coming out forcefully against the practice. Table 7.1 summarizes the positions of several education agencies on tracking in science education

TABLE 7.1
Summary of Interpretation of Policy Stances Regarding Ability Grouping

Organization	Favor "detracking" heterogeneous grouping	Neutral	Favor programs for gifted and talented: homogeneous grouping
The Bush Administration—America 2000		X	
National Governors' Association		X	
National Science Foundation		X	
National Science Teachers' Association	X		
American Association for the Advancement of Science	X		
National Research Council	X		
U.S. Department of Education—Eisenhower Project		X	
U.S. Department of Education—Office of Civil Rights	X		
National Association for the Advancement of Colored People	X		
Carnegie Council on Adolescent Development	X		
U.S. Department of Education—Jacob Javits Gifted and Talented Education Program			X
National Research Center on Gifted and Talented Education			X

Note. From *Ability Grouping and Science Education Reform*, by S. Lynch, 1994.

reform (Lynch, 1994). Most of the policymaking organizations are wary of tracking, and indeed, this concern has resulted in detracking becoming a major focus in school restructuring efforts. The result has most often been the elimination of lower level classes (Gamoran & Weinstein, 1995).

Quantitative Research on Ability Grouping

The body of quantitative experimental research focused specifically on tracking in *science* education is in short supply (with the exception of Hoffer, 1992; see also Lynch, 1994, for a more complete review). Yet, there is an abundance of empirical research and meta-analyses on the tracking issue *in general*. Although much of this work is equivocal and advocates often selectively cite studies that support their positions (Loveless, 1995; Lynch, 1994), the results can be summarized in this fashion: When the mean achievement measures for all students taken together under either grouping condition are compared, the differences are minimal (Hoffer, 1992). Further examination shows that students placed in lower track science classes generally achieve somewhat less well than their counterparts in heterogeneously grouped classes. Students placed in higher track science classes achieve somewhat better than they would have had they been heterogeneously grouped. This is especially true if the curriculum is accelerated or in some way specially differentiated for these students (Kulik & Kulik, 1991). The achievement scores of middle-range students are not much affected under either condition, homogeneous or heterogeneous grouping.

Qualitative Research on Ability Grouping

A substantial body of qualitative research on tracking provides a more disconcerting and less equivocal picture. Students in lower track classes have fewer resources and experience science very differently than students in higher track classes. To be specific, Oakes (1985, 1990b) and others showed (using very large databases) that students in lower track classes are taught less material at lower levels of expectation by less qualified teachers who have less access to education resources in classroom environments that are characterized, not unsurprisingly, by less motivated students and teachers and more discipline problems. For students in upper tracks, the opposite conditions exist. Students in the middle tracks fall in the middle of most of these measures.

It is, of course, an equity issue when some students within a school get fewer or inferior resources, especially if these students are not performing well to begin with. Yet, an even greater problem is not disparate per pupil expenditures, it is the fact that students in lower track classes often are cut off from high-status knowledge, the important concepts and skills that lead to educational attainment at upper levels:

> Students who are thought to be of low ability are far less likely to be placed in traditional academic courses. . . . These disparities undoubtedly reflect earlier and broader conditions that fail to develop the skills . . . of disadvantaged students rather than overt discrimination in the enrollment process. But the net effect is that . . . [they] . . . have considerably less access to knowledge that is considered necessary either for science or mathematics careers or for becoming scientifically literate, critically thinking citizens and productive members of an increasingly technological workforce. (Oakes, 1990b, p. 45)

Track placement seems to determine teacher expectations and exposure to higher order thinking skills, especially in mathematics and science (Raudenbush, Rowan, & Cheong, 1993). Researchers have shown how variations in course selection of gateway science and math courses (e.g.,

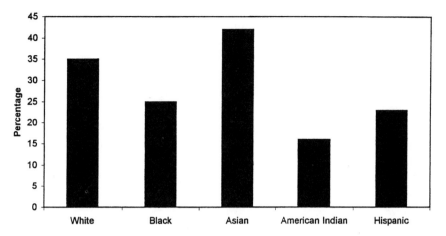

FIG. 7.2. Percentage of 1990 10th-grade students enrolled in college preparatory, academic, or specialized academic programs by race or ethnicity. *Note.* Hispanics may be of any race. From *Women, Minorities, and Persons With Disabilities* by NSF, 1994.

chemistry, geometry, etc.) for females and underrepresented groups result in these students being locked out of upper level courses (see Fig. 7.2), thereby limiting their opportunities to pursue science, mathematics, and engineering further (Gamoran & Berends, 1987; Oakes, 1990a). The finest curriculum based on reform principles taught by the best prepared teachers using the most elaborate equipment will not result in equitable science, if some students are excluded from access or ignored by administrators and other decision makers. For example, in one high school of an suburban school system, 80% of the very diverse student body takes physics—equal numbers of boys and girls and good representation from every ethnic group. Almost everyone takes a science course every year; it is cool to do so at this high school. A few miles away in a school with almost identical demographics, less than 25% of the students take physics. A glance into the physics classrooms of the second school reveals that most of the students are White male students and Asian Americans of both sexes—there are very few underrepresented students or White females, despite their presence in large numbers at the school. This situation seems to bother no one.

RESTRUCTURED SCHOOLS AND THE TRACKING PROBLEM

This research evidence has led to school reform measures that minimize tracking or attempt to eliminate it altogether (Oakes & Wells, 1996). It has been easier for schools to eliminate lower level classes than upper level ones (Gamoran & Weinstein, 1995). For instance, a NSF (1996c) report on the Urban Systemic Initiatives indicated that several participating urban school districts initiated their reform of science and mathematics education by eliminating the lower level classes (e.g., in Baltimore, Cincinnati, Phoenix, and Dade County) such as consumer math, and by raising high school graduation requirements (e.g., in Baltimore, Chicago, Cincinnati, Dallas, El Paso, and Dade County). In Baltimore, 80% of the eighth graders were placed in algebra.

Simply changing graduation requirements may be sufficient to push some students into a more rigorous high school program that positions them better for college and prepares them more effectively for interesting jobs. This is a cheap fix for improving science education and one whose merits should not be underestimated. However, simply setting standards or raising the bar will not alone bring all students to science literacy. Some will need additional support in order to meet rigorous standards in science and mathematics. This is something that even Bart Simpson of the television series, *The Simpsons*, can recognize. In one episode, the Simpson family moves to another state where Bart finds himself behind the other students in school and is placed in a remedial class. Bart, although no genius, quickly recognizes that he is never going to catch up with the kids in the other classes if all the remedial teacher ever does is dwell on the first three letters of the alphabet or provide self-esteem building exercises such as musical chairs with an excess of chairs. This seems so obvious, yet when one examines science classes designed for students having difficulties, rarely do we see serious efforts to actually close gaps, something that could easily require more time and resources for science, not less.

In a noteworthy exception in the area of mathematics, California and New York both have created transition courses to bridge basic and college preparatory math. For instance, a Stretch Regents class in Rochester, New York covers in 2 years what the typical Regents math course covers in 1. The class replaces the non-Regents sequence of General Math and Consumer Math. Although the pace is slower in Stretch Regents, depth is not compromised. Given that the student population targeted is low-achieving students whose prior math experiences were less than optimal, this approach makes a great deal of sense. A study of seven high schools in New York and California providing such bridge courses indicated that students in these classes were much more successful than those in the general track in obtaining college preparatory math credits, had greater achievement gains, and showed greater interest and self-confidence in mathematics (White, Porter, Gamoran, & Smithson, 1996). There were problems for English language learners, however, because the bridge courses required a higher level of English proficiency than many of these students attained.

There are obvious equity implications for science education reform efforts where the goal is science literacy for all students within a school. Students must have access to the same high status knowledge defined in the NSES and Benchmarks. Yet, there may be more than one path to achieve these outcomes. Some students may take longer than others, especially if their previous experiences in science vary greatly, and this may require some ability grouping. However, other types of compensatory measures such as afterschool tutoring, Saturday classes, or summer study may also be options that reduce the stigma of grouping and put more responsibility on the student to catch up or to use regular class time more wisely.

Science teachers are not at all unanimous in their attitudes toward ability grouping (see Fig. 7.3), with high school science teachers being far more supportive of tracking than elementary and middle school teachers. This may bolster the stereotype of high school science teachers being far more interested in teaching their subjects than students, or it may reflect the fact that by the time that students enter high school, differences in their background knowledge are so great that it becomes increasingly

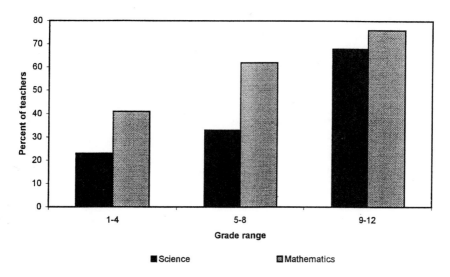

FIG. 7.3.   Percent of science and mathematics teachers agreeing that students learn science or mathematics best in classes with students of similar abilities by subject and grade range: 1993. Note. From *Indicators of Science and Mathematics Education: 1995*, in NSF (1996a).

difficult to effectively teach all students in a heterogeneous group. Is it possible to offer high quality, authentic science instruction to all students in detracked schools?

In a study of 300 restructured schools by Gamoran and Weinstein (1995) that focused primarily on grouping patterns for mathematics and social studies, 92% of the schools reported that students spent most of their time in heterogeneous groups. All had eliminated low level or remedial tracks. However, on further probing, the researchers found that less than one half made extensive use of mixed ability grouping. Rather, most schools (especially the high schools in the study) had between-class grouping for math and social studies and also had sections of honors math. The researchers selected 24 of the most innovative, restructured schools for intensive study in order to explore how restructuring had affected the quality of instruction. In many of the schools, the detracking efforts resulted in a loss of academic rigor, with some teachers gearing their pedagogy and content to their low expectations for lower achieving students. Others provided more challenging and engaging instruction to students, no matter what the grouping situation. Researchers found high-quality instruction to be idiosyncratic, varying among teachers according to their commitment to intellectual rigor, rather than driven by school-wide implementation of high standards (Gamoran & Weinstein, 1995).

There were two exceptions to this pattern, noteworthy not only because of the quality of instruction, but also because the schools took very different approaches. One secondary school with an ethnically and socioeconomically diverse 7th- through 12th-grade student body, successfully and completely detracked all courses through the 10th grade. It offered some choice variations in Grades 11 and 12. The school was distinguished by a visionary principal, a self-selected and committed teaching staff, small class sizes, individualized and personalized instruction, and substantial extra funding for support. The standards were high for all students, and if a student fell behind, it was understood that the student should seek the extra help provided by the school. For instance, there were tutoring sessions offered on Saturdays.

The other successful school was also characterized by a high quality of instruction for all students, but in marked contrast, was built around the philosophy of personal choice and a passionate commitment to teaching and learning. At this middle school, students could choose from various levels of courses. In this sense, they were self-tracked. However, the instruction in even the lowest level was challenging (more challenging than in higher track classes in other schools in this study). Students were constantly given opportunities to regroup themselves in every discipline and high standards were upheld. Teachers rotated teaching assignments, but were encouraged to become passionately involved in their subjects. The result was an instructional climate of richness and depth, no matter how differentiated the levels, rather than one characterized by fragmented knowledge.

Because only 2 schools out of 300 restructured schools were able to demonstrate a climate of high level, authentic learning for all, this study shows that restructuring schools neither results in the elimination of ability grouping, nor is likely to remedy the ills of stratified opportunity to learn that characterizes tracked schools. Restructuring must be accompanied by substantial changes to the school's intellectual environment and a clear vision of high standards for all.

COMPETING MANDATES AND EQUITY

Education reform initiatives at the state level have encouraged or even coerced some schools to reexamine their policies for tracking students in science. High stakes testing and new graduation requirements lead to accountability for student achievement that, in the past, may have been nonexistent. In science, schools have been able to ignore the fact that some students have not learned much science because there is no state-mandated assessment of science achievement or because substantial numbers of students are regularly excused from taking such tests when they are available (LaCelle-Peterson & Rivera, 1993).

This is a grouping issue that has been swept under the rug—students with disabilities and English language learners who receive their science in sheltered classes are taught by special education or ESL or bilingual education teachers with little or no background in science. Although such within-school administrative arrangements may be well-intentioned, based on my observations of such classes, they can be generally characterized as light on science and heavy on reading and language skills instruction, as the following examples illustrate.

The instruction in one special education science class seemed to be a bad parody of traditional science instruction. In one instance, a special educator taught all of Newton's Laws in a single class period to six middle school students with multiple learning and physical disabilities. Three of the students had central nervous system (CNS) disorders and were in motorized wheelchairs. As the teacher flashed overheads of Newton's Laws, students highlighted the corresponding lines on their individual copies of the teacher's notes, as if a stroke of yellow highlighter across the words on paper could sweep in understanding. An experienced science teacher would know that teaching these concepts for understanding requires much more time and a very different approach. A creative science teacher might develop a wonderful series of activities on velocity, acceleration, and momentum built on students operating their wheel-chairs—ideal motion carts with a well-regulated rheostats. This probably would have been a welcome change for these students. Their chairs could become the center of a science activity and useful tools, rather than an accommodation to reduced mobility.

Although special education and ESL or bilingual education teachers may have significant, crucial expertise in their specializations, the dearth of knowledge about science or science teaching can result in instruction that requires only low-level memorization of vocabulary or hands-on activities that seem to lead nowhere, rather than building conceptual understanding. Yet, these teachers are drafted into teaching science. They may lack not only factual knowledge, but also have little notion of important science concepts to emphasize, nor the instincts (pedagogical content knowledge) to create lessons to get them across. Sometimes, the science taught is simply dead wrong—as when such a teacher told her high school students that jellyfish (lowly coelenterates) and squid (more evolutionarily advanced mollusks) must be closely related because both have tentacles. This example demonstrates more than a factual error; it points out an important misconception of the nature of evolution. In other instances, the science taught was accurate, but perhaps not worth teaching, as when another teacher asked her class of students with severe multiple learning and communication disabilities to memorize the parts of a flower from a diagram in the text—ovule, stamens, pistils, etc.— rather than explaining the function of a flower in plant reproduction or providing flowers and seeds for the students to examine.

Just as special educators and ESL or bilingual education teachers are placed in situations in which they insufficiently prepared to teach science, so are the science teachers often out of their depth when they are recruited to instantaneously become effective teachers of students with disabilities or of those who are learning English. Whereas 40% of teachers reported having English language learners in their classes, only 29% said that they had some training to teach them (National Educational Goals Panel, 1994). As for preparation to teach students with disabilities, only 27% of high school science teachers considered themselves well-prepared, 46% of middle school teachers, and 50% of elementary school teachers (NSF, 1996b).

Yet, as long as specialized training for teaching science to students with disabilities or English language learners is not specifically required, many science teachers will find themselves floundering in their efforts to reach diverse learners. For instance, in one high school science department, a science teacher volunteered to take on a general science class for English language learners. The course was designed to be a transition course between the ESL program and the mainstream and was to run over the course of 2 consecutive years. On the day that I was invited to observe the class, the teacher lectured for 80 minutes straight (the school had block scheduling). He seldom used visual aids, and when he did, the transparencies were illegible, a problem that no student pointed out. This lengthy a lecture would be a boring proposition for any group of high school students, but for students who have only partially mastered English, it had to be exhausting if they were seriously trying to follow him. In addition, all speaking of the students' first languages had been banned from this classroom, even though this type of exchange might have been used to clarify concepts or directions. Project-based work and performance assessments had been eliminated in favor of multiple-choice tests. All of this was well-intentioned and had a rationale—the teacher was preparing them to take the high stakes state science examination for high school graduation and was concerned about job opportunities for these students if their English was poor—but it was also contrary to recommended practices in ESL or bilingual education or the goals of science education reform. Had this teacher some substantial, formal training in ESL or bilingual education (which usually consists of a series of courses, including linguistic theory, methods, and multicultural approaches to teaching), his classroom practice likely would have been very different. In what other profession but education could a person shift major assignments without additional specialized preparation?

The teachers in these examples were trained for a school organization system that is becoming increasingly obsolete. They are caught up in competing mandates—new academic standards, high stakes state assessments that may or may not match curriculum frameworks, school-to-work standards, the special education inclusion movement, and bilingual education and ESL directives. In addition, in-service teacher training efforts float down from on high, promoting a variety of innovations such as team teaching, increased use of technology, integrated or thematic instruction, portfolio assessments, and so on. Yet, without a cohesive, collective vision for improved science education, this rain of initiatives can result in confusing school organization policies and practices that deliver good news–bad news results as schools attempt to improve education for diverse learners.

In one high school, a science teacher and special education teacher teamed up to teach a (special) section of science for students with learning disabilities. Such team teaching holds a great deal of promise because it provides the combined skills of the special educator with those of a science teacher. The science teacher, although inexperienced, seemed creative and energetic, and the special educator was skilled and knowledgeable. The two teachers were happy with the arrangement and were collaborating well. However, the school administration had not scheduled them with a mutual planning period. As a result, they divided up the teaching workload so that the science teacher took on most of the planning and all of the teaching, and the special education teacher did all of the grading—hardly an optimal arrangement for science instruction responsive to students' developing conceptual understanding. Worse yet, all of the students in this class had been mainstreamed the previous year, so this special science class represented a huge step backward for them in terms of inclusion. It seemed to be organized to accommodate the mandate for team teaching and the teachers' schedules. It also relieved the other science teachers in the department of the responsibility of working with students with disabilities.

At another school, science teachers team taught heterogeneous inclusion classes with ESL or bilingual or special educators, but it often appeared that the teachers, in attempting to work together, had developed a science curriculum that had been "dumbed down." In some cases, the science teachers reported dropping projects and activities involving inquiry or technology, and replacing them with worksheets, word searches, and study guides. Science, a class with so much potential for learning through interaction with physical phenomena, had devolved into a class centered on English language skills, the ability often in shortest supply in these inclusion classrooms. Group activities focused on writing and vocabulary, and were often structured so that the less able students were supported by the more able to the extent that it was not clear that they were learning anything at all, although they were getting good grades. Teachers created accommodations designed to get students who had difficulties with language through a course loaded with language, rather than adjusting the course so that it was less language dependent or offering a menu of activities that relied, to varying degrees, on language skills. (These observations are consistent with a large study of teaching higher order thinking skills in science classrooms, where the researchers found that expectations connected to academic track were more salient than teacher preparation or administrative support; Raudenbush et al., 1993.)

In some team-teaching situations, the science teacher takes on the brunt of the course load, while the special educator acts more like a teacher's aide, assisting students with their homework during the odd moments of the class, rather than teaching portions of the class or helping the science teacher to plan and structure activities to accommodate a range of learning styles and abilities. This leads to resentment on both sides of the teaching fence—the science teacher feels overburdened and the special educator or ESL teacher feels diminished and sometimes bored. What might be a resource-rich, collaborative, imaginative team is reduced to an uncomfortable and ineffective compromise.

These examples are not intended as condemnations of either science teachers or special education and ESL or bilingual education teachers involved. Rather, these teachers are valuable resources, but resources that are misused by a school organizational structure that responds to competing mandates with no coherent vision. This is an unflinching portrayal of the circumstances in which teachers can find themselves, like it or not, as mandates shift, but where support systems and resources do not always accompany them. Not only do the students suffer, but it also creates a environment of uncertainty and frustration for the teachers, many of whom openly acknowledged the problems just described.

THE EQUITY SCHEMA
AND SCHOOL ORGANIZATION

When we speak of science literacy for all, are students with disabilities and English language learners included? Can they achieve the outcomes described in the science standards documents? Both groups contain students with the potential to operate at the highest levels of science achievement, well beyond the thresholds called for in science literacy standards. Consider, for example, Stephen Hawkins or Albert Einstein. Yet, we must also acknowledge that there are also some students with substantial cognitive disabilities for whom formal operational reasoning will always be elusive. In addition, older students who have recently immigrated to the United States from countries where they had little formal schooling may find that science standards at their grade level may be nearly impossible to achieve in a short time. However, for the vast majority of students with disabilities and English language learners, progress toward these literacy goals makes as much sense as for any other student. Given the high-stakes testing tied to high school diplomas and employment opportunities that are being called for in many states, we need to develop some protective policies or alternative routes for students who cannot achieve these outcomes in a standard curriculum. We badly need more research in this area in order to better understand how to help these students attain the science literacy goals or recognize circumstances under which it may be unreasonable to expect a given student to reach these goals.

Within School Equity Issues

Just as we used the equity schema (Fig. 1.1) as a way to assess the fairness of resource distribution across school districts in chapter 6, it may also be used to analyze the conditions of science learning within the individual school situations, such as those that were previously described. At Level 1, we ask if students in a particular class or group have reached the threshold outcomes outlined in the Science Standards (NRC, 1996) or Benchmarks (AAAS, 1992). When students are tracked into low level classes that do not seem to teach much of anything well and lock them out of future opportunities, the equity issue is obvious. As a result, many schools have already eliminated such classes.

Yet, we are less likely to be able to answer this achievement question for students with disabilities and those who are learning English because many are routinely exempted from large-scale assessments (LaCelle-Peterson & Rivera, 1993). This, in turn, is a monstrous equity issue because selectively excusing individual students from assessments means that the school organizational structure is also excused from accountability through evaluation. It allows schools to turn a blind eye to the efficacy of instruction for some students, as it is easier to pass them along rather than figuring out ways to effectively teach them science. It seems reasonable to suppose that if the school's progress in teaching science to students with disabilities and English language learners were monitored, then many of the conditions described in the previous pages would be improved.

Next, we turn to Level 2 of the equity schema, and ask if the basic level of resources within the school are equitably distributed? Do all groups of students have appropriate curriculum materials, access to certified science teachers, laboratory space, and technology? Sometimes, adequate facilities are not provided for students with disabilities or English language learners, although they exist in the school. The answer often is "no" with regards to access to certified science teachers or to teachers who have specialized training to work with students with special needs. As the inclusion movement in special education gathers momentum and more English language learners enter our schools, we will need science teachers with the skills to better teach these students. Admittedly, some exceptions exist. One of the best science teachers I know is a middle school ESL teacher with no formal training in science (but whose father was a research scientist) who works on a middle school team that provides him with excellent science materials to adapt for his ESL students. I also have observed some creative and flexible science teachers concoct wonderful adaptations for their diverse students, but these seem to be more the exception than the rule. If we are indeed serious about the goal of science literacy for all, there are two reasonable solutions to these problems: either require dual certification in science and special education or bilingual or ESL education and be prepared to fund this added requirement or provide teams of teachers who together have the requisite skills and knowledge and be prepared to pay for two teachers working together in a classroom. Such teachers will also require some substantial training in team teaching and will need to be provided with administrative arrangements that support collaborative work. Anything less sets up the students and teachers for failure, especially given the demands of science education reform and high stakes accountability.

Yet, under other circumstances, such as the team-teaching arrangements described in this chapter, decent basic resources are available and certified teachers were present. Therefore, we must address equity issues at Level 3 of the schema, attempt to evaluate the situation in terms of its basic fairness, and be prepared to make trade-offs. For instance, in the case of special education students who had been removed from the mainstream and placed in a team-taught, homogeneously grouped class to accommodate school organizational practices, the school's decision makers should reconsider the trade-off that has been made. The current situation—disinclusion—may solve one school organization problem, but perhaps at the expense of students' best interests. Obviously, more details are required to fully understand the reasoning behind this arrangement. According to federal guidelines and the field's view of best practice, inclusion is the priority. However, a decision to mainstream these students could mean that more science teachers would have to learn how to accommodate students with disabilities and that the special educator as a resource would have to be deployed differently.

Moreover, there is a concern about how the inclusion of students with disabilities will affect other students in the class. Without adequate support, the pace of instruction might be slowed. On the other hand, many of the accommodations recommended for students with learning disabilities, such as instruction that uses multiple modalities, teaching methods other than lectures, and emphasis on laboratory work, group work, and alternative assessment, are consistent with science education reform goals and could improve the instruction for all students.

Equity Vectors for Science Education Reform

In order for schools and teachers to make sound decisions about how to approach the myriad trade-offs that need to be made, Fig. 7.4 provides a series of equity vectors for school organization that all aim in the same direction—best practice for diverse learners in science education. The logic behind many of these equity vectors has already been discussed, or is addressed more fully in chapters 8 and 9. Figure 7.4 is designed to alert educators to bedrock principles of improved education for diverse learners, as they weigh the within-school allocation of resources in science education. These equity vectors are not absolutes—rather, they point the

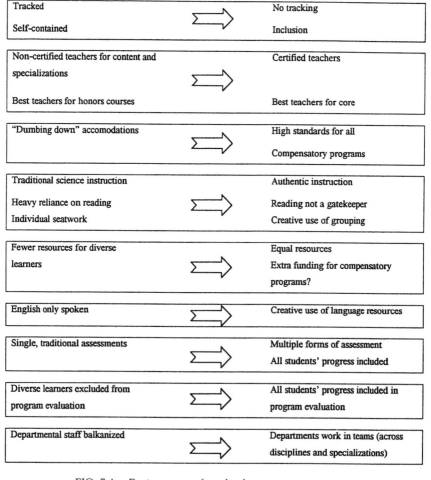

FIG. 7.4.   Equity vectors for school science organization.

way toward equitable recommended practices that may in fact be very difficult to actually achieve.

The first item in Fig. 7.4 aims at conditions in which it is preferable to organize classes that are inclusive and heterogeneous, rather than tracked and ability grouped. This may mean the following:

- Eliminate low-level classes and their ambience of disappointment or despair (Gamoran & Weinstein, 1995).
- Reduce the number of levels of classes.
- Frequently regroup students.
- Design alternative routes so that students are not locked into a track that excludes them from opportunities.
- Intervene when it becomes apparent that certain students are being unfairly disadvantaged by groupings. It may mean that some science teachers may need substantial professional development experiences that help them to develop instructional practices that can both challenge and meet the needs of a heterogeneous group. Perhaps class sizes should be reduced or a wider variety of curriculum materials made available (e.g., texts written at different reading levels or levels of sophistication).

The second item in Fig. 7.4 points toward the goal of having all students taught by teachers certified in science as well as areas such as special education or ESL or bilingual education as necessary. Moreover, class assignment priorities are shifted so that the best teachers teach the core courses. This benefits those students in the middle, the majority. It may require new organizational arrangements such as team teaching, the hiring of additional teachers, or substantial, long-term professional development for members of the current staff, but how can we seriously countenance a goal of science literacy for all students as long as some are taught science by teachers who themselves are not scientifically literate?

The third item suggests vigilance about the types of accommodations made for diverse learners so that course material is not "dumbed down," but that adjustments are made with a clear eye toward science literacy standards. This, in fact, may be the most important single equity vector of all. Sometimes, troubled urban schools are awash with offers for help and special programs, resulting in scrambled priorities. Teachers or science departments may be lured into experimenting with innovative curriculum materials, extraneous to the science standards. Teachers who are intrigued with new technologies may be vulnerable to the siren call of new software. These opportunities, for all their merits, represent detours from the central goal of science literacy. This vector calls for a steady and clear focus on curriculum standards. If interesting sidetrips are to be undertaken, the teacher should be aware of it and be able to provide a rationale.

The fourth vector (to be discussed in more detail in chap. 8) suggests that in order to better meet the needs of diverse learners, teachers must depart from traditional lectures, heavy reliance on reading and work-sheets, and move toward instruction that is more experiential, engaging, and relevant. Students should learn through activities that are not solely based on verbal presentation, but work directly with science phenomena whenever possible. Such instruction may often rely on students working together in groups. However, if the groups are constructed so that the burden falls on one or two members while the others go along for the ride, then this is a problem. The composition of the groups, the nature of the group assignments, and the assessment system all must be orches-trated until it is clear that group work results in the participation and progress of each student.

The fifth vector suggests that in cases where diverse learners have access to fewer resources or to resources of lesser quality, the situation can be improved to the point that resources are at least equalized. A substantial amount of time and professional effort must be devoted to reviewing materials for their capability to effectively teach targeted stan-dards and meet the needs of diverse learners. A reallocation of resources, or a hard look at existing organizational patterns, may be necessary. Moreover, this is where important trade-offs or compensatory programs should go on the bargaining table.

The sixth vector points toward science education that uses language resources creatively in schools where there are large populations of Eng-lish language learners. This implies that the science teacher is aware of the nature of the second language acquisition process and is willing to group and regroup in various ways that may or may not allow use of the students' first language. In schools where there are sufficient numbers of students with a common first language, a bilingual science program may be considered, although this would require trade-offs that a school or community might not support (e.g., segregated classes for English lan-guage learners, hiring a competent bilingual science teacher, etc.).

The seventh vector suggests that assessment take multiple forms (to be discussed further in chap. 9), rather than relying solely on current traditional forms that often test students' reading ability more than their understanding of science concepts. Of course, multiple forms of assess-ment take more time, are more difficult to grade, and raise validity and reliability issues. Yet, as large-scale exams add performance-based components (as in the 1996 NAEP in science; Sanchez, 1996), science teachers will ineluctably change their assessment style.

Hand in hand with the assessment vector is the eighth vector that points away from the exclusion of diverse learners from program evaluations and toward the measurement of their progress in order to give feedback to science education decision makers within the school about how to create more effective instructional environments. If standardized assessments are inappropriate for this purpose, then other program evaluation methods must be found.

Finally, the last vector points toward school organization patterns that allow teachers to work together across departmental lines to meet the needs of diverse learners. The ESL or bilingual and special education departments are especially important in discussions about science education standards and equity issues. Moreover, if a school seriously intends for all to achieve ambitious and comprehensive standards, it seems apparent that the departments of mathematics, social studies, and technology education must be involved in curriculum coordination. Much of the science curriculum connects very naturally with these disciplines, and it is hard to imagine all of these science concepts being taught for deep understanding in the confines of a science program alone.

In summary, Fig. 7.4 is designed to focus a response to competing education mandates or trendy professional development schemes in ways that provide a clear target: science education reform that attends to equity principles. As the reform moves forward and its powerful ideas are implemented in schools, evaluation practices that specifically address equity issues are being developed that go hand in hand with science reform. They include many of the guiding principles illustrated in Fig. 7.4 as well as other aspects of equitable school organization for science teaching. They help alert schools to group differences in patterns of course assignment, grading, test scores, attitudes, post-high school jobs and college majors, participation in activities such as science fairs and clubs, community support and practices within classrooms. (Some examples of these equity checklists may be found in *Science Education Reform for All*, George & Van Horne, 1996.)

SCIENCE EDUCATION REFORM AND GIFTED AND TALENTED EDUCATION

It seems impossible to write an honest chapter on tracking and science education reform without discussing gifted and talented education, an entity that includes the happy situation of talented and motivated students eager to learn science, as well as powerful advocacy and lobby groups that influence local, state, and national education policy. It may be equally impossible to say anything about the matter that has not already been said, many times.

The basic tension between science education reform and education of the gifted and talented is that the aim of the former is to raise the standards and increase access and instructional quality so that all students can become science literate, whereas the latter's goal is to is to develop the exceptional talent of a few. Science literacy for all should result in a better educated citizenry, the closing of achievement gaps, better representation in science careers for underrepresented groups, and a workforce that has the demanding basic skills to maintain the U.S. position in the global marketplace. Gifted and talented education in the context of science should result in the encouragement and intellectual development of those who show exceptional early talent and interest in science and who may go on in science-related careers and make contributions for the greater good. Gifted and talented education is seen as an individual, personalized response to students who may need unusual educational services to keep them challenged and engaged, services that a school may have difficulty providing in the regular program. Who could argue with the merit of either of these goals?

The twin goodness of these goals, however, is often overshadowed by the fact that resources are a limited commodity in schools, with the interests of one group weighed against those of others competing for them. Moreover, changing one child's education program is not a neutral act—it has effects, positive or negative, on other students. According to *National Excellence: A Case for Developing America's Talent* (U.S. Department of Education, Office of Educational Research and Improvement, 1993), the 1988 National Educational Longitudinal Study (NELS) study found that 8.8% of American eighth graders participated in gifted and talented programs. That included 17.6% of all Asian American students, 9.0% of White, non-Hispanic students, 7.9% of Black students, 6.7% of Hispanic students, and 2.1% of American Indian students. These statistics show that Asian Americans are overrepresented by a factor of nearly 2, and Hispanic and Black students are somewhat underrepresented. American Indian students are underrepresented by a factor of about 4. The report points out that states that use IQ scores as identification measures are likely to have greater ethnic disparities and within local school districts, the underrepresentation of Blacks, Hispanics, and American Indians can reach even higher proportions (Maker, 1996). However, as discussed in chapters 2 and 3, SES is more salient than ethnicity and probably underlies some of the ethnic disparities. The report says that:

> Economically disadvantaged students were significantly under-served. . . . Only 9% of the students in gifted and talented education programs were in the bottom quartile of family income (under-represented by a factor of nearly 3), while 47% of the program participants were from the top quartile in family income (over-represented by a factor of about 2). (p. 17)

Thus, those who are best situated in terms of SES, are most often the recipients of the extra resources for gifted and talented education at schools. The more a child is removed from the middle-class mainstream culture, the less likely for the student to be identified and served by gifted and talented programs (Subotnik, 1996). Although the direct line-item expenditures for gifted and talented education are relatively modest—only 2¢ for every $100 spent on education (U.S. Department of Education, Office of Educational Research and Improvement, 1993)—within schools, students seen as having high ability often have access to better teachers, facilities, and an improved learning environment, compared with students who are seen as average or less. (Extra resources are also often available for other groups of students through Title 1 or through special education services, but these programs just do not have the same cache as gifted and talented education.) Often at issue is the problem of ability grouping because it seems to confer some achievement advantages to those in the upper tracks (where gifted and talented children are likely to be placed), but disadvantages those who are not.

Politics, Rhetoric, and Ethics

The real question is whether heterogeneous science classrooms can be constructed so that the intellectual development in science of all students can be enhanced. This includes those who enter a course with considerable background knowledge and interest in science as well as those who do not. The problem, of course, is the rigid dichotomy that emerges as soon as we begin using this type of language and make this type of distinction—those who have it versus those who do not. Science literacy is too complex a construct, and students' background and motivation are too variable. Disproportionate representation by ethnicity and social class among programs for the gifted have sometimes made gifted and talented education a ferment of distrust, despite the fact the gifted and talented educators have tried for years to develop identification measures and design programs that cast a wide net to include diverse groups (Borland &

Wright, 1994; Maker, 1996). However, as we have seen, socioeconomically advantaged children, who are most often White and Asian American, are still the main recipients of the label and the services.

This situation has been interpreted by critical theorists in education
as a struggle by parents of White and wealthier families who have political
power to shape the system to their interests, creating closed classes for
children with similar backgrounds and values. Thus, tracking is seen as
a means of maintaining power and advantage in a stratified society, and
its advocates are characterized as traditionalists or selfish guardians of
privilege (Bowles & Gintes, 1976; Loveless, 1995).

Certainly, many educators hold this belief. I recently asked a science
coordinator of a large urban school district why the city schools seldom
grouped students by ability, whereas in the surrounding suburbs there is
an elaborate system of magnet schools for children talented in science
and math as well as tracking schemes within schools. Without pausing
for a breath, she eloquently and forcefully denounced the magnet school
approach as a means of allowing rich, powerful White parents to keep
their children from attending classes with students of color or poor students. However, in the same discussion, she allowed that she had removed her own son from the urban school system and placed him in a
private school. She saw no similarities in the two situations.

Tom Loveless (1995) of Harvard University, a political scientist who
explored the detracking of middle schools in the state of California in the
late 1980s, offered a different explanation of the politics of tracking.
Loveless could not entirely dismiss the interpretations of the critical
theorists as to the motivation of tracking advocates—class-based self-interest. However, he argued that an equally plausible explanation is the
politics of aggregation (see Green, 1980, 1983). This involves the conflicting goals of two different social institutions—the family and the state
educational system. When school systems initiate detracking measures,
the impetus is most likely to come from educators who are agents of the
state and act in the best interests of the groups of students, all students.
Their goal is equality of opportunity. Parents, on the other hand, are most
concerned with making the best decisions for their individual children
and are less likely to have equality of opportunity as a goal—they want
their own children to get the best education possible and that may mean
that their son or daughter receives more resources than other students
(Green, 1980). Loveless (1995) added:

> Because of these differences, we do not consider good teaching and good
> parenting to be synonymous, or ideal teachers and ideal parents to be inter-

changeable. Each fulfills a distinctive role in the child's life and the social structure. A conundrum emerges from serving as the guardians of groups versus the guardian of individuals . . . conflicts of aggregation. (p. 11)

Thus, Loveless suggested that the important differences in the tracking debate are not rooted in a division between the wealthy and the dispossessed or the selfish and the altruistic. Rather, the breach is between the purposes of family versus the purposes of the state systems of education, a dilemma that animates all policymaking in education.

This raises the issue of equity and parental advocacy. Ethnicity, proficiency in English, and length of residency in the United States are all factors that influence parent advocacy. Thus, it may be especially important for educators, in addition to parents, to energetically advocate for underrepresented students where ethnic groups have not consolidated political power. The U.S. educational system expects parents to be interested and involved advocates for their children. Parents who are familiar, comfortable, and successful with the public school system are certainly advantaged. For instance, in one study of new students' placement in high school honors English classes, it was found that lower class students and students of color were judged more rigorously on standardized tests for access to honors classes than their White and middle-class counterparts who were more often assisted by their parents' intervention (Gamoran, 1992).

Interestingly and contrary to other studies, Loveless did not find, in his study of detracking in California, that low SES parents were silent and disempowered in the state detracking initiative. Principals of the lowest SES schools reported the most dominant parent influence, more than the high SES schools, but the thrust of their influence supported the detracking policies, which was the opposite of what occurred in wealthier schools.

Both the critical theorists' analysis of gifted and talented education and Loveless' "conflicts of aggregation" explanation seem viable hypotheses for the politics of gifted and talented education and ability grouping. One does not wish to be naive in assessing the effects of the differing distribution of education resources among groups or the dog-eat-dog social Darwinism that seems to animate powerful sectors of the voting public and their politicians. In the end, perhaps it does not matter what motivates people, class-based self-interest or the individual concerns of parents for their children. Perhaps, we are all motivated to some degree by both, although we clearly have the capacity to act on behalf of *all* children. As educators, we are obligated to do so.

IMPLICATION OF SCIENCE EDUCATION REFORM
FOR THE GIFTED AND TALENTED

Implications of Science Education Reform
for the Gifted and Talented

For students who show exceptional talent and ability in any area—sports, the arts, academic subjects, or leadership—it seems only natural that schools would provide venues and outlets for these young people to joyfully pursue and develop their interests and abilities. Few would want a science education reform that could not provide for this and some worry that current reform will bring the achievement level of the top students down to close the gap, rather than bringing the bottom ones up.

However, one can speculate that even students identified as gifted and talented might not achieve the science standards, Level 1 of the equity schema (Fig. 1.1). Although once again we run into the assessment problem, it seems likely that despite high scores on standardized tests, mastery of NSES or Benchmarks requires a type of reasoning, conceptual understanding, and process skills unusual in today's science classrooms. In *Science for All Americans* (AAAS, 1989), the authors stated:

> Cognitive research is revealing that even with what is taken to be good instruction, many students, *including academically talented ones*, understand less than we think they do. With determination, students taking an examination are commonly able to identify what they have been told or what they have read; careful probing, however, often shows that their understanding is limited or distorted, if not altogether wrong. (p. 185; emphasis added)

The *Private Universe* film series discussed in chapter 5 aptly illustrated that the MIT and Harvard graduates (who almost certainly would be classified as gifted and talented and must have had high test scores in order to get into these prestigious universities) could not explain basic science concepts such as the cause of the seasons or the carbon cycle. Rather, they held tenaciously to their misconceptions.

There is some misconceptions research on gifted and talented high school juniors and seniors who attended the Virginia Governor's School for the Gifted in Science and Technology at the College of William and Mary (Bass & Reis, 1995). Students selected to attend this summer academic program were tested using a number of age-appropriate problems (including NAEP questions), designed to measure their understanding of specific scientific principles. On the whole, the group scores often were not high, and few students could answer two forms of the same problem, raising comprehension and transfer questions. There was a great range of variability in the adequacy of response in both concept and process problems, including a lack of mastery of key experimental design problems. This is exactly the type reasoning called for in science education reform documents, which are represented as baselines or thresholds, albeit ambitious ones. The researchers concluded that, even gifted students are not necessarily equal with respect to their ability to *solve different kinds of scientific problems*, speculating that the heterogeneity within this group of students at a school for the gifted suggests that they need special small group or independent learning activities (Bass & Reis, 1995). This sounds a little like tracking and remediation and probably would not be popular among students who have been told they are gifted. It also implies that conventional ways of identifying students as gifted in science may lack validity. If performance in science inquiry were used as an identification measure instead of standardized test scores, grades, or teacher recommendations, a different population might emerge (Borland & Wright, 1994; Maker, 1996)

However, leaving identification issues aside for now, there is little question that the range of human variability will mean that some students will be able to achieve the standards with greater ease or sooner than others. Science education reform holds a great deal of promise for such students. For instance, a comprehensive, valid assessment system, well aligned with standards, could be used to show that a student has mastered the standards for his or her grade band and is ready to move ahead. Students who can voraciously learn arcane facts and vocabulary, acquire sophisticated nuances into science concepts, or explore advanced topics seem to have much to gain and little to lose from the range of ambitious thresholds provided by Benchmarks and NSES. This assumes that schools loosen lockstep grade patterns. If a student can show mastery of the standards for his or her grade band, then the student could engage in challenging design projects or small-group or individual inquiry. Elective courses beyond the standards are another option. This is more or less consistent with James Rutherford's (the former Director of Project 2061) view of curriculum described in chapter 5. Another scenario has the precocious child charging straight through all of the standards, then branching out to electives such as traditional AP courses, other sorts of electives, college-level courses, or mentorships.

New technologies hold promise for individualization in the event that a student is ready for more advanced work as well as being a benefit to students other than the high achievers. Some students with disabilities would also be served well by technology if they needed to progress more slowly. The current educational structures for K–12 science education, both physical and administrative, do not accommodate the full range of human variability across developmental levels. The most serious impediment is the lock-step grade structure with the concurrent development of curricula and materials on a grade-by-grade basis. This can create unrealistic expectations for the teacher and result in the presentation of curriculum content inappropriate for students with disabilities (Cawley, 1994; Stefanich, 1994), as well as for academically talented students.

Currently, in most American schools, advanced science is synonymous with The College Board's AP programs. These courses replace college freshman survey courses in the sciences. Such university courses are often infamous for the mind-numbing quantity of material covered and act as hurdles that keep all but the most dedicated out of science. Although reform science would not preclude the AP programs for those who have achieved science literacy, one could readily conceive of other types of science courses as culminating or extended science experiences. At some magnet schools for science, mathematics, and technology, advanced courses take the form of full-year courses where the emphasis is on students doing creative, inquiry-based science or challenging design projects. These are independent projects done individually or in teams requiring the integration of concepts and skills to solve nontrivial real-world problems (Barth, 1994).

Assuming that it will eventually be possible to ascertain that some students have reached the science standards early, schools will still need to provide science beyond the core curriculum. Care should be taken to make sure that these additional courses do not gobble up resources and the best teachers, leaving the core depleted. Indeed, if there is a group of students who may not require the best teachers in the standard sense, it is the gifted and talented (James Rutherford, personal communication, December 18, 1996). Highly talented and motivated students may flourish with a type of coaching that relies more on relationships that develop with mentors who are experts in a particular science discipline, and the resulting sophisticated involvement with the subject matter.

Trade-Offs

Schools are incredibly resistant to change. Reforms that do not require major upheavals in the way that business is done may stand a better chance at implementation (National Center for Science Teaching and Learning, 1994). Consequently, changing rigid practices such as ability grouping is bound to be met with resistance, unless the school community can be convinced that it is practical and that all special interest groups of students will have something to gain. Sometimes, schools have been detracked without a great deal of thought as to the consequences. They do not have measures in place to accommodate diverse student needs or evaluation efforts for measuring the effects (Lynch, 1994). The documentation and evaluation of detracking efforts as schools implement science education reforms, such as the study of the effects of school restructuring on mathematics and social studies done by Gamoran and Weinstein (discussed earlier in this chapter), is exactly the type of research that is needed in science education. Trade-offs are more palatable when they are being negotiated in an atmosphere that allows understanding of their impact on various groups. Although it does not seem pollyannaish to think that improved science achievement and participation for all really could be the product of this reform, we do not know that this is the case. Moreover, the increasing use of disaggregated assessment data may help to convince parents committed to public education that their children are progressing well in detracked or highly diverse schools or suggest areas for improvement.

Equity and Attitudes Toward Scholarship

The thrust of this chapter has been on how we might organize schools to focus on science literacy for all, especially those who have been underrepresented in science in the past. An issue not yet addressed is how the school climate supports students who are excited about learning science. Can we imagine schools as supportive of educational excellence as they are of their football teams? Unfortunately, this has not been true for students who are interested in scholarship and intellectual pursuits, in general, or in science, in particular.

For instance, I recently judged a science fair in a city where the majority of the students are Black Americans and poor. The science fair finalists, 14 in all, were mostly White, mostly male, mostly middle to upper class, and mostly from private schools. At first blush, this seemed to be another demonstration of the science achievement gap between affluent and poor children, Black and White. Yet, the truth is more complicated. Comparing the entire pool of science fair participants with the winners, the winners seemed to represent the demographics of the schools that submitted projects—mainly private and parochial schools and public schools that were academic magnets. Few of the regular neighborhood high schools sent participants, indicating that they had not sponsored school-level fairs or required science fair projects of their students. Did the neighborhood high schools see their students as unable to compete in the science fair or uninterested?

Two researchers with a long history of work with mathematically precocious youth, Benbow and Stanley (1996) discussed the impact of anti-intellectual attitudes toward high achieving youngsters:

> We hear much today about teaching students to appreciate diversity, in particular cultural diversity. Why is intellectual diversity not included? We wonder if Americans would allow any other group in our society to sustain and endure the abuse that highly achieving precocious students children face on a daily basis in their schools . . . School climate should be free from taunts and jeers based upon race, gender, age, ethnicity, religion, sexual orientation, disability *and* high ability. (p. 260)

To increase the participation of underrepresented groups in science, schools must be more than free of discriminatory behavior toward students who excel in academics. They must support them, celebrate their accomplishments, and find ways to make academic accomplishment as socially rewarding as athletics. This involves a conscious effort on the part of the school's leadership with the creative input of students and staff.

Given the richness of the new science standards and the breadth of the topics included, it seems extremely unlikely that the division of students into categories such as *gifted and talented* and *not gifted and talented* is useful. Rather, some students are likely to be much better at some things than others, and some talent is bound to emerge from untapped pools of students. This can only happen if the entire enterprise of science education is viewed as one of talent development rather than of talent identification, just as, in the scenario that opened this chapter, Coach Herrington viewed his football players.

8

Teachers and Teaching: Understanding, Courage, and Change

*Our teachers care so much because a lot of them have lived here a long time. A lot of them went through this school. I do feel like the discipline and the expectations that every child in the classroom will do as well as the one sitting next to him, regardless of how much money his mama and daddy have, what color he is, or anything else. I don't know of a teacher out here that doesn't feel that way . . . If they didn't care, they . . . **wouldn't go through the changes they go through.***
—Parent and substitute teacher at Springlake Junior High School (quoted in Charles A. Dana Center at the University of Texas, Austin, 1996c, p. 24)

TALES OF URBAN SCIENCE CLASSROOMS

Tom, a middle-aged, chemical engineer, taking on a second career in teaching, is an intern in an urban high school participating in a major reform effort. He has been placed in the chemistry classroom of Mr. B, who had to be persuaded (coerced) into taking on a student teacher for reasons that soon become apparent. Before long, Tom discovers that Mr. B does not really teach much at all. Rather, Mr. B assigns his students busy work that he seems to dream up in the first 5 minutes of class. For example, "Here are 10 sentences. Locate them in the chapter and write out the paragraph that you find them in on your papers and turn them in at the end of the hour." Day-to-day activities are often unrelated. However, the class is quiet and relatively free of conflict, an accommodation having been silently reached—the teacher will not ask much of the students and they will not give him a hard time (a bad bargain for the students, especially).

Mr. B also seems to have serious gaps in his basic content knowledge. He entered the education system through emergency certification measures and never student taught or worked directly with an effective science teacher. Although he subsequently accumulated sufficient credits to legitimately certify as a science teacher, this piecemeal education has not made much of an impact on his practice as a teacher.

In the last year, Mr. B attended mandatory professional development sessions to explain the school district's new science curriculum and its relation to the science standards. He has a set of the promising, new chemistry textbooks designed to help him implement it, but he maintains that the new books are not challenging enough for his students and he does not intend to use them.

The intern, Tom, who has a masters' degree in chemistry and has worked in a research lab in his first career, is frustrated and wants out of the placement because the only thing he is learning is how not to teach. Tom has come to see the students as poor urban kids who do not read very well, have problems understanding abstract ideas, and come from uncaring homes in a crime-ridden neighborhood. It is apparent that the students, mostly low SES Black American ninth graders in a troubled urban school system, stand as much of a chance of learning chemistry in this classroom as Tom does learning to teach there.

The university supervisor sees that this bleak situation must change, at least for Tom (she has no control over the situation for the high school chemistry students beyond sending an oblique message to the principal that something is wrong). She arranges for Tom to student teach with Susan, a Grade 10 earth science teacher who has been working extremely successfully in a nearby high school with similar demographic characteristics. Susan recently completed her masters in science education and is a committed, even zealous, constructivist. In Susan's classroom, Tom observes students engaged in a connected series of activities that she designed to build an understanding of the movement of tectonic plates and energy conversions—friction and heat energy and their potential effects on geologic formations. Susan's students are enthusiastic and involved and learning some sophisticated science concepts, as well as facts about geology. They love Susan and their earth science class. Tom does not view this group of students as bundles of deficits and is eager to teach at this school, although there really is no difference between these students and those at the first school. Rather, it is the teacher who has made the difference.

Simple? All a teacher must do is know his or her content area and how to teach in order to be successful with urban students. Unfortunately, not so.

James, a graduate of the same program and a contemporary of Susan's has a similar constructivist philosophy, but he is having a terrible time in his first teaching position, a science department in a school where virtually all of the students are Black Americans and more than 80% qualify for the free and reduced lunch program. Although James is an expert in his subject area, just shy of a doctorate, and has all of the mechanics of well-structured, hands-on science classroom neatly in place, he has constant problems with discipline, which sometimes blow up into major events such as vandalism, fighting, and serious insubordination. Students do not relate well to him and vice versa. It is hard to exactly put a finger on the problem here—in his university classes, James seems personable, interesting, and has a fine, ironic sense of humor.

Yet, in his science classroom, James finds that when he meets his students' questions with other probing questions (inquiry-based teaching), the students take this as a sign of his disrespect for them. His ironic remarks are sometimes construed as insults, as when he teased a student for not knowing about powdered hand soap and the student thought he was being told that he was not clean.

The first thing one sees upon entering James' classroom is a bulletin board prominently featuring those famous dead White males of Western science. This is not a huge issue, of course, but how easy it would be to exchange these pictures for the ethnically diverse collection of contemporary scientists other teachers sometimes manage to find and display on their walls. Also problematic is James' difficulty in targeting his instruction to his students' conceptual backgrounds in science (a common problem for first-year teachers). Sometimes his lessons are too childish and sometimes too sophisticated. The students are frequently caught off balance and lose confidence in themselves and the class. Because the basic trust is not there, science takes a back seat to discipline issues. James will stick it out here for 2 years, then take a position in a more affluent suburb where the majority of the students and teaching staff are White and middle class. This is where Ms. E teaches.

Ms. E is a master teacher of science with more than 20 years of experience. She is teaching sixth graders in a magnet school program for gifted and talented students. Despite the affluence of the community as a whole, this school is highly socioeconomically diverse. The gifted and talented science program has been constructed so that its population mirrors that of the immediate neighborhood, and there is proportionate representation of males and females, Black Americans, Hispanics, Asian Americans, and Whites across SES groups—the best and the brightest that could be found for this special program.

On this particular day, Ms. E gives her students an overview of their new unit, where they will be asked to work in teams of four to solve a particular problem over the course of the next several weeks. She constructed the individual student teams for maximum diversity in terms of ethnicity and gender. The teams must first plan their particular approach and give it to Ms. E in writing for approval before they proceed. As she turns her students loose to begin planning, she can readily see who quickly takes charge within each of the eight teams. It appears that in every group but one, White males assume the leadership position. In the exception, a Black American female quickly establishes her role as the leader. Although all of these students have been specially selected for this program on the basis of exceptional talent and the instruction consists of challenging, student-centered inquiry, the classroom dynamics present a constant issue for Ms. E. She struggles to find ways to rearrange a pecking order that she recognizes as a problem. She wants all of her students to have a chance to engage in thinking, planning, and doing, but has to work against a social dynamic that many of the students seem to readily accept.

CHARACTERISTICS OF SUCCESSFUL SCIENCE TEACHING FOR DIVERSE LEARNERS

These stories are illustrative of the challenges of teaching science in diverse classrooms in the midst of education reform. In the first case, Mr. B simply did not have the tools to teach successfully—neither a sound background in content knowledge nor a repertoire of pedagogical skills that allowed him to structure successful science experiences. Although professional development classes for new curriculum materials consistent with reform efforts were available to him, it has made little difference to his practice. He seemed unwilling or unable to change. His students will receive the usual array of As, Bs, and Cs, despite having learned very little. It is classrooms like this that prompted one educational wag to remark that the smartest students are those who have dropped out of school and are on the streets.

A mile away, Susan and her students prosper. The system, however, does not distinguish between her and Mr. B.

Despite his strong background in science and education, James, the new teacher, must come to grips with classroom management problems. For lack of better terms, rapport and trust seem to be an issue for him, and the cultural differences between his students and himself may contribute to the problem. He needs to find a way to reach them and this requires changes in his everyday interpersonal interactions with his students.

In the case of Ms. E, a master teacher of science who had excellent rapport with her students, change is also going to be necessary. She is sufficiently sophisticated to be aware of the problems in the classroom dynamics, where others may have seen none. She knows that she must develop some new strategies for working with her diverse students in order for them to achieve optimally in an adolescent social system that stratifies opportunity to learn within her class.

In summary, teachers' openness to change is crucial if the goal is science literacy for all. The aforementioned stories illustrate the teacher characteristics necessary to implement science education reform in classrooms with diverse learners. These characteristics, diagramed in Fig. 8.1, are placed in two broad categories, *Just Plain, Good Teaching*, general traits of effective science teachers, and *Specialized Traits* for reaching diverse learners. This chapter summarizes some of the principles of *Just Plain Good Teaching* and discusses the means of achieving them through professional development programs. It also focuses on the research supporting the *Specialized Traits* and discusses how to recruit new teachers and design preservice programs that encourage the development of all the characteristics in Fig. 8.1.

Just Plain Good Teaching

Content Knowledge and Pedagogical Skills.   Chapter 6 of this volume made the case for the importance of teachers' expertise in their content areas, and chapter 7 delved into individual science classrooms to further demonstrate how this factor plays a role in opportunities to learn for various populations of students. A teacher must have a sound understanding of the nature of science, science concepts, science themes, habits of mind, and process skills, especially as the grade levels of the students increase. Lee and Fradd (1998) made distinctions among science classroom activities that require students to *know science*, *do science*, and *talk science*. A teacher who has had extensive background in doing science, either through formal education or career experiences, is far better equipped to move students from low-level, fact-oriented, know-science exercises, to do science and talk science. Doing and talking science, in turn, actually lead to a deeper understanding of science concepts—knowing more science.

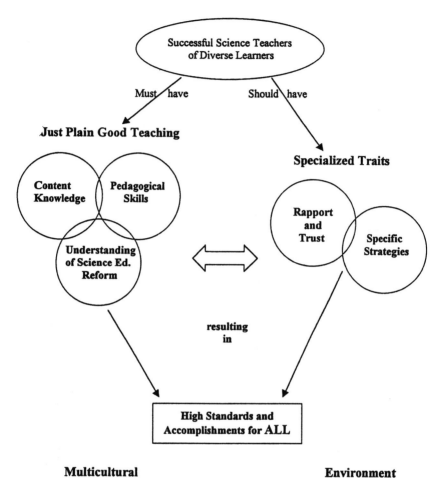

FIG. 8.1.   Characteristics of successful teachers of diverse learners.

So there is an interaction between content knowledge and pedagogical skills, indicated by the overlapping circles in Fig. 8.1 that may be particularly important in schools where the students do not automatically buy into the value of learning science. The *pedagogical skills* include understanding constructivist teaching, a cornerstone of science education reform, which means that individual students create their own understanding of science concepts when they are deeply engaged in significant thought:

> The essential point is that in order to learn the sorts of things envisioned by reformers, students must think ... By "think" we mean the students must actively try to solve problems, resolve differences between the way

they initially understand a phenomenon and new evidence that challenges that understanding, to put collections of facts or observations together into patterns, to make and test conjectures, to build lines of reasoning about why claims are or are not true. Such thinking is generative. It literally creates understanding in the mind of the thinker ... Students don't get knowledge from teachers, or books, or experience with hands-on materials. They make it by thinking, using information, and experience. No thinking, no learning. At least no conceptual learning of the kind reformers envision. (Thompson & Zeuli, 1997, pp. 8–9)

Yet, it is not as if a teacher can simply waltz into a classroom, exhort students to think deeply, and suddenly do creative work in science. This is especially true if students have been accustomed to science classes consisting of worksheets, vocabulary drills, lectures, and labs that require physical activity, but none of the generative thinking just mentioned. In such schools, a great deal of groundwork needs to be laid for classroom management systems that promote thoughtful activity without dissolving into chaos.

For instance, in a study of science teaching in an urban middle school, Meadows (1998) reported that successful urban science teachers must be able to develop routines for laboratory work. Cooperative learning must be explicitly taught. Teachers must help students make personal connections with the material and establish clear accountability and reward systems. Although these pedagogical attributes of *Just Plain Good Teaching* are standard yet challenging grist for preservice teacher education programs, the Meadows' study shows that in-service teachers also need assistance in honing these basic teaching skills.

Understanding Science Education Reform. The literature on science education reform emphasizes the importance of aligning teacher beliefs with reform goals (Czerniak & Lumpe, 1996; Lynch, 1997). Teachers need to understand the reform, believe in it, and be willing to change their practices. Yet, it is clear that many teachers are unconvinced about the reform goals and their instructional emphases may run counter to reform recommendations (Weiss, 1997). For instance, in a study of five local school districts undergoing science education reform in Michigan, researchers found no evidence that these districts were promoting a hands-on approach that remotely resembled the Project 2061's notions about science habits of mind or the scientific enterprise. Rather, some districts seemed to regard hands-on science activities as motivational or memorization aids rather than as a means to learning (Spillane & Reimann, 1995). These school districts had undertaken significant changes in their science curriculum documents, but the attempt to align science topics with standards tended to mask the fact that there were few substantive changes to programs.

This may not mean that educators resisted the reform. Rather, they simply did not understand it, which implies that they had not had opportunities to come to grips with its implications for their instruction. The field is coming to understand that education reform may depend on experiences far different from the 1-day, one-shot in-service workshops that have characterized many professional development activities in the past.

Professional Development That Promotes Just Plain Good Teaching

Assuming that teachers have adequate content knowledge and the skills to manage groups of students in science classrooms, they must understand the intent of the reform and how it differs from the usual kinds of activities that may have passed for science teaching and learning science in the past. Descriptions of the type of teaching imagined by reformers may be found throughout the NSES, in chapter 13 of *Science for All Americans*, throughout the *Benchmarks for Science Literacy*, or any number or recent teacher education policy documents such as those from the National Board of Professional Teaching Standards (science) or the National Science Teachers Association's Standards for Science Teacher Education (1998). NSES especially emphasize the role of inquiry as a means of learning science because through authentic inquiry, students are challenged to think in ways that cause deep restructuring of their science knowledge.

Inquiry is often associated with hands-on learning and laboratory work. Indeed, a longitudinal study (NELS: 88) that used a large, nationally representative database indicated that students learned more in science classes in which they were regularly engaged in lab activities (Burkham, Lee, & Smeardon, 1997). Interestingly, although this positive result was applicable to both boys and girls, it proved especially effective for girls taking physical science and helped to reduce the gender gap. However, hands-on science may only indicate a potential for reformed science teaching, not the actual fact because it is possible to have laboratory work without students engaging in inquiry or much thought at all.

Teachers need the time to think about standards, to contextualize them in terms of their practice in their schools, and to have examples of effective curricula aligned with the standards. This is probably best done collaboratively. An example of an ambitious professional development program that has shown signs of having a positive impact on student achievement has been undertaken by Detroit public schools in conjunction with Wayne State University in Detroit's Urban Systemic Initiative funded by NSF. This program has already reached a large number of K–12 teachers (an average of 800 per year for 3 years) and routinely has more applicants that it can handle (Stein, Norman, & Chambers, 1998). The program is built around constructivist teaching principles. Each school sends a team of science and mathematics teachers and administrators to a summer institute where participants engage in focus sessions (e.g., alternative assessment, family math and science, technology), lectures from scientists, science content area workshops, and perhaps most important, team meetings where action plans for the academic year are developed. About 70% of the action plans are actually implemented. This professional development extends beyond the summer and into the schoolyear. There is accountability and follow-up. The principles woven into the institute design were as follows:

- Keep the focus on student learning.
- Recognize that change affects staff members in personal ways.
- Change the organization's culture at the same time that individual teachers and administrators are acquiring new knowledge and skills.
- Use a systems approach to change.
- **Provide content-specific staff development that addresses both the deeper forms of content knowledge and instructional strategies most effective in that discipline.**
- **Make certain that the learning processes for teachers model the type of instruction that is desired.**
- Provide generous amounts of time for collaborative work and various learning activities.

The principles in boldface correspond roughly with the findings of an extensive evaluation effort on the relations among policy, professional development, and student achievement in mathematics conducted in California (Cohen & Hill, 1998). Researchers examined a number of different types of professional development programs. They found that most teachers only spent a nominal amount of time in professional development activities, with a small fraction indicating that they attended workshops lasting at least 1 week or longer. Most of the activities taught general pedagogical skills or content knowledge rather than being grounded in student curriculum. The most successful professional development, in terms of students' outcomes that matched the intents of the reform (i.e., higher achievement test scores) were programs where teachers learned about the concepts that their students would study and about the teaching methods that went along with it. In other words, curriculum-based professional development that extended for 1 week or more seemed to result in the greatest positive changes in student outcomes.

The Texas State Systemic Initiative also provides an impressive example of effective professional development in science education reform. The researchers at the Charles A. Dana Center at the University of Texas at Austin (1996a) chose only high poverty schools for their evaluation of reform efforts, focusing on 26 schools that had more than 60% of their students eligible for free and reduced lunches, but had managed to get at least 70% of their students through the reading and mathematics sections of the Texas Assessment of Academic Skills. The thrust of these professional development efforts seemed to rely on the internal capacities of individual schools, characterized by an unyielding, even bullheaded confidence in the individuals within the schools and their ability to get the job done (i.e., "When there's a will there's a way"). The researchers identified the following themes as common to all of the high-poverty–high-success schools:

• Focus on the academic success of every student. This meant that almost every decision about the selection of instructional materials, the adoption of staff development strategies, the use of fiscal resources, the scheduling of the school calendar, the assignment and use of teachers, support personnel and volunteers, the use of classroom, playground and building space . . . was guided by the mission of ensuring academic success of every student. Teachers knew the objective they were teaching and why the particular instructional approach was most likely to work with their students. (pp. 3–4)

• No excuses. Educators . . . tended to believe that they could succeed with any student regardless of the home situation . . . the student's previous performance or diagnosis, . . . or other constraints that might confront the school. This might have meant having the student do homework at school, calling to provide a wake-up call on mornings when the mother worked the night shift, allowing students to take extra portions of lunch home so that they could have dinner, or showing a mother how to read to a pre-school child. (pp. 5–7)

• Experimentation. If an approach was not working with one student or a group, teachers were allowed, expected, and encouraged to try different approaches. Entire school staffs explored new ways to stimulate achievement. (p. 7)

• Inclusivity. Everyone is part of the solution. Teachers at all grade levels and in all content areas supported the goals, as did the professional and non-professional staff, asked to assist in cooperative learning or peer tutoring. (p. 8)

• Sense of family: There was a powerful sense of family that included teachers, students, parents, and other school personnel such as social workers, school nurses, and counselors whose roles were blurred as they did what ever was required to help the students in ways that included and went far beyond the academic. (pp. 9–10)

• Collaboration and trust: The school personnel worked and learned together collaboratively, and when disagreements arose, they were able to express their feelings without fear of reprisal. (pp. 11–12)

• Passion for learning and growing: The schools in this study, although having achieved a great deal, were not content to rest on their laurels, but rather to push on to even higher goals. (pp. 12–13)

Summarizing these three studies of successful professional development for education reform, the critical factors are a focus on building the teachers' content knowledge and pedagogical skills in context of curricula aligned with high standards; building a critical mass of inquiring and dedicated teachers within a school; and creating a professional community that believes in the students and understands the promise of the reform. This requires substantial time for ongoing, professional development and a structure for change within school districts that supports the changes—knowledgeable, effective management. Professional development costs money and some school districts are creatively adjusting current resources to meet these needs. The finances of professional development and school reform is an important equity issue, along with who has access to the professional development and who leads it:

> Inequitable policies and practices in school funding can create unequal opportunities for professional development. Just examining the variation in how Eisenhower funds are distributed and then used in different school districts is enlightening. Resource-rich schools, which are unlikely to be serving underrepresented groups, can better support the learning of their staff, considered by some to be a luxury or frill when lab equipment and books are in short supply. Access to professional development is restricted when teachers do not have the resources to buy new materials the professional development program requires or recommends. (Loucks-Horsley et al., 1998, p. 205)

Beyond Just Plain Good Teaching: Specializing
for Individuals and Groups

Much of the science education reform literature, although acknowledging
the central importance of equity issues, discusses the reform in a colorblind fashion (Cochron-Smith, 1995; Ladson-Billings, 1995; Rodriguez,
1997) rather than acknowledging that different students, different combinations of students, and different education settings, all may require
responses far beyond *Just Plain Good Teaching*. In chapters 6 and 7, the
equity schema included certified teachers, reasonable facilities and materials, and effective, knowledgeable management. Assuming that these
minimums are in place, a review of literature on effective science teaching
for diverse learners consistently suggests that two other factors should also
be considered. On the right side of Fig. 8.1, these are labeled, *Specialized
Traits*, including *Rapport and Trust* and *Specific Strategies*, resulting in *High
Standards and Accomplishments for All*, at the bottom of Figure 8.1. This is
best accomplished in a multicultural environment, such as that envisioned by Banks (1994). Banks' model includes the following:

- *Content integration*, the extent to which teachers use examples and
  content from a variety of cultures and groups to illustrate key concepts.
- *The knowledge construction process*, or how well teachers help students
  to understand the implicit cultural assumptions and biases within a
  discipline influence the ways that knowledge is constructed within it.
- *Prejudice reduction*, which focuses on students' racial attitudes and
  how they might be modified by teaching methods and materials.
- *An empowering school culture and social structure*, which empowers
  students from diverse groups by examining grouping, achievement,
  sports participation, and interactions among students and staff.
- *An equity pedagogy*, whereby teachers modify their teaching, including
  a variety of teaching styles to increase the achievement of students
  from diverse groups.

In short, Banks' model acknowledges that ethnic and cultural differences exist within schools that have serious consequences for power
relationships and education outcomes. Consequently, educators, including science educators, must take action to insure all students have an
equal opportunity to learn and achieve. Equal opportunity does not mean
a uniform approach to teaching and learning, however.

The Relationship Between High Standards and Rapport and Trust. If one watches a good coach teaching children to do something difficult or dangerous (e.g., gymnastics, rock climbing, or football), it becomes apparent that even very young children quickly size up the competence of the coach and if he or she is deemed trustworthy and knowledgeable, are increasingly willing to take the risks necessary to learn the sport. The sports situation seems analogous to diverse learners in science classrooms. The education reform is built on the premise that all students can achieve high standards. In order to make this something more than a slogan, students who have been unsuccessful in science in the past or otherwise received a message that they are members of a group that does not do science must believe that their teacher is asking them to learn things that are within their reach and worth learning. Rapport and trust between teacher and students are crucial. This is especially true if students are members of communities where they are not likely to encounter important others who successfully negotiated their way through the science pipeline and are engaged daily in work related to science. Thus, the teacher is likely to be the first mediator to the world of science, with its particular values, methods, attitudes, and rites of passage. At the same time, the teacher conveys a respect for and acknowledges the importance of cultural competence—a way for students to maintain their cultural integrity (Ladson-Billings, 1995). Insistence on high standards, without rapport and trust, is likely to place both students and teacher in an untenable position, as was the case of James in the scenario that opened this chapter.

Much of the literature on effective teaching of science for students in underrepresented groups implies that that there is a psychosocial-emotional component to the teaching and learning process too important to ignore. The background experiences, knowledge, and beliefs of the learner are crucial and, by extension, so are the learner's culture, gender, SES, and myriad other factors. As the child moves toward adolescence, his or her predilections toward science seem to be increasingly a factor. So the social context of the science classroom is crucial, and here, the teacher is the engineer, coach, social director, and arbiter. If the classroom seems unfriendly or ill-structured, then the knowing, doing, and talking science critical to students' restructuring of knowledge seems less likely to occur.

For example, in Colburn's study (1997) of the beliefs driving an exemplary urban science teacher, Colburn quoted the teacher as saying, "it takes a quarter to develop control, cooperativeness, *rapport* to make most kids feel that they can be successful, establish the expectations . . . you have real good warm relationships at the end of the year" (p. 5, italics added). Similarly, after spending 1 year in urban science classrooms, Meadows (1998) cited *teacher warmth* as a key facet of effective pedagogy. A study by Luft, da Cunha, and Allison (1998) described two teachers successful (high enrollments and high achievement in science) with Hispanic students and other students of color, as *valuing* their students and *really wanting to help*. Vasquez (1988) used the term *warm demanders*. Kahle spoke of the importance of *nurturing* relationships, and Benedict of effective schools that provide a structure for *caring teachers* and counselors (as cited in Murphy, 1996). Haberman (1995) described a humane, respectful, caring, and nonviolent form of *gentle teaching*.

In the literature on effective science instruction for females, persons with disabilities, students learning to speak English, and urban students, this characteristic comes forth loud and clear: Teachers who care deeply about their students are most effective. By building rapport and trust, teachers connect not only with the students themselves, but they also build student–student interactions—science discourse—in the context of substantive science content and activities. As a result, students are more likely to attend their classes, have more positive attitudes toward science, and, not surprisingly, show higher achievement (Van Sickle & Spector, 1996).

This rapport and trust, or caring, or teacher warmth is not exactly the same, it would seem, as teaching methods that encourage the teacher to connect the material with the lives of the students, or to understand the home and cultural backgrounds of students that are clearly called for the NSES (pp. 29, 46). Certainly, understanding and connection are necessary to constructivist teaching and are logical, methodological approaches for effective teaching of diverse learners. The point here, however, is that in addition to this intellectual aspect of teaching, an affective component needs to be considered (Murphy, 1996).

The considerable research on gender differences in science and mathematics achievement and attitudes provide support for the importance of rapport and trust. Teachers play a major role in either creating or perpetuating gender differences in self-perceptions of ability, molding expectations for success, and encouraging students to develop their interests in math and science (Eccles, 1995). Extensive observations in preschool, primary and secondary school, and college classrooms have led several investigators to conclude that the quantity, quality, and type of interactions boys and girls have with their science teachers and professors are often very different, depending on gender. In general, teachers interact more frequently with boys than girls, especially in mathematics and sci-

ence classes (American Association of University Women, 1992; Eccles
& Blumenfeld, 1985; Parsons, Kaczala, & Meece, 1982). As early as
second grade, boys get more math instruction than girls, and girls get
more reading instruction (Leinhardt, Seeward, & Engel, 1979). In high
school, math teachers are more likely to encourage the academic abilities
and interests of the boys, to joke with the boys, and to make public
statements indicating high expectations to the boys (Becker, 1981).
Moreover, although the majority of the secondary school science teachers
are male, these tendencies have been documented in both male and
female teachers.

Can science teachers be trained in caring? Can rapport and trust
become a policy recommendation? Certainly anyone who believes in
Gardner's (1983) theory of multiple intelligences understands that the
ability to effectively communicate interpersonally is not evenly distributed
among us. Although this is likely to be a highly fallible process, a policy
that develops and nurtures rapport and trust between science teachers
and their students may begin with selecting people as teachers of diverse
students who perceive themselves as caring individuals. Teacher education and professional development environments should provide these
teachers with the breathing room to care and the resources to act on a
student's behalf. For instance, the teachers in a Baltimore high school
that was a member of the Coalition for Essential Schools, after studying
and discussing the goals of the Coalition over several years, decided that
professional development had to be in house, continuous, and rely on
internal resources. This was necessary if the learning community initiated
under Coalition principles and implemented by the teacher leaders was
to be sustained (Lynch, 1993). This meant reorganizing the schedule and
teaching loads so that teachers had time to meet to discuss individual
students and their needs and to implement changes that supported the
learning community. It allowed them to develop context-specific strategies to improve student learning.

It is also important to nurture the spirits of the dedicated teachers
endeavoring to implement science reform. This is no easy task in the best
of circumstances and for teachers who work in underresourced schools in
poor communities, it can be especially daunting. Many of the school
reform efforts stressed the punitive aspects of the reform—school takeovers by the state, teachers losing their jobs, and students being held
back. In contrast, the state of Texas provides recognition and incentives
for schools that foster high achievement for diverse learners. The NSF-
sponsored State Systemic Initiative for science and mathematics reform
published profiles of 26 high-poverty–high-success schools. For instance,

one of the featured schools is the Nixon-Smiley Middle School, located in a rural farm community. The majority of the students at this school are Hispanic and about 70% are eligible for support for free and reduced-price lunches. Despite the low incomes of the students, passing rates on key state exams range from 73% to 82%. The school is also nationally recognized as a high achieving Chapter 1 school, and won the Texas Successful Schools Award for significant gains in 1994 and 1995. The school attributes its success to high expectations, coupled with the support systems such as tutoring, independent study, and the Accelerated Reading Program that allow the expectations to become reality. A sixth grade teacher says: "We have lots of teachers that have really high expectations of students. . . . The attitudes of the students have changed. They know that teachers expect a lot of them. . . . There's no reason to expect mediocrity when you can expect excellence" (Charles A. Dana Center, 1996b).

Specific Strategies.   In addition to *Just Plain Good Teaching* and trust and rapport, science educators search for effective strategies for reaching different groups of diverse learners, often in very specific contexts. There is a crucial need for more systematic research on specific methods to teach science more effectively to diverse learners (Lee & Fradd, 1998). Although good teachers find or develop strategies to help their students all the time, these responses are seldom recorded in the research base.

For example, in a recent course for student-teaching interns, five high school chemistry teachers were asked to identify a problem that was creating difficulties for the diverse learners (loosely defined) in their chemistry classes. Three of the interns identified the chemistry textbook as the significant problem. This text had just been adopted and was being used for the first time in this school district. Its format was busy, flashy, and nonlinear. Students had to be able to extract information from a splash of figures, tables, and text, and make sense of it. This seemed to create particular problems for students with disabilities and English language learners, or in fact, for any students whose science abilities were less than optimal. The student teachers, independently of one another, were able to find and implement three different research-based strategies that promised to help their students to more effectively read the text and process the information it contained.

Although this was a very specific response to a specific situation, more general strategies for improving science teaching and learning for diverse learners are available in the professional literature. A small sample of these more general strategies are discussed in the following sections.

Although these strategies evolved from a focus on specific groupings, such as gender or other students with disabilities, oftentimes the responses can be generalized to other groups of diverse learners.

Gender

The research on gender equity in science classrooms (Eccles, 1995) shows that even if overt gender bias by teachers is eliminated, other factors impinge on girls' opportunities to learn science. Teachers must develop strategies to deal with these factors. In many math and science classrooms, a few students, usually White males, dominate the teacher–student interactions and assume the leadership roles in laboratory activities. These same students often monopolize the laboratory equipment and computers, effectively denying the females the opportunity to use these tools and develop confidence in their ability to master the skills involved in laboratory sciences. Under such conditions, females tend to withdraw and become observers, rather than active participants. It is clear that merely providing hands-on activities and group work (*Just Plain Good Teaching*) is insufficient for an effective and equitable classroom environment. Rather, teachers must create classroom dynamics that allow (require?) all students to learn how to use equipment, operate computers, develop and test their ideas, and discuss observations and results. Girls participate more frequently and achieve better when teachers use noncompetitive teaching strategies; give extended examples of applications from medicine, engineering, and so on; stress the creative components of math and science rather than facts and endless word problem sets; provide extensive hands-on learning experiences; and are actively committed to nonsexist education (Eccles, 1995).

Perhaps the most effective method to convince teachers of these problems and encourage change is by creating opportunities for the teachers themselves to document patterns of gender-differentiated responses in the classroom. By using classroom interaction coding techniques or videotaping lessons for examination later, teachers can examine the patterns of behaviors that lead some students to success in science, whereas others are discouraged. Science teachers have proven to be more open to change when convinced that inequitable interactions tended to occur in their own classrooms (Scantleberry & Kahle, 1993), given the opportunity to reflect on the data, and suggest modifications in the classroom learning environment

Virtually all of these strategies for gender equitable science classrooms have three things in common: They reduce stereotyping, mitigate traditional power arrangements, and create conditions whereby students who have had less prior experience and background knowledge in science are given a chance to catch up. For instance, students (perhaps working in small groups) are provided direct experiences with the physical phenomena, equipment, or techniques.

English Language Learners

Educators who work with English language learners want science teachers to be able to understand the needs of students who are learning English and to develop or adopt strategies, materials, and activities that help such students. Bernhardt (1995) provided a rationale for specialized strategies, saying that, regardless of the polemics and politics around ESL or bilingual education, three facts are at hand:

1. There are children who do not speak English well despite their successful exiting of English support services.
2. Given that it takes 6 to 8 years to develop proficiency in English that is competitive with English-speaking peers, these children must receive content instruction in English anyway.
3. Classroom-based research shows that non-English-speaking children are frequently ignored in content classrooms (i.e., they are often relegated to doing busy work until they learn enough English to participate). (pp. 1–2)

Bernhardt (1995) analyzed science education methods texts and found that English language learners are either hardly mentioned or placed in the context of multicultural education or special needs. Some texts lumped English language learners together under the grouping of *disadvantaged, culturally impaired,* or *emotionally problematic.* She concluded that one could read all of the formal education materials about English language learners contained in popular science methods texts in about 30 minutes. Bernhardt pointed out that there is very little specific information about the learning of science through a language over which students do not have full control.

As an example of specific strategies for English language learners in science classrooms, in a 1995 journal article, Spurlin suggested that teachers should regularly engage in the following activities:

1. Analyze written materials used in science instruction for semantic, syntactic, and pragmatic problems.

2. Adapt and simplify written materials.
3. Embed cognitively demanding material in context (hands-on).
4. Use constructivist approaches.
5. Observe English language learners in schools, noting how they are treated and the kinds of instruction they receive.
6. Observe how language is used in instruction.
7. Identify how teachers can bring in the backgrounds and cultural experiences of diverse learners into the science classroom.

Such lists are not useful, however, unless science teachers, especially those who are likely to work with substantial numbers of students who are learning English, have an understanding of the basics of language acquisition, and some specific instruction in how to implement these strategies. The model used in special education inclusion classrooms, teaming a science educator with a special educator, could also be productive for ESL or bilingual education teachers and science educators. The National Clearinghouse Bilingual Education is a good resource for specific teaching strategies. There are also texts available on this subject, such as Barba's (1995) textbook, *Science in the Multicultural Classroom: A Guide to Teaching and Learning*.

Students With Disabilities

Probably the richest, most profuse literature on strategies for diverse learners comes from the field of special education, which has traditionally seen its role as developing strategies for students with disabilities to learn subject matter disciplines. Students with learning disabilities have difficulty acquiring an understanding of science in traditional science classrooms where they get stuck in a morass of vocabulary and the goal is coverage rather than conceptual understanding. Yet, there are some important differences of opinion on the best way to teach science to students with disabilities. It is generally true that many of the strategies approaches used by special educators in the past were mnemonics, designed to help students with learning disabilities cope with vast amounts of material to be memorized in science classrooms. However, as the reform proceeds and alters science instruction so that there is a greater emphasis on deep understanding of concepts, experiential learning, inquiry, and habits of mind, then adaptations beyond mnemonics will be required. Promising teaching methods include hands-on instruction, discovery teaching, theme-based instruction, cooperative learning (Cawley,

1994), and content-enhancement routines (Fisher, Shumaker, & Deschler, in press). Grossen (1995) recommended:

1. Teaching big ideas in both content and processes (including inquiry).
2. Teaching conspicuous strategies for problem solving using visual maps that refute common misconceptions.
3. Scaffolding the acquisition of meaningful learning by moving from teacher-directed learning to student-centered learning.

The inclusion movement has expanded the need to develop strategies for students with disabilities in the context of the regular education classroom. Resources from the Council for Exceptional Children (CEC) provide both general and very specific strategies for adapting classroom practices for students with disabilities. Following the CEC website to the Educational Resources Information Center (ERIC) data base search (using the descriptors *science, students with disabilities*, and *K–12*) resulted in a listing of 427 articles in June 1998. Although only about 1 article in 10 focuses exclusively on science education, the level of specificity is encouraging. For instance, one can find materials on how to adapt the science classroom to students with hearing impairments, websites suitable for students with learning disabilities, curriculum materials for students with mild disabilities, and research that systematically explores a particular strategy.

It is a powerful truism that adaptations and strategies for students with disabilities improve the quality of the instruction for all students in the classroom. For instance, a teaching strategy that evolved from research on students with learning disabilities is "The Unit Organizer Routine" (Lenz, Schumaker, & Deschler, 1995) developed at the University of Kansas. The *unit organizer* is primarily an elaborated advance organizer (cf. Ausubel, 1960) that uses a concept map and other explicit organizing devices to provide students with an overview of a teaching unit and cues them to the important concepts, a unit schedule, organizing questions, and the unit's relation to prior and successive units (see Fig. 8.2, as an example). By providing the unit organizer to students on the first day of a unit, referring to it frequently as the unit progresses, expanding the concept map to reflect daily lessons, teachers provide a sort of roadmap that explicitly guides students graphically through the course of study.

Having seen success for students with learning disabilities, the University of Kansas researchers introduced the planning and organizing strategy to in-service secondary science and social studies teachers who used the unit organization in their regular classrooms and found that student achievement improved. At George Washington University, we experi-

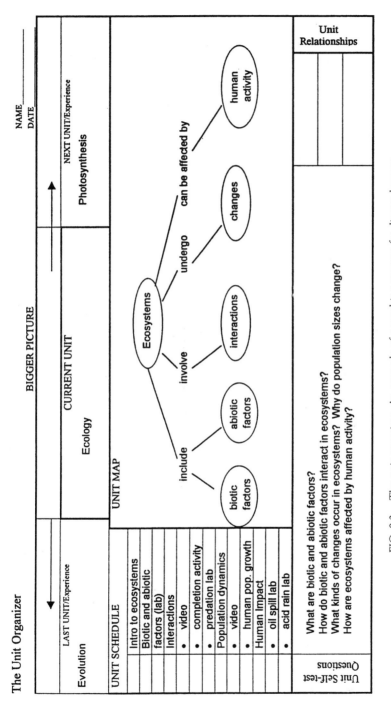

FIG. 8.2. The unit organizer: An example of a teaching strategy for diverse learners.

mented with the unit organizer as a way of focusing preservice teachers on concept teaching aimed at specific science education standards and are convinced of its efficacy as a planning and organizing tool for new teachers who will work with diverse student populations (Lynch & Taymans, 1998).

Although lists of recommendations for strategies for students with disabilities are common, there are fewer research studies to validate them. In a article that reviewed strategies alleged to be effective for students with learning disabilities, Fisher, Schumaker, and Deschler (in press), found that only 29 studies of 14 strategies met their criteria for empirical adequacy. The authors recommended that future research on inclusive practices for students with disabilities have the following features:

1. Report the effects of the practice on all students in the class, not just those with disabilities because in some cases, the strategy was more effective for nondisabled students.
2. Indicate if the effects are socially significant for students with disabilities (i.e., result in a grade of C or better), not just statistically significant.
3. Indicate if extra support is needed outside of the regular classroom (i.e., some strategies seemed effective but required more time).
4. Make clear the status of the students with disabilities—mainstreamed, full-inclusion model, etc.
5. Describe the amount of professional development time required of teachers to prepare them to use the strategy.
6. Describe if the practice supports or supplants the standard curriculum.
7. Report both teacher and student satisfaction with the strategy.

These recommendations for research on science-teaching strategies for students with disabilities can be generalized as research recommendations for other groups of students by ethnicity, English language learners, gender-related issues and others.

Social Class, Ethnicity, and Geographic Location

There is a substantial research base for strategies for teaching science to female students and students with disabilities, and a developing one for English language learners, but we need more research on effective strategies for teaching to other varied groups. Classroom observations lead one to conclude that although there are some universal principles of *Just Plain Good Teaching*, developing successful methods and strategies for specific contexts is also an important aspect of teaching that defies simple summaries. For instance, groups of students who are primarily of one ethnicity, such as American Indian students of a particular tribe, multiethnic classes of students who have recently immigrated to the United States, urban students, high SES suburban students, or students who live in remote rural areas all may have some common learning needs. Yet, each group may also require some specific adaptations not readily located in the research base.

Science educators need to proceed cautiously, but with open minds. Lisa Delpit (1988), a Black language arts educator who openly questioned the conventional wisdom of the powerful education establishment's views of whole-language approach to teaching reading (acknowledging that there never was an establishment consensus on this topic), made the point that what is good for middle-class, White children might not always be the best for other people's children. More recently, teacher educators, James Fraser and Jacqueline Irvine (1998) questioned the principles for teaching embedded in the still very young National Board for Professional Teaching Standards. After having viewed initial data showing that Black teachers achieve Board certification less frequently than their White counterparts, Irvine and Fraser suggested the possibility that the review process contained a deeply flawed cultural bias in favor of White, middle class teacher norms—and against the norms which are seen by many African American educators as most effective.

Anyone working in education for any amount of time can recount examples of unconventional teaching practices that students seem to love and that are effective in certain contexts. Clearly, there is a need for a great deal more research on the teaching of science to diverse learners, especially because much of the reported research assumes a colorblind point of view. However, as gender studies research has shown, there are dangers in either approach. If we suppose that we are all just the same, we may be ignoring differences that could lead to improved education for some students. On the other hand, if we assume that some groups are fundamentally different from others, we also leave open the door to bias and stereotyping.

Cheche Konnen: Just Plain Good Teaching and Special Traits. Figure 8.1 presented an overview of the components that go into the rich stew of effective science teaching for diverse learners. An inspiring and well-documented example of science teaching and learning that seems to embody all aspects of this diagram can be found in the work of Rosebery,

Warren, and Conant (1992). These researchers, who work with English language learners, believed that equality of educational opportunity in science cannot be achieved simply by importing mainstream science into classrooms where the students are anything but mainstream. In their *Cheche Konnen* (i.e., *search for knowledge* in Haitian Creole) project, Haitian immigrant students in an urban school engaged in collaborative inquiry to solve real problems. These students studied local aquatic ecosystems throughout the schoolyear, focusing on determinants of water quality.

In one of their explorations, the Cheche Konen group investigated the belief widely held among the school's junior high students that water on the third floor of the school was superior to that of other fountains (Rosebery et al., 1992). These secondary school students in a bilingual education program engaged in doing science and talking science, similar to practicing scientists. They posed their own questions, planned and implemented their own research, created and revised explanations, drew conclusions and acted on their results. In the water fountain investigation:

> Students conducted a blind taste test to confirm their belief that water from one water fountain in the school, the one they always drank from, had "better" water than the other fountains. When the results of their tests showed that most of them actually preferred the water from the "worst" water in the school, the students were shocked and suspicious of their results. . . . When their second test confirmed the results of the first, the students wanted to find out why one fountain was preferred over the others. To answer this, they analyzed the school's water fountains for differences along several chemical, biological and physical dimensions. (p. 63)

As the investigations continued, students developed a hypothesis. They thought that the reason one drinking fountain was preferred over others was because its water was actually colder, due to its location on the first floor. They developed a theory that because the water sat underground and was naturally cooled, it arrived at a lower temperature to the preferred fountain, but had warmed in the school's pipes by the time it reached the less desirable fountains on the upper floors.

This study is interesting for many reasons, but perhaps most important was the documented development of the students' scientific reasoning through the selection of problems that had real meaning to them. Interestingly, the teacher team involved here was unusual in that it included Haitian Creole bilingual teachers with no formal training in science, as well as the researchers. This is a study that is well worth reading in entirety, as it exemplifies *Just Plain Good Teaching* listed in Fig. 8.1, as well as special strategies for the Haitian Creole students involved.

PRESERVICE TEACHER EDUCATION,
EDUCATION REFORM, AND EQUITY

Because the focus of this volume is on equity and science education reform, it avoids huge and legitimate general problems, such as preservice science teacher education and the mismatch between how science is usually taught in undergraduate programs and how new teachers are being asked to perform in constructivist science classrooms. These crucial issues are left to other publications because they are beyond the scope of this text (cf. The chapter on teacher education in *Blueprints for Reform* by the AAAS, 1998; the original papers by the National Center for Research on Teacher Learning, 1994; or the National Science Teacher Association's draft on Standards for Science Teacher Education, 1998). Instead, the focus of this section is teacher education and equity—learning to teach diverse groups of students.

Science education needs more science teachers who care about their students, who define their roles as teaching science to all students, and who have the potential to develop the attributes listed in Fig. 8.1. The number of science teachers who will retire in the next 10 years means that there will be a substantial turnover in the nation's K–12 science faculty. What sort of people will these new teachers be?

My university has specialized in recruiting *mid-career changers*—teacher candidates who are highly qualified in science—former engineers, scientists, technicians, and military officers (who often hold degrees in engineering). Some of the people who interview for the program (but who are not necessarily admitted into it), however, harbor philosophies of education better suited for the Cold War than the inclusive classrooms of the 1990s. We have actually heard platforms for education from some candidates that include: more kids should fail because it is character building; the age of mandatory schooling should be decreased to get the less able out of schools sooner; English language learners should stay out of classrooms until they master English; and most prominently, a teacher cannot be all things to all students or cannot really hope to teach all children, but will be sustained by occasional rare child who see the beauty of science. That people applying to a teacher education program actually make these statements during interviews in which they are trying to impress provides an inkling of how some sectors of the American public view our children and our schools and how far we have to go in order to teach science to all. Moreover, in our geographic area, the need for science teachers is so great that virtually all these individuals—even the most negative—can easily get jobs through emergency certification channels.

Recruiting a More Diverse Teaching Population

If there were more science teachers of color, there would be more role models for students in the schools, but perhaps more important, science departments might have a collectively more balanced and comprehensive understanding of our diverse populations of students, and develop more effective ways to teach them. Yet, as we have pointed out in chapter 4, the statistics indicate otherwise and the situation is getting worse. No state save Hawaii has a representation of teachers of color that is similar to the ethnic background of the students (NSF, 1994). This is not to say that the most effective teachers of students of color are teachers of color, or that there should be a match between the ethnicity of students and their teachers. What little evidence there is for this, seems to suggest no relation between the teacher's ethnicity and student achievement. Rather, the point is that achieving a positive, multicultural environment for science teaching and learning is likely to be greatly enhanced by a multicultural and highly qualified teaching staff.

There is not much mystery in recruiting persons of color to teach science; the problem is how to pay for their education. For instance, an ad in the *Washington Post* for a George Washington University science and mathematics teacher education masters' program focusing on District of Columbia public schools produced more than 200 responses, with approximately two thirds of the respondents being persons of color (Linda Tredway, personal communication, August 22, 1995). The program provided free tuition for teaching interns during the first year, a $500 per month stipend, and the promise of a regular teaching contract after 1 year. In our experience, many persons applying for such programs are well-qualified candidates, but they may be financially unable to attend a university teacher education program without substantial aid. Many have families to support, are paying off undergraduate student loans, or do not have the financial backing of their White middle-class counterparts.

Haberman (1995) believed that preparing effective teachers to work with poor children, regardless of the ethnicity of the teacher candidates, is 80% dependent on the selection of good candidates and only 20% dependent on the rest of what happens in a teacher education program. He and his colleagues at the University of Wisconsin, Milwaukee, identified three related truths regarding selection:

1. The odds of selecting effective urban teachers . . . are approximately 10 times better if the candidates are over 30 rather than under 25 years of age.

2. There is no problem whatsoever in selecting more teachers of color, or more males, or more Hispanics, or more of any other "minority" constituency if training begins at the postbaccalaureate level.
3. The selection and training of successful urban teachers is best accomplished in the worst schools and under the poorest conditions of practice. (p. 778)

Haberman believed that if teachers are trained in professional development centers placed in some of the worst conditions, then they are ready for anything in their first teaching jobs. Effective urban teachers are those who have a coherent vision—a humane, respectful, caring, and nonviolent form of gentle teaching. These teachers believe that regardless of the life conditions of their students, they as teachers bear the primary responsibility for sparking their students' desire to learn. Successful teachers care deeply about their students' physical, emotional, and social well-being.

Haberman's message is remarkably similar to that of special educators. The inclusion movement for students with disabilities requires science teachers who have the skills and understandings to effectively modify curricula. Teachers have to come to grips with a broader definition of their roles, especially those teachers who work with middle school students whose social and emotional needs are so great. Stefanich (1994) suggested that the effective, inclusive science teacher must:

- Be able to modify instruction so that every student, with full participation, can have a successful learning experience.
- Model accepting every student socially as well as academically in the classroom.
- Be skilled in conflict–resolution strategies based on nonconfrontational methods.
- Collaborate with other professionals in the school to develop inclusive, effective classrooms.
- Support every child's development of basic skills.

Preservice Teacher Education

Once this diverse, caring, mature, and qualified population of teacher candidates is found, the nature of the teacher preparation program deserves consideration. George Washington University is currently experimenting with a professional development school centered at an urban high school where all of the teacher candidates obtain dual certification in both general and special education. They have substantial time to teach, a supervised internship over two semesters. Because 20% of the students at this school had been identified by the school district as having disabilities prior to the initiation of the teacher education program, the dual certification enabled the new teachers to understand the principles behind inclusive classrooms, and through the program, asks them to implement these principles. Dual certification in ESL or bilingual education and science education is another combination that holds some promise.

Second, teacher education for diverse learners ought to provide the interns the opportunity to explore effective teaching strategies in context by exploring the research base and attempting to implement specific strategies in an organized and systematic fashion—action research. This helps solve the problem of *timing* of the delivery of the knowledge base with *need to know*. For example, a method (the unit organizer routine, mentioned earlier in this chapter) that was introduced to preservice science teachers at the beginning of their program was greeted politely, but without much enthusiasm. Six months later, the student teachers saw a similar approach as a major breakthrough when they rediscovered and implemented it independently, in response to a classroom problem. The difference of course, was their need to know in the context of their science classrooms, as well as the action research component that helped to prove to the interns that it would improve their teaching.

Third, although the teacher education programs in which I work have not yet adequately developed this component, it seems important that student-teaching interns be provided with some opportunities to see teaching in action that embodies the principles of the science reform, consistent with the components of Fig. 8.1. Most important, this exemplary teaching should be done with populations of diverse learners, with diversity defined as broadly as possible. Interns should spend some time in classrooms like the ones described in the Cheche Konen project or in Susan's or Mrs. E's classrooms from the scenario that opened this chapter.

Fourth, the multicultural education component of the preservice program should be geared to the content to be taught. The goal is to help teachers understand the relation between science and culture and to increase their capacity to meet science standards and the particular needs of the diverse student populations by exploring how cultural values and ways of understanding can effect science learning and teaching (adapted from Weissglass' work in mathematics in Loucks-Horsely & Hewson, 1998). Teacher educators can design assignments for preservice teachers that help them understand these relations. Probably most promising, is the individual case study approach, where a student teacher is asked to choose an individual student and through interviews and observations, try to understand how the student approaches science and the barriers to learning. What this approach lacks in generalizability, it more than makes up for in the richness of understanding that emerges as student teachers come to see the schools from their students' viewpoints. (Examples of well-developed cases, not specific to science classrooms, however, can be found in Nieto's, 1996, text, *Affirming Diversity: The Sociopolitical Context of Multicultural Education.*)

Finally, although this chapter discusses preservice education and professional development, the weak link in the educational system, especially for teachers of diverse learners, is likely to be the induction years, the 3 years during which the new teacher attempts to reconcile the expectations espoused in the university or college teacher preparation program with the realities of teaching in the schools. Many give up and leave the profession. About 22% of all new teachers leave the profession in the first 3 years because of lack of support and a sink-or-swim approach to induction (National Commission on Teaching and America's Future, 1996). Others stay in the profession, but become disillusioned, advising new student teachers to "forget everything that they told you in your teacher education classes." For others, like James in the scenario that opened this chapter, there are happy endings. James returned to his university to report substantial accomplishments in his new teaching environment. The skills he learned in both education courses and his challenging urban classroom eventually brought him success and recognition, as well as some nostalgia for the students who had given him such a hard time, but who needed him more than the affluent students in his new school.

School systems, particularly those with diverse student populations, are probably going to have to do more to support new science teachers (who statistically are most likely to be White and of different ethnic and socioeconomic backgrounds than their students) in their induction years. Mentoring programs are one answer. Some schools of education are experimenting with extended induction networks and seminars. This is one area the federal government might support through research opportunities and training grants that extend well beyond initial traditional teacher preparation.

CONCLUSIONS

This chapter discussed the attributes of successful science teaching for diverse learners by categorizing practices into the two broad categories shown in Fig. 8.1. The left side of the diagram, *Just Plain Good Teaching,* corresponds roughly, it must be admitted, to Shulman's (1986) classic model of professional knowledge for teachers, consisting of: content knowledge, pedagogical content knowledge, and curricular knowledge. In this case, however, curricular knowledge has been changed to *Understanding Science Education Reform* because it is clear that the reform principles ask something new of science teachers—reaching all students in order that they achieve high standards.

Yet, Fig. 8.1 also suggests something beyond *Just Plain Good Teaching* and the research base provides clues about these other attributes. Rapport and trust between science teachers and students allow students who have been bypassed by science to see themselves as capable of knowing, doing, and talking science—and wanting to do so. Teachers need to build rapport and trust as part of their jobs and have the resources to act as caring, effective individuals, rather than as demoralized, distant purveyors of knowledge.

There is one unavoidable and obvious conclusion: Science learning environments are as unique as the individuals who inhabit them. This suggests that effective teaching and learning will be enhanced if science educators—preservice and in-service teachers, curriculum specialists, university teacher educators—understand that a crucial part of our roles is to build the knowledge base on specific strategies for diverse learners. Science methods texts, as well as this volume, are not going to be enough. Fortunately, if formal inquiry and teacher action research are inevitable parts of the solution, then as science educators, we ought to be well prepared to take on the challenge.

9

Assessment, Equity, and Science Education Reform

I'd rather set the [standards] bar high and have us look at how we're going to help the student get over that bar, than set the bar low and know that when she or he got over it, it didn't mean a darn thing.
—Sidney Thompson (Superintendent of Los Angeles Unified School District as quoted in Linn, 1994, p. 2)

Outcomes are what counts. Process measures help us to understand why we see or do not see improvement in a subject, but outcome measures tell us what students know and are able to do, and who those students are.
—Luther Williams (as quoted in NSF, 1998, p. 7)

Just because you know how to weigh a pig better doesn't mean it will get fatter.
—Unidentified state policymaker, engaged in a discussion about improving assessment (as quoted in Massell, 1998)

Peter, a Russian child adopted by American parents, was having a hard time in third grade. After 2 years of special ESL instruction, he had been moved out of his ESL classes, more by reason of longevity than accomplishment. In the mainstream, he was having difficulties understanding and communicating in English and with all of his schoolwork, save the playground, where he excelled. His parents and teachers were beginning to suspect learning disabilities. Then, one day, Peter mysteriously found himself back in an ESL classroom. When his parents asked about the reason for this strange turn of events, Peter's teacher explained that the ESL placement was only temporary, about 2 weeks, during the state performance assessments in science (and other subjects). The teacher said that Peter would experience a loss of self-esteem and be frustrated if he participated in the tests. Peter wondered what he had done so wrong that he was sent back to ESL. His parents inferred that the school wanted to keep its test scores as high as possible, in order to avoid sanctions. As Peter was not likely to boost the group mean, he was excused. In their minds, given all of Peter's problems, this was not worth a fight with the school system. Yet, no one learned anything about Peter's progress toward achieving science standards or the school's role in his accomplishments or lack thereof, although he had been in the school since kindergarten.

THE PURPOSES OF ASSESSMENT
AND SYSTEMIC REFORM

Nowhere is the politics of education reform more hotly contended than in the area of student testing, where the "rubber meets the road" or, at least, that is the wistful intention. Political battles are waged over what counts as knowledge (e.g., "how to learn" or the "cannon"), the format of testing items (e.g., multiple choice or performance-based), the labeling of the results (e.g., *achievement scores* or *outcomes*), the reporting of data (e.g., disaggregated or not), and the stakes involved (i.e., high, middle, or low). Equity issues figure strongly in the mix.

Assessment is both central to systemic reform in science and mathematics and is an index for judging its success. The assessment system is intended to stimulate reform by communicating standards and holding schools and students accountable for them (Land, 1997). One of NCTM's three volumes on mathematics reform focuses solely on the topic of assessment, *Assessment Standards for School Mathematics* (1995). The NSES has a chapter devoted to assessment, and examples of nontraditional assessments linked closely to instruction can be found throughout this document.

When state-mandated assessment results are used to leverage reform within a particular school by determining future resources, interventions, or state takeovers, this is referred to as *middle stakes testing*. "Teachers (singly or in groups) could be rewarded or punished if students did not meet performance goals. Whole schools could be reconstituted if student performance did not meet certain norms over extended periods" (Wyckoff & Naples, 1998, p. 4). *High stakes testing* is the term used for assessments that determine if a student is retained in a grade or allowed to receive a diploma and graduate. When high stakes tests are enacted, students and their parents have powerful incentives to make sure that schools are providing opportunities to learn so that students can meet educational standards.

Although it seems harsh to hold students accountable for what they have not had an opportunity to learn; the alternative, little or no accountability, is not serving the best interests of students either. It may most particularly hurt children whose parents are unable to provide accessory educational experiences at home when schools are not meeting their needs. On the other hand, these same students may also be the ones whose parents lack the wherewithal to challenge a school system that fails to teach their children. The equity issues behind middle and high stakes assessment are the main focus of this chapter.

Student assessments are used for many purposes beyond assigning of grades. The goals of assessment can be characterized as *internal* to the school, including feedback for teachers, parents and students or *external* to the school, including administrators, policymakers, and the public (to say nothing of the real estate agents whose sales are made or broken by a local school's test results). To elaborate, according to the Assessment Chapter in Blueprints for Reform (AAAS, 1998), the internal purposes for assessment include:

- Conveying to students expectations about what is important to learn.
- Providing information to students and parents about student progress.
- Helping students to judge their own learning.
- Guiding and improving instruction.
- Classifying and selecting students. (p. 162)

External purposes serve the needs of those on the outside of the school looking in and include the following:

- Providing information for accountability systems.
- Guiding policy decisions on funding, staff development, and so on.
- Gathering information for program evaluation.
- Sorting and classifying people for admissions, certification or hiring. (p. 162)

Although these are general purposes of assessment, because of the expense and difficulty in constructing, securing, and maintaining valid and reliable assessment systems credible to the public, states may seek to create one assessment system that can simultaneously serve multiple purposes. According to the Consortium for Policy Research in Education (CPRE; 1995), new assessments are used for:

> providing good data for comparing the performance of schools, providing diagnostic feedback to help teachers improve their practice and meet the needs of individual students, and providing strong incentives for desired changes in practice. This may seem reasonable on its face, but is difficult in practice. Assessments measuring individual student achievement and providing instructional feedback may not be good tools for accountability. And it may be hard to keep multiple purposes of in balance. Thus, a high stakes assessment may drive curriculum in unanticipated and undesired directions, while resulting in short-term improvements in performance undermining long-term goals for improving practice. (p. 9)

External Purposes of Assessment

Who Takes the Tests?

Needless to say, in the scenario that opened this chapter, excusing little Peter from a thoughtfully constructed test of science achievement served none of the purposes of assessment just listed. How widespread is this practice? James Ysseldyke at the National Center of Educational Outcomes at the University of Minnesota says that "people try to keep low functioning kids out of the picture" by sending them on field trips or telling them to stay home, because teachers' and administrators' merit raises, promotions, and bonuses are based on test scores (Kantowitz & Springen, 1997, p. 60). About 27 states track the participation of students with disabilities in statewide assessments and within these states, only about 50% of these students are tested. Forty-four out of 48 states (having assessment programs) reported allowing exemptions for English language learners. The criteria for exemption and the proportion of the students exempted varies.

On the national level, NAEP reported a 41% to 44% exclusion rate for students with disabilities and English language learners (O'Sullivan et al., 1997). Although it is certainly true in severe circumstances that some students cannot meaningfully participate in an assessment, a study conducted by the National Academy of Education in 1993 (National Center for Educational Statistics, 1996) found that many students excluded from NAEP were capable of participating, especially if some accommodations and adaptations were offered. In the 1996 administration, NAEP provided criteria designed to include rather than exclude students, but the results from the 1996 mathematics NAEP and eighth-grade science NAEP indicated that the revised inclusion criteria had little overall effect on the percentage of total population assessed or the percentages of students with disabilities or English language learners assessed.

In contrast, the provision of accommodations and adaptations on the 1996 NAEP resulted in a modest increase in participation rates in the mathematics assessments at Grades 4 and 8, but not Grade 12. Students with disabilities had accommodations that included the provision of large-face booklets and calculators, Braille booklets, talking calculators, and modifications of test procedures such as unlimited testing time, individual or small group administrations, extended time, directions read by a facilitator, allowing students to give answers orally, and using special mechanical apparatus. Spanish-speaking English language learners were provided with a Spanish–English bilingual version of the mathematics NAEP. Similar trends were noted for the science assessments but were not as pronounced, perhaps due to the limited range of accommodations offered for the science NAEP (i.e., a Spanish–English glossary of scientific terms that few students seemed to use and extra time were provided). Only for Grade 12 was a significant reduction in exclusion rates (36%) found for a combined group of students with disabilities and English language learners.

In addition, for both science and mathematics NAEP results in 1996, a *switching phenomenon* was noted—a portion of the population of students with disabilities were tested with accommodations when they were available in one assessment, but the same students switched to standard assessment conditions when special administration procedures were not provided. The results obtained with accommodations may be more valid, but switching can complicate the interpretation of trend results. The switching effect was not noted for English language learners, however, who had similar participation rates under any conditions. A report on the efficacy of the accommodations on test scores is planned (O'Sullivan et al., 1997).

Within states, there are a variety of criteria used to excuse English language learners from taking various state assessments, and modifications are made to allow such children to show what they know and are able to do (see Tables 9.1 and 9.2). Although these variations raise important test validity issues—test results of students who had accommodations may not be comparable to those without—the impact of assessing students who may have been pushed aside and ignored in accountability systems in the past should not be underestimated. If these students count in the evaluation of the reform, more attention to effective teaching and curricular responses will not be far behind (see chaps. 6 and 7).

Some groups of students are more likely to have difficulties on large-scale assessments than others, and consequently, their data are disaggre-

TABLE 9.1
Criteria Used by States to Exempt LEP Students

Exemption Criterion	States reporting each exemption criterion (N = 44)	
	Number	% of total
English language proficiency level	27	61
Time in United States or school district	20	45
Teacher/administrator recommendations	16	36
Special program participation	15	34

Note. From *Statewide Assessment Programs: Policies and Practices for the Inclusion of Limited English Proficient Students* by C. Rivera, C. Vincent, A. Hafner, and M. LaCelle-Peterson, 1997. Reprinted with permission.

TABLE 9.2
Most Frequent Test Modifications Reported by States

Type of modification	No. of states using (N = 27)	% of total
Extra time	22	81
Small group administration	20	74
Flexible scheduling	17	63
Simplified direction in English	15	56
Use of dictionaries or word lists	14	52

Note. From *Statewide Assessment Programs: Policies and Practices for the Inclusion of Limited English Proficient Students* by C. Rivera et al., 1997. Reprinted with permission.

gated from the totals for purposes of comparison and diagnosis. States frequently report disaggregated data by gender, ethnicity, and SES. (The test scores of Title 1 students or those who receive free and reduced lunches from the federal government due to low-income levels are often reported separately.) Some states disaggregate or exempt the data of students who have recently transferred into the schools because schools understandably do not want to be held responsible for the achievement of students whom they did not serve directly over time.

For instance, the assessment data provided by the state of Texas on its website includes results by ethnic group and disaggregated by SES. The results show the progress of economically disadvantaged students over time (Texas Educational Agency, 1997). (Readers of this text are urged to update assessment data included herein by checking appropriate websites.)

Disaggregated data present a detailed picture of the test results landscape. Yet, it can, in a sense, let schools off of the accountability hook because the implication can be, "See who we have to teach and the problems they bring to school? No wonder we such low test scores." Malik Chaka, the head of a Black American parents group in Maryland says of this rationale, "It's a cop-out. It provides a ready-made excuse for public schools' failure to educate some children . . . that some kids can't achieve because they are poor, black or Hispanic" (Nakashima, 1998, p. B1). As high stakes testing is being instituted in the state of Virginia, the Chairman of the Alexandria School Board says that he has no problem holding every student to the same standard, but he will urge the state to change its plans to use the same benchmark for assessing each school, making special allowances for schools with large numbers of students who are low income or whose native language is not English. "The fact is . . . that we may be doing a tremendous job [with] children who come to us as some of the most needy and ill-prepared" (Benning, 1998a, p. B4). Although there is a valid point about the challenge of teaching students from low-income homes or who are English language learners, how can school officials require children to be held accountable for standards that bear the highest of stakes, while stepping back from the responsibility themselves?

Assessment results with disaggregated data can also make it clear that schools with similar student demographic profiles are achieving very different results. For instance, the state of Texas compares high-poverty schools in their performance, showing that some schools are far more effective than others, recognizing and rewarding the high-achieving schools. Here, assessment results are linked with access to resources and to school improvement efforts. Disaggregated achievement test results from the state of New York showed that the schools with low achievement were most likely to have the fewest certified teachers and other resources, as well as the most low SES students (Lynch, 1998). This kind of information may serve as a diagnostic–prescriptive service, albeit one that may not be entirely welcome by the educators in low-performing schools. Disaggregated data allows policymakers to direct funds strategically to areas that need extra resources, as well as to determine how those funds are to be provided and spent. However, accountability systems that provide bad news, but that are not attached to a plan and funding for improvement, are likely to be more demoralizing than helpful.

William Sanders, the director of the University of Tennessee's value-added research center, has developed a statistical procedure that weeds out wealth as a differential factor among schools, using each child's change in performance level on tests as the basis for the evaluation of school effectiveness (Nakashima, 1998; Sanders & Horn, 1995). He contended that this levels the playing field for schools by requiring all schools to be judged on the basis of individual student improvement, which affects schools with affluent and poor children more equally.

Alignment of Learning Standards
With Assessments

In the equity schema introduced in chapter 1 and used throughout this volume, Level 1 examines educational outcomes, the assessment of students' achievement of national science standards. If some identifiable groups of students are falling short of the goals on assessments, we turn to other levels of the equity schema, examining opportunities to learn and contemplating interventions. A problem with this approach is that Level 1 supposes that there is an adequate assessment system for measuring the equity goal of achieving high outcomes for all. Unfortunately, the development of student assessment systems has lagged behind the development of standards. (Standard-setting logically should precede the construction of assessments, although this has not been the case in many states.) There is no one recognized assessment that tests the national science standards. The NAEP comes closest, but is dependent on the voluntary participation of each of the states, and the science NAEP is only given every 6 years. Also, it is not designed to yield individual student test scores, but provides state-level scores.

Furthermore, the NAEP has recently come under criticism for the manner under which it has set its cutoff scores to define levels of performance expectations (Pellegrino, Jones, & Mitchell, 1998). The 1996 science NAEP results are particularly suspect because they seem to be based on a different philosophy and process of standard-setting than in the past, one that was fraught with disagreement and controversy. Some test experts believe that the result of these changes is that the scores reported on the 1996 science NAEP are artificially low, that is, the performance level expectations set by NAEP were set too high and do not seem reasonable. "There has been a lack of correspondence between NAEP ... results and external evidence of students' achievement, such as course-taking patterns and data from other assessments (for example the advanced placement examinations), on which higher proportions of students perform at high levels" (Pellegrino et al., 1998, p. 167). Of course, students of color and low SES students are likely to be most affected by artificially high standard setting because the test scores of these students tend to cluster in the lower levels of the test. Because the NAEP is *the nation's report card* and is a *policy-relevant metric*, it is important that it provides comparable methods of data collection and achievement level setting over time. Changes in test-score reporting (as reflected in changes in the way in which the cut-off scores for various levels of proficiency are set) create an impression that things are worse than perhaps they are, especially after nearly 10 years of reform efforts to boost science achievement.

It is no small task to make a credible, fair science assessment. If the science NAEP, funded by congress and administered through NCES, provides a questionable view of achievement due to how its standards were set, how will individual states with far fewer resources and less expertise in testing create valid, reliable, and equitable assessments? Further complicating matters, although the most recent science NAEP was revised to align with national standards, each state has adopted its own science standards that have varying degrees of fidelity to the national standards. Each state also has its own assessment system. The state-mandated tests typically carry more weight than the NAEP because they set the stakes within the state. Some of these state assessment systems are old and borrowed from bygone eras, bearing little relation to the goals of science education reform (CPRE, 1995; Land, 1997). Other states have developed new tests that seem well-aligned to measure student achievement in a particular state, whereas other states have new assessments of dubious quality.

Types of Assessments: Performance Versus Traditional

Over the years, large-scale testing in the United States has changed from standardized (which refers to the conditions under which the test is given), multiple-choice, *norm-referenced* (designed to compare students) tests; to standardized, *criterion-referenced* (standards set by a panel of experts) tests; to standardized, *performance* assessments. Because U.S. science education has been criticized for its emphasis on facts, the shallowness of instruction, and the huge number of topics covered, researchers and reformers are asking if the introduction of new performance assessments can break the pattern and serve as a powerful lever for shaping instruction and catalyzing reform (Firestone, Mayrowetz, & Fairman, 1998). Performance assessments were also know as *alternative* or *authentic* assessments, although there is disagreement over the use of these terms (Newmann, Brandt, & Wiggins, 1998; Terwilliger, 1997). This chapter uses the terms *traditional* and *performance* assessments as relatively value-neutral terms to describe these types of assessments.

Performance assessments in science are designed to provide students with the types of realistic, messy problems that they encounter in (some) school science laboratories or in life, in general. Students are often required to work with materials to solve a problem, making observations, taking and analyzing data, and explaining and justifying results. This may be done individually, in groups, or in combination. For instance, a retired Maryland performance assessment for fifth graders asks them to build a simple hydrometer, take some salinity readings, predict results, and apply what they found to salinity charts in order to design a salt-water aquarium. The task has proved to be challenging and engrossing to graduate students (in science methods courses) and there is little doubt that fifth graders would also find it so.

Educators have built up a lot of hopes for performance assessment and have anticipated positive effects. Performance assessments are thought to encourage curricular reform, provide better alignment with curriculum standards, emphasize higher order skills, offer better models of instruction, contribute to staff development, and improve communications with parents (Stecher & Klein, 1998). Unfortunately, there is little research to confirm or refute these projected benefits.

In addition, performance assessments were seen as a way to reduce achievement gaps in test scores. Because some groups of students have not performed well on traditional tests of science achievement, such as the NAEP, ACT, SAT-science achievement tests and AP science exams (Rodriguez, 1997), it was thought that group differences would diminish or disappear altogether in a different kind of testing environment (Darling-Hammond, 1994; Stecher & Klein, 1997). Performance assessments provide students with equipment and a context in which to demonstrate science reasoning. This could (it was hoped) level the playing field and reduce achievement differences because performance tests would be less dependent on background experiences and knowledge obtained outside school.

In some cases, performance-based tests have resulted in new patterns of achievement data. For instance, in the 1996–1997 Maryland School Performance Assessment, females tended to outscore males at most grade levels and within most ethnic groups. Yet, unfortunately, the scoring patterns of various ethnic groups on this assessment are consistent with those reported on more traditional measures of science achievement (Maryland State Department of Education, 1997). This has generally been the case throughout the United States (Stecher & Klein, 1997).

From the standpoint of equity and accountability, instead of a test that measures science aptitude or background knowledge (both of which are linked to social class), one would want an assessment that measures a student's science achievement. Achievement in this sense is the result of effective learning experiences in the science classroom. It is curriculum and instruction that ought to level the playing field. In a detailed study of the reliability and validity of performance assessments in science, Shavelson, Baxter, and Pine (1992) found that performance tasks had to be carefully crafted in order to measure more than science aptitude. Tasks that were closely linked to instructional experiences (i.e., tapping both procedural and declarative prior knowledge) seem most sensitive to equity concerns. For example, a performance task such as a *batteries and bulbs* (assuming that students have had classroom experiences with the equipment and discussed the underlying concepts) assesses an understanding of electricity through the building of circuits, providing students with the background experiences to learn.

The issue of transfer is important. Although educators may expect students to transfer concepts learned to different contexts, it is not clear whether this transfer is tapping into deep conceptual understanding or to prior experiences that may advantage some groups of students over others. Consequently, in terms of equity, it seems wisest to link assessment closely to classroom instruction and experiences. Shavelson et al. (1992) found that a combination of performance assessments taken together (with varying degrees of linkage to prior experience), in aggregate, had about the same correlation coefficient with aptitude as the standardized multiple-choice achievement test. This seems to suggest that if both instruction (content and processes) and assessment were carefully aligned with standards, then a student's chances of success would increase a great deal with a good performance assessment system. If assessments do not reflect prior experiences, then it is just as well to give a cheaper and easier to administer norm-referenced standardized test. Shavelson et al. (1992) also found that interrater reliability on the performance tasks was high, so high that a single rater can provide a reliable score. Yet, intertask reliability was much harder to obtain—some students scored high on some tasks but low on others, suggesting that in order to estimate student achievement accurately, a number of tasks would be needed and this would be expensive.

Hamilton's (1998) conclusions as a result of an analysis of the science items on the National Educational Longitudinal Study of 1988 (NELS: 88) were similar to those of Shavelson et al. (1992), although this test was traditional rather than a performance assessment. Hamilton was primarily interested in understanding the gender differences in science achievement (favoring males) on NELS: 88, factoring in student background, school characteristics, and instructional experiences. For the multiple-choice items on the science assessment, she found that the gender differences were primarily on items that required spatial–mechanical reasoning, whereas gender differences on items that required quantitative skills or background knowledge were minimal. In addition, participation in an ESL program was negatively correlated with spatial–mechanical reasoning and background knowledge, but had no effect on quantitative skills. For constructed response items (short essay responses to specific prompts, e.g., asking students to compare and contrast fossil fuels vs. nuclear energy), the gender differences were similar. In examining background variables, it appeared that the items that showed the largest gender differences were those that had not been taught directly in schools, but picked up informally (e.g., an item on solar and lunar eclipses). The items that showed the smallest gender differences were those that students said were based on in-school experiences. Students in ESL programs and Hispanics had negative relations on the multiple-choice format, but not on the constructed response format. The multiple-choice test showed a stronger relation with math reasoning and reading than the constructed item response test.

Hamilton (1998) concluded that the gender differences seem less dependent on differences in general or scientific reasoning ability than they were on outside-of-school experiences, particularly those that promote visual or spatial reasoning. When test items were closely tied to school curriculum experiences, females in this study performed as well as males. She suggested that schools could address the discrepancy in test scores by providing opportunities for all students to participate in relevant hands-on activities during school hours. "These findings have implications for efforts to reduce the racial/ethnic and socioeconomic group differences because these also tend to be larger on test items that call on outside knowledge or experiences" (p. 192).

In order for assessment systems to fulfill the external purposes of assessment and provide accountability, they must include the diverse learners who have been excluded from testing in the past. Because one of the purposes of assessment is to create a feedback mechanism that gauges the effectiveness of the reform, state assessments must be closely aligned with state standards, and the tests must be carefully constructed in order to capture as accurately and fully as possible the interventions introduced to improve the school-learning experiences of the students tested. However, the evaluation of systemic reform in science and mathematics has proven to be a more burdensome and perplexing problem than anyone anticipated. It seems for all our reliance on the engineering metaphor for systemic reform (see Fig. 5.4), many state assessment systems have been notoriously poor in providing the kind of information that helps reformers measure the impact of their efforts.

NSF's Statewide Systemic Initiatives:
Evaluating Systemic Science Education Reform

The validity of program evaluation depends on alignment of content standards with the assessment system. States that have received federal funding through NSF's Statewide Systemic Initiatives (SSI) are under some pressure to demonstrate the effectiveness of their SSIs in a number of ways. The most crucial outcomes are documented gains in student achievement in science and math, while closing the achievement gaps. Since 1991, NSF has invested $6 to $10 million dollars in each of 24 states (i.e., Arkansas, California, Colorado, Connecticut, Delaware, Florida, Georgia, Kentucky, Louisiana, Maine, Massachusetts, Michigan, Montana, Nebraska, New Jersey, New Mexico, New York, North Carolina, Ohio, South Carolina, South Dakota, Texas, Vermont, and Virginia) and the Commonwealth of Puerto Rico to develop SSIs to improve mathematics and science education. States receiving these funds are asked to demonstrate increased student attainment in science, mathematics, and technology.

Program evaluation efforts within the 25 SSIs have proved to be daunting. In a study commissioned by NSF, only 7 SSIs (i.e., Kentucky, Louisiana, Montana, New Mexico, Ohio, Vermont, and Puerto Rico) were deemed as likely to generate the most credible evidence that student achievement has risen (Laguarda, 1998). On the whole, these states were able to attribute only small, statistically significant increases in student achievement to the SSI interventions. However, somewhat more encouraging was the fact that the SSI activities, in many instances, particularly benefited historically underserved students, and shrunk, but did not close, achievement gaps. Four of the SSIs—Louisiana, New Mexico, Ohio, and Puerto Rico—made equity a central focus of their evaluations, collecting data to examine specific gap questions by gender, ethnicity or race, and poverty level. These SSI evaluation results are so important to the theme of this volume that each is summarized in the following sections. More details may be found in an NSF-funded evaluation by Laguarda (1998) or within individual state evaluation documents.

Louisiana. Assessment data from Louisiana's SSI, *LaSIP*, showed that, overall, LaSIP students showed greater gains on the state assessment than non-LaSIP students, although the gains were quite small. However, disaggregated data by ethnicity or race and poverty level suggest that Black students, especially those having free and reduced-lunch status (poor children) may have profited more from the SSI intervention than their White or middle-class counterparts, reducing the performance gap.

In addition, LaSIP students reported more variety in science and math experiences, more hands-on learning, and field trips. They seemed to be more able to see applications of science and math outside the classroom and experienced more variety in teacher-made assessments.

New Mexico.   New Mexico's SSI, called *SIMSE*, targeted students in K through Grades 12. Each year for 3 consecutive years, new schools were added to the SSI, but the patterns for evaluation results were inconsistent. Promising results came from the first cohort of schools participating in SIMSE, 90 in all, which showed gains on the ITBS in science and mathematics that were greater than the state average. When compared with baseline data collected from SIMSE schools before the SSI was initiated, the gains were also significant. Unfortunately, subsequent cycles of SIMSE (Years 2 and 3) did not show similar patterns of achievement results, probably due to differences in the schools participating in the reform as time went on.

New Mexico has substantial numbers of Native American (10%) and Latino (46%) students. SIMSE reported that "almost all gender and ethnic groups demonstrated consistent and considerable gains in science and mathematics in the two years following the baseline year" (Laguarda, 1998, p. A-36). Although all ethnic groups and genders had gains, the gaps between Anglo and both Hispanic and Native Americans for the lower grades remained the same or increased slightly, although at the eighth grade level, the gaps decreased between Latinos and Native American boys compared with Anglo boys, especially for Native Americans. Overall, however, there was much inconsistency of the direction of results from grade to grade and year to year, suggesting that more long-term study of the effects of the SIMSE is necessary. Yet, this is the type of analysis that helps us to understand the effects of science and mathematics education reform on different groups of students over time.

Moreover, it is hard to know what to make of these data because the ITBS (a norm-based, multiple-choice, standardized test) is hardly the ideal instrument to evaluate the success of an initiative that sets as its goal the kinds of changes in instruction and learning envisioned by science and mathematics reformers. However, it is encouraging that SIMSE students' test scores did not plummet on this traditional measure. Yet, what kinds of science achievement results might have been captured with a test better aligned with SIMSE?

Ohio.   The evaluation results for Ohio SSI, called *Project Discovery*, are in many ways the most interesting and most informative for equity concerns. Project Discovery targeted students in Grades 5 through 8 in

TABLE 9.3
Results of Discovery Inquiry Tests by
SSI Participation, Race, and Gender: 1995

				Raw percent correct								
	Discovery				*Match*				*Difference*			
	African American		White		African American		White		African American		White	
Subject	F	M	F	M	F	M	F	M	F	M	F	M
Science												
(n = 610)	44%	40%	60%	54%	35%	31%	50%	50%	9%	9%	10%	4%

Note. From *Assessing SSIs Impacts on Student Achievement: An Imperfect Science*, by K. G. Laguarda, 1998.

science and mathematics. Because of Ohio's privacy laws, the evaluators were not able to use the state achievement tests, so they created inquiry-based tests in science and math, using retired NAEP items. It is apparent that the evaluators took greater pains than most states to construct an evaluation with a well-structured research design that included reasonably matched comparison groups (students in the same schools who were taught either by Project Discovery trained teachers or by those who had no special training). The evaluation was designed to determine the effects of Project Discovery by gender and ethnic group (in Ohio, Blacks are the second largest ethnic population, after Whites). Unfortunately, although the design was commendable, it included only a small number of schools due to cost and logistics.

Project Discovery set closing achievement gaps as a major goal, along with raising achievement for all through participation in the SSI. Table 9.3 shows the results of one iteration of several similar evaluation studies of the Ohio SSI. From this table of results, good news is immediately apparent. By comparing Project Discovery students, broken down by gender and ethnicity with their counterparts in the comparison or match group, Project Discovery students showed consistent gains for every comparison (see Table 9.3). White females showed the greatest gains.

Because African-American students in Discovery classes scored significantly higher than their peers in non-Discovery classes, and because girls taught by Discovery teachers scored higher than males in their racial group, Kahle and Damnajanovic (in Laguarda, 1998) theorized that the inquiry-based, cooperative learning techniques introduced in Discovery science classrooms—techniques designed to engage students who have traditionally been socialized away from science—may benefit minority students and girls disproportionately. (pp. A-45–46)

However, despite these achievement gains for SSI students within ethnic and gender groups, Project Discovery seems to have been less successful in closing achievement gaps by ethnic group. For instance, the 1995 evaluation showed a 17-point gap in science, favoring Whites for the Project Discovery group, versus an 11-point gap in the match group (Laguarda, 1998, p. A-44). Looking at Table 9.3, and examining the achievement gaps by ethnicity within genders, we see that the gap has shortened somewhat for males—a 14-point gap favoring White males in Project Discovery group versus a 19-point gap in the match male group. For females, the gap remains about constant, a 16-point gap favoring White females in the Project Discovery group versus a 15-point gap for the match group.

Project Discovery assessments resulted in unexpected gender gaps between White females and males, favoring the females, whereas for Black females and males, the gender gap favoring females remained approximately the same for Project Discovery and match groups. The researchers' interpretation was that the Project Discovery classroom interventions were successful in appealing to females and teaching science more effectively than traditional classrooms. The issue of achievement gaps is an important and vexing one because one should not assume that improvements to curriculum and instruction will have the same impact on different groups of students. The Ohio study did not examine the effect of this inquiry-based curriculum on students with disabilities or English language learners. Some educators reserve special doubts about the efficacy of inquiry-based instruction for students with learning disabilities. Project Discovery's emphasis on cooperative learning and hands-on techniques may counter students' difficulties in making inferences, which is so important to the inquiry process. However, the costs and design challenges make comprehensive evaluation efforts difficult.

Puerto Rico. The SSI in Puerto Rico, *PR–SSI*, initially targeted students in grades 7 through 9, although it has currently expanded to include Kindergarten through Grade 6. A major equity issue in Puerto Rico is poverty. Almost all of the island's middle-class students (i.e., 19% of the student population) attend private or parochial schools, whereas the rest attend the public schools. Within these public schools, about 78% of the students are eligible for free and reduced-lunch rates. PR–SSI contracted to have the NAEP translated into Spanish and adapted for Puerto

Rican students, and this assessment instrument formed the basis of the evaluation of the SSI. In addition, PR–SSI used data from the territory's own testing program, did attitudinal studies of students involved in the PR–SSI, and conducted student focus groups.

The initial results are very promising. Students in PR–SSI schools significantly outperformed in science and mathematics their counterparts in non-PR–SSI schools and made progress in closing the gap with the private schools. In the one area, geometry, the SSI students matched the scores of private school students. As the PR–SSI continues, the data gathered should be useful and interesting because the evaluation design is sound. However, it should be noted that the cost of such evaluation efforts are substantial, estimated to be about $500,000 per year to administer and score the tests (after the initial costs of translating the NAEPs that were considerable). This is about 25% of the annual budget of the SSI.

Other Evaluation Difficulties

The previous discussion points out systemic reform's differential effects on various groups, as well as the substantial evaluation problems encountered when attempting to gauge the success of reform effort costing millions of dollars across 25 states, each with its own unique educational environment and policies. Because the United States has neither a national curriculum nor national assessments, each state must design its own. Creating a system that has *logical integrity* (alignment among standards, curriculum, and assessment) and that can accomplish the evaluation goals of the NSF-sponsored SSIs has been no easy task. Some additional problems of the evaluation are presented in the following sections.

Alignment and Timing Issues. In some states, the grade levels and specific curriculum changes targeted through the SSI did not match the state assessment system in terms of timing, even if there was some overall content alignment of assessment and standards across grades. The timing of the state assessments (some states have predetermined cycles that do not allow the testing of students in science and math every year or at every grade level) did not match the reform implementation schedule (Laguarda, Breckenridge, & Hightower, 1994).

Privacy Issues. In some states, the achievement data proved useless if the state restricted the release of data in a manner that would not allow distinguishing treatment and control groups. Some states implemented the reform by targeting particular teachers for professional development as opposed to schools or school districts (Laguarda et al., 1994). Concerns and regulations about student confidentiality made access to individual or classroom level results difficult or impossible to obtain. Data were reported only down to the school district level, so there was no mechanism to gather data on students in the specific schools or classrooms affected by the SSI.

Comparison Group Contamination. As the SSI reform trickled down through the system and affected more teachers through informal channels (shared lessons, etc.), it was difficult to separate the effects of the SSI on students who were exposed to SSI interventions versus those who were not (Laguarda, 1998). The dissemination of the reform through these indirect channels was a positive intent of the reform, but messy for evaluation purposes. In 1994, a NSF-sponsored evaluation of the 25 SSIs in existence at that time concluded that only five states (i.e., California, Connecticut, Kentucky, Maine, and Texas) had assessment programs that could deliver reasonable data for science reform evaluation (Laguarda et al., 1994).

Disaggregating Data. A chilling prospect for anyone concerned about a reform whose intent can be summarized as "higher standards and science literacy for all" is whether the reform could result in even greater gaps between those proficient in science and those who are not. Another possibility is that the reform could succeed in raising achievement overall, but the gaps between various groups would remain about the same. The third possibility, the ideal, would be to close the gaps (i.e., NSF targets the reduction in attainment differences between those historically underserved and their peers) as achievement levels increase for all (Laguarda, 1998). In order to address this NSF goal, states must gather assessment data so that it can be easily disaggregated, but some states do not administer tests in such a way. It is difficult and expensive to determine the impacts of the reform on various subpopulations of students in states that have not created systems for disaggregated data. Because of cost, technical challenges, and credibility issues, it is desirable to avoid a situation where evaluators have to develop and administer their own assessment instruments as was done in Ohio (previously discussed). Although the Ohio SSI evaluation was well designed, it only affected a handful of schools and did not provide sufficiently large samples of students for compelling evaluation evidence (Breckenridge, Goldstein, & Zucker, 1996).

As the nation engages in science education reform efforts (be they NSF-sponsored or not), it is clear that new accountability systems in the form of medium stakes testing will play an important role. For students who have been historically underserved by science education by a system that inequitably distributes resources to schools and ignores the results, medium stakes testing would seem to hold some considerable promise, provided it was used to leverage educational improvement where it is most needed. Too often, statewide accountability systems seem designed to congratulate schools lucky enough to have high income, high achieving students. On the other hand, *high stakes testing* (holding students accountable for achieving high standards) raises many opportunities to learn issues that, if accompanied by wise funding policies, could boost achievement for low SES students.

High Stakes Testing—Holding Students Accountable

On the face of things, it seems ridiculous to institute a system of reform that holds educators accountable for school improvement, without also extending responsibility to students and their parents. It is reasonable to ask students to attend to the betterment of their own education and for parents to assist in the process. High stakes testing is being proposed to drive the system toward improvement because nothing seems more likely to get students' (and their parents') attention than being held back a grade or failing to obtain a high school diploma.

To what extent are high stakes testing policies being implemented? In 1996, about one sixth of 12th-grade students reported that they had to pass a state or school district science test in order to graduate (O'Sullivan et al., 1998). Yet, the performance of students having such a requirement was no different on the science NAEP than those who did not. In a policy study that had 100% participation rate (50 states and the District of Columbia), Rivera and Vincent (1997) found that 17 states had high stakes assessment programs in place during the 1993 through 1994 school year. Of these, 5 included tests in science. In a more recent study, Wyckoff and Naples (1998) reported that 18 of 30 states that they studied either have, or plan to have, high stakes tests for students. This is a trend across the nation and it appears that high stakes tests in the sciences will increasingly be the norm. For instance, the state of New York has recently moved to an all-Regents examination system that will require all students to take and pass the Regents examinations for a high school diploma, which includes passing exams in two science subjects (Lynch, 1998). Maryland and Virginia also plan to require high stakes tests in science and will be phasing in these requirements in the next several years (Benning, 1998b; Grasmick, 1998). As raising the number of science courses required for high school graduation has resulted in improvements in student achievement (Chaney, Burdorf, & Atash, 1997), it seems likely that high stakes tests will also result in improvements in students achievement (Bishop, Moriarty, & Mane, 1998).

High stakes testing in science raises interesting psychometric questions as well as important equity concerns. What is acceptable high school, exit-level performance in science? Setting high standards may spur achievement overall, but what does such a policy do for students who simply will not be able to meet them? Because as a nation, we have a minimal experience in testing science performance for all children, this seems to be a very open question (even the New York's Regents examinations in science have been taken by a limited portion of the population). Setting educational standards for what students ought to learn is one thing, but holding young people's futures hostage to a nascent assessment system that attempts to quantify what they actually have learned and have also had the opportunity to learn is quite another.

Determining Acceptable Performance Levels on High Stakes Tests

As discussed earlier in this chapter, the one test that had the best reputation and track record as a national assessment of science achievement, the NAEP, has recently been criticized for the methods used in determining performance standards, particularly for the 1996 science NAEP (Pellegrino et al., 1998). For criterion-referenced tests, the method most frequently used to determine acceptable performance levels probably is the *Angoff procedure* (Bob Mislevy, personal communication, November 9, 1998), which employs panels of trained raters to determine cut-off scores. It is important to note that this technique is based on the supposition that experts can decide what students should be able to do in terms of conceptual understanding and related skills. In the 1996 science NAEP, the public representatives on the standard-setting committee consistently set higher cut-offs than the professionals on the committee. Given the disagreements, the NAEP eventually turned to a different procedure, called *behavioral anchoring techniques*, which seems essentially normative in that cut scores were based on students' actual performance on the 1996 NAEP—what students did know and were able to do rather than what they should be able to do. There is a huge difference in the suppositions underlying these two approaches, and this is what has fed the controversy (Pellegrino et al., 1998).

Although the NAEP is administered nationally, it is a relatively low-stakes test (only used to compare the states' progress toward achieving national goals). The issue of how performance standards are set becomes even more important within each individual state because it is at the state level that the most influential decisions in education are made. Each state decides whether to initiate high stakes testing with grade retention and high school graduation hanging in the balance for students. There are very real threats of lawsuits from students who have not had the opportunity to achieve the standards (Rivera & Vincent, 1997). Court rulings have gone both ways, with states and local school districts prevailing if they could show that the material on the test aligned with state standards and the student had the opportunity to learn it in class. The Mexican American Legal Defense and Education Fund filed a federal lawsuit, with results pending, alleging that the state of Texas' graduation exams discriminate against minority students (Benning, 1998c). Legal challenges are also likely to be mounted when the testing processes are perceived to be arbitrary or unfair, if values or attitudes appear to be assessed, or if accommodations for students with disabilities have not been offered (Linn & Herman, 1997).

In Maryland, high stakes tests will be phased in gradually and implemented by the year 2003 (Grasmick, 1998). Maryland currently uses a method of establishing criterion performance levels on its current middle stakes test in science that was described by Bill Schaefer, the State Director of Assessment, as a combination of expert judgment guided by student performance (personal communication, November 10, 1998). The mean scale score on a cluster of items around a particular performance task is calculated, .6 of a standard deviation is added to that score, and cut-off is designated as the *Satisfactory Level*. This cut score becomes the goal for 70% of students to obtain. In addition, a panel of experts determines a second cut score, the *Excellent Level*—25% of the students achieving within 70% *Satisfactory Level* are to reach *Excellent Level*.

At first blush, it seems surprising that the method used to determine performance levels is so normative. Yet, upon further reflection, it seems reasonable to examine how a group of students actually performs on average, raise the bar somewhat higher in a consistent way (using standard deviations), and then ask schools, through increased focus and attention on curricular and instructional matters, to get 70% of students over the bar.

However, in establishing high school graduation criteria, the state would probably want to get more than 70% of the students to reach criterion competencies, something closer to 100%. This assumes that students are reasonably motivated and industrious, that the schools' curricula are closely aligned with the assessment, and curriculum and instruction are effective. In Maryland, at the present time, the prognosis for getting virtually all of the students to pass a rigorous science test (and others) in order to graduate seems doubtful. In 1997, only about 92% of students passed Maryland's low-level functional tests currently required for graduation (including four subject areas, but not science). These tests are scheduled to be phased out because they are not sufficiently challenging and do not include subjects such as science. Only about 50% of Maryland eighth graders passed the science performance assessment (Maryland State Department of Education, 1997).

The percent of Maryland students of African American, Hispanic, and American Indian/Alaskan Native descent passing the functional tests or science performance assessments was lower than the group mean. For these groups, the dropout rate was higher on average. Imagine a distribution curve, however irregular in shape, with proportionately more students of color generally falling to the left half of the curve. As the standard for satisfactory performance is pushed to the right, these children have further to go on average, than White or Asian/Pacific Islander children who are concentrated on the right half of the curve. If the reform is successful (improved opportunities to learn following from the higher standards), then it is children of color who have the most to gain in two senses. They will have the most ground to cover to achieve a satisfactory score for the high stakes, but they will have access to a much better education, and as a consequence, they will be better positioned to receive the rewards of education than they are currently.

Given the discussion regarding how the content of questions and the format of responses differentially affects how a group of students may expect to perform on a test, the issue of test bias is important. Maryland's State Assessment Director, Bill Shaeffer, reported that for the state performance assessment in science, there were some patterns of differences in question bias for Hispanic and Asian American students, compared with that of the entire population (personal communications, Oct. 27 and Nov. 10, 1998). Yet, this was only a middle stakes test. When high stakes graduation tests are constructed, the questions will have to undergo a rigorous expert evaluation for bias or potential source of bias.

If Maryland's procedures for standard setting can be seen as somewhat normative, Virginia's method for setting high school graduation requirements, at least as reported in the newspapers, seems frightening. The new multiple-choice tests, based on Virginia's Standards of Learning (SOL), were given to students for the first time in 1997 as a pilot study. However, the criteria for passing were set without regard to students' performance. Rather, panels of teachers and parents were convened for each test and provided to the state's Board of Education a range of scores that panel members estimated students could achieve. The Board of Education, in most cases, chose the highest score in the range provided by a panel (Benning, 1998c), perhaps representing the opinion of a single person on a test panel. Comparing the cut scores eventually selected by the Board of Education with the actual scores of students in the pilot test group shows that the Board of Education's cut scores were about equivalent to the pilot students' mean scores (in 10 of 27 tests, the Board of Education's scores were somewhat higher than the students' mean scores). Reflecting on the psychometric implications of this decision, this means that about one half of the students in the state would have failed any one of the exams on the first round, and no doubt the majority would have failed to graduate, given that a combination of tests needed to be passed. There has also been much discussion about the large number of English language learners in Virginia who, some educators believe, will be wiped out by the new high standards. Schools with large populations of immigrant children fear that they will lose their accreditation because they must be able to show a 70% pass rate on the new tests.

Politically, it may be easier to justify setting performance criteria by creating panels of experts to make these decisions rather than using criteria based on actual student performance on a test that is normative and generally seems to be perceived negatively. Yet, the panels of experts, mostly teachers, must base their judgments on the performance of students that they have taught, and in this sense, is also normative. This procedure is also suspect as it is possible to question how panel members were selected, the representativeness of the students that they teach, and the value placed on each panelist's judgment as important decisions are made.

The advent of high stakes testing in science raises a number of psychometric issues related to the lack of experience with large-scale testing in science, the difficulty in establishing acceptable cut scores to determine competency, test bias problems, and group differences in performance that burden some children more than others because they have so much ground to gain. Rivera and Vincent (1997) offered some guidelines to facilitate equitable and fair assessments that help to insure that assessment results have a positive backwash on the curriculum and instruction for those who have been underserved by science education. Given the special jeopardy in which English language learners are placed in high stakes testing, Rivera and Vincent recommended the following for states instituting high stakes tests:

1. Carry out studies to evaluate the impact of high school graduation requirements on all student populations and use disaggregated data

(e.g., ethnicity and race, SES, gender, classification as past or present LEP, or disability status) to determine access to content, dropout rates, test repeat performance, the types of accommodations used, and the effectiveness of interventions.

2. Use deferrals from test administrations sparingly (deferrals defeat the diagnostic capabilities of tests and delay interventions).
3. Make judicious use of accommodations in testing with clear policies established for local educators' reference.
4. Develop native language tests if students received instruction in their native language or in bilingual classes.
5. Develop assessments well-aligned with instruction.

This last recommendation is particularly important because it helps level the playing field for students whose out-of-school science experiences may not align with school science expectations for achievement.

Bob Mislevy, an assessment expert at the ETS, believed that educational improvement in the context of high stakes assessment would be best served if states worked much harder in specifying the kinds of desired skills and knowledge from the very beginning and designing assessments to hone in on them. Rather than basing a serious decision about high school graduation on a single test, performance requirements should be syllabus-based and responsive to instruction, as they are for AP or International Baccalaureate (IB) assessments, but aimed at a level set for high school graduation. Cut points for a final exam would be based on classes where the material was actually the basis for instruction and they would be determined by a panel of teachers directly involved and supplemented by other experts. The result would be a well-grounded, attainable assessment rather than one "dropped from the sky" (personal communication, November 9, 1998, representing Mislevy's own views and not those of ETS). For high stakes tests, curriculum-based assessment seems to hold the most promise. Curriculum rather than assessment should be the master of the assessment enterprise (Nitko, 1995), but this is not how state-level assessments are usually designed. This approach is more labor intensive and requires considerable expertise.

In addition to these sensible recommendations about the high stakes test construction and cut-score determinations, equity concerns demand that the students and teachers who are involved in the creation of curriculum-based assessments represent salient population characteristics across a state. In other words, one would need to be assured that students in this assessment standard-setting process reflected the state's diversity. Moreover, the assessment should be based on what students actually demonstrated having learned under conditions of reasonably good in-struction. This is not an issue ordinarily discussed by assessment experts who tend to take a colorblind approach to criterion-based test construc-tion, determining questions, cut scores a priori. However, high stakes testing and equity demands that these realities are confronted in the planning phases of assessment design.

Internal Purposes of Testing

Although much of the emphasis in this chapter has been on the external purposes of assessment because this gives us the best clue about the effectiveness of science education reform and the thorny problems faced by groups of diverse learners, the efficacy of the reform for internal purposes of assessment is also important. Assessment results should be used to improve classroom instruction and provide information to stu-dents and parents about what is important to learn and the student's accomplishments.

Improving Practice Within Science Classrooms

Anecdotal evidence seems to imply that the reform is affecting how science teachers assess their students, which influences the quality and nature of the information available to classroom teachers. This, in turn, may lead to better instruction. A graduate student intern reports that:

> In biology, the types of assessments are endless (about one per day). This is because (the students) are freshmen and we are trying to give them as many chances to do well as possible. We have oral presentations, drawing diagrams, tests, homework outlines, creative stories, journals, and so on. Basically if the kids do it, we grade it. It might be unethical, but how we often grade (except tests) is we look through the papers and make four piles—great, good, okay, and "missed the boat." By using this method, we are gauging the kids on what they received out of the lesson, instead of what we thought they should get. Plus, it tells us how we should adjust for the next day. (Penny Panzer, personal communication, November 23, 1998).

As encouraging as this sounds, this intern also noticed that chemistry teachers in the same department only assess using traditional tests and lab reports.

According to data gathered on the 1996 science NAEP (O'Sullivan et al., 1998), the teachers of 61% of fourth graders and 53% of eighth graders have had professional development experiences with alternative methods of assessment. Yet, NAEP results showed no relation between these professional development experiences and students' scale scores. Of course, there are several links between efficacy of professional development in alternative assessment, implementation in classrooms, and gains in student achievement. Forthcoming further analysis of the performance-based NAEP scores may yield a more promising picture or shed some light on this situation.

A study of the internal effects of a low stakes and medium stakes performance assessment programs in Maine and Maryland, respectively, indicates that the power of performance assessments in mathematics to influence school reform may be overrated (Firestone et al., 1998). There was more of a response in Maryland, where stakes were higher, than in Maine. When statewide science performance assessments were first introduced in Maryland, one sometimes heard that the assessments provided more demanding and engaging activities than did the regular classroom teaching. Some teachers and administrators, understanding that the performance assessment was not going to go away, began to initiate changes in curriculum and instruction that required more reasoning and problem solving in interesting, contextually rich settings. That, of course, was the point, and state science coordinators have provided opportunities for professional development and written materials that encourage classroom instruction that not only focuses on content standards, but also captures the kinds of high-level, problem-solving activities that characterize the Maryland performance assessment (Householder, personal communication, October 27, 1998). Although science test scores have been increasing steadily, it is difficult to know how widespread and comprehensive the changes have been.

Researchers studying the effects of the performance assessment on the middle school mathematics curriculum found that most of the activity was focused on the test itself—teachers taught test-taking strategies—rather than on improving day-to-day instruction (Firestone et al., 1998). There was some evidence of better curriculum alignment—teachers began to provide more instruction on the content and processes included on the test. There was less evidence of changes in basic instructional practices, however, with many of the math teachers maintaining an approach to teaching that emphasized practicing on many small problems and on shallow coverage of topics. The researchers found that additional teacher professional development opportunities were not increased as a result of the new assessment demands, but available opportunities were better focused. These researchers concluded that the problem was a lack in teachers' grasp of content and pedagogical content knowledge that performance assessments alone cannot change. Anecdotal evidence yields a more promising picture. Performance assessments can influence classroom practice over time, at least for teachers who become open to change and who are sufficiently reflective to understand their benefits in the context of reform. In addition, as teachers become more efficient in providing this sort of assessment to their students, they will likely view it more positively. In summary, assessments well-aligned with reform content and that have high contextual validity may provide a necessary, but not sufficient, substrate for reform.

There are conditions that seem to encourage the adoption of alternative forms of assessment within schools. One of the most important factors is allowing teachers to see actual examples of performance assessments in practice. Teachers need real-world practical examples to model before they can readily implement them (Heather McGavin, personal communication, November 23, 1998). Linn and Herman (1997) reported that providing opportunities for teachers to grade the performance assessment is effective professional development in Maryland. Teacher involvement is the cornerstone for the ongoing success, as teachers develop Maryland School Performance Assessment Program (MSPAP) assessment tasks following state specifications and score the tests in four regional centers managed by an outside contractor. Teachers also helped MSPAP set up content and performance standards. Although Maryland makes serious efforts to collaborate with teachers for the state-testing program, only so many can be directly involved. In addition, the Maryland Assessment Consortium, a voluntary teacher professional organization, is a network for teachers to create and share performance assessment for classroom use, resulting in increased understanding and enthusiasm for this new type of assessment.

Providing Information to Parents and Students

Assessment should provide parents and students with feedback about how well the student is doing. Parents of children on the margins of school success might reasonably want to know how their child is performing in comparison with others. Although the discriminating focus of norm-based testing has lead to abuses and overemphasis on competition, there are instances where objective and straightforward measures of a student's progress are useful.

The Washington Post (Matthews, 1998) ran a fascinating account of a youngster in a poor, urban elementary school whose test scores on the Stanford Nine were at the lowest deciles at the end of first grade. His mother, a teacher's aide, knew better than most parents what the scores forebode and embarked on a program for her son that included close attention to homework, reading with him daily, turning off the television during weekdays, summer school, and some occasional formal tutoring. At the end of second grade, his test scores had improved, as did nearly everything concerning his schoolwork. Although the Stanford Nine is a traditional test, it had its place in this child's education and perhaps will spur changes at his school as well.

In another instance, a colleague with a daughter in special education at an affluent suburban school was concerned that the child seemed not to be learning much in seventh grade, as evidenced by a lack of homework and projects and a decline in the child's interest in school. However, the child was bringing home As and Bs in both mainstream and special education classes and made the honor roll. At the close of the schoolyear, when the results of the state- and district-level mandated assessments were provided, the parents' fears were realized—no progress. Additional assessments by a former private reading tutor indicated that the student was no longer using the strategies they had developed—small wonder as she had not been doing much reading.

Why the stark discrepancies between the test results and report card grades? The teachers said the child did not test well, but delving deeper into the situation, it appeared that the students with disabilities were not being assessed by the mainstream teachers nor according to mainstream standards. Rather, special education teachers were providing grades based as much on seat time and student cooperation, rather than a reasonable standard of accomplishment. The parents were positive that their daughter was capable of a higher standard of work, but it had been hard to argue a situation where the child was making the honor roll and proud of her good grades. The child's program was adjusted, she started to study, and test scores began to creep up—none of which may have happened were it not for those test scores.

Parents of students with disabilities, English language learners, and children in poor schools can be lulled into false senses of accomplishment, unless there are reasonable standards and a comprehensible accountability system. The issue is how to make assessment fair and equitable, as well as valid and reliable, as the system moves toward reform goals.

CONCLUSIONS

One of the purposes of assessment listed earlier in this chapter is for sorting and classifying people for admissions, certification, or hiring. Business and industry want an educational system that prepares students better for an Information Age workplace and have been a major impetus behind education reform, especially in science, mathematics, and technology. For example, in Maryland, the rationale for high stakes testing given by the state superintendent is that schools must "help prepare students for an increasingly competitive world" (Grasmick, 1998). Grasmick cited a survey of 1,000 Maryland companies indicating that job applicants need better skills for the more challenging workplace and to succeed in college. High stakes testing is being used to drive the system toward improvement because nothing seems more likely to get parents' and students' attention than being held back a grade or failing to obtain a high school diploma.

This kind of reasoning supposes that it is a lack of motivation or effort that keeps students from achieving. There are at least three other possibilities: insufficient opportunity to learn; a lack of instrumental competence that allows students to link educational experiences with foreseeable, tangible rewards, immediate or distant; or psychometric issues (i.e., Can science tests be constructed that accurately and fairly measure the accomplishments of all the students taking them?). Concomitantly, because high stakes tests are meshed in a web of societal rewards and punishments (e.g., jobs, salaries, opportunities for advanced education, and status), it is important to monitor how the system is responding in a reasonable and fair way, especially to students who have not succeeded in science in the past.

Madaus (1994) pointed out that although the potential benefits of new technologies such as high stakes testing are enormous, all technologies simultaneously create problems, open up new ways to make mistakes, alter institutions in unanticipated negative ways, and have a negative impact on certain populations. Although technology is not by nature socially unjust, it is inextricably intertwined with wealth, ethnicity/race, and gender relations. Madaus noted that most Americans do not ask if and how a proposed test might produce an undesirable set of consequences or about the values and biases made by the technical elite who create such tests: "The ways that individuals and groups are hurt by testing must become the central focus of evaluating the design and the implementation of every proposed . . . system of tests" (p. 81).

There is a need for more accountability in science education, especially for students who have not been served well in the past. An equitable assessment system should do the following:

1. Assess all students who are taking instruction in schools in order to understand the effectiveness of the teaching and learning environment.

2. Disaggregate data in informative ways not only including gender and ethnicity, but also by SES and for students with disabilities and English language learners.
3. Develop accommodations as needed and if test validity is a concern, disaggregate the data with the appropriate caveats.
4. Design curriculum-based assessments for high stakes tests closely aligned with students' school experiences. Cut scores should be determined by what has been actually demonstrated as possible for students to do across representative samples of the state's population.
5. Accompany high and middle stakes tests with a plan and funding for improvement, both for the individual student and for the school as a whole.
6. Involve teachers in the development, updating, and scoring of the assessments in order to link the system more closely to school improvement efforts within classrooms and to increase credibility.
7. Encourage people of color to enter the field of testing and evaluation and develop state-level committees for test oversight with the expertise and sensitivity to understand not only the technical aspects of testing, but also the wide-ranging social, political, ethical, legal, and economic issues (Madaus, 1994).

Finally, when determining accountability structures, the needs of business and industry and those of state politicians out to make a name for themselves by appearing to be tough-minded must be balanced by the needs of students in schools. "Science for all Americans" has been a terrific slogan. It was hard to argue with higher and better science standards for all or with the advent of systemic reform that promised a means to achieve them. However, now, a dose of reality is in order.

The higher the standards, the more students who are likely to be left behind. Some children will pass any test set before them, and a small percentage of children with very limited cognitive abilities will not be able to pass any test. Others will fail some of the tests, study more, and pass. Yet, there is likely to be a fourth group of students, those who will pass some tests in some disciplines, but not in others, given any reasonable period of time or accommodations. If a high school diploma is contingent on passing combinations of really substantial, rigorous tests in a number of subject areas, including science, some individuals simply will not be able to do this. We know this from the experiences of school systems abroad that have been administering high stakes tests for decades. In addition, experience within the United States tells us that these students will most likely be people of color and/or poor.

Will other avenues for further education and decent jobs be open to those who do not achieve the high stakes diploma? As in Europe, these students will need other ways of demonstrating various intellectual competencies, skills, and suitability for meaningful employment or continuing education. Madaus (1994) pointed out that for equity reasons, the number and level of European exams was greatly expanded to 30 or more subjects so that students who were not university-bound could leave high school with some credentials. In the United States, obtaining a high school diploma is mostly a binary decision—either one receives one or one does not. A different type of diploma system is needed. As the country relies more on high stakes testing and demands that students achieve more, more also should be demanded of parents, employers, and others who will have to understand complex patterns of student achievement and what they mean in context. Educators will continue to struggle with balance between high standards for all and the recognition of individual differences or multiple intelligences.

10

Families, Peers, and Community: How They Influence Student Learning and Resiliency

"Publius" insisted that it was not climate and heredity that were decisive for the formation of human societies, but the consciously willed elements of law, morality, and government. The peculiar virtue of human societies lay not with those aspects that have been circumscribed by nature. Instead, humanity's uniqueness—and certainly its capacity for political distinction—was owed to its capacity to transcend what is naturally given, to shape life according to the designs of higher human ends.
—Wolin (1998)

Important as family and friendship are to children, across the political spectrum, there is a growing consensus that both children and parents depend upon wider nets of social ties, on communities.
—Weissbourd (1998)

A group of 20 preservice teachers who just completed their student-teaching internships was posed with the following situation (which was bound to be poignantly realistic for at least some of them): Suppose that in the course of student teaching, you taught a unit of study that you developed yourself, working long and hard on it. It represented your best work and you thought that it would be effective, engaging, and intelligent. You expected your students to enjoy the material and to learn a great deal because you were introducing them to wonderful new ideas and useful skills. Unfortunately, when you calculated student grades for the unit following the final assessment, you found that most of the students not only received low scores, but also clearly failed to grasp the material. Whom would you blame for the many failures?

To their credit, many of the student teachers said that they would place the responsibility for the students' poor performance on themselves as novice teachers and that they would have to analyze the problems and reteach the material. Yet, they admitted that if a somewhat smaller, but still substantial proportion of students failed to learn, they would be likely to attribute the failures to problems within the students themselves—a lack of motivation or background knowledge and skills—rather than poor instruction. They also might lay responsibility at the feet of parents who had not supplied the children with sufficient support, structure, or incentives. The student teachers reasoned that if the majority of their students learned from the unit of study, then all students should and it was not the teacher's fault if some did not take the opportunity to learn. Now, if these failures were evenly distributed among ethnic or socioeconomic groups, then this would not be so much an equity issue as a generic instructional problem. Yet, we know from chapters 2 and 3 that this is not often the case, and lower achievement tends to follow lines associated with ethnicity, SES, or other groupings.

School administrators, who are under increasing pressure to deliver high test scores due to the standards movement and high stakes testing, often ascribe achievement problems plaguing their schools to changing demographics. This is code, meaning that they have more students of color or English language learners than in the past or that they recognize what most of the large-scale studies show—the strong relation between SES and achievement.

With shifting student populations, educators realize that old assumptions and teaching methods may no longer apply and struggle to find ways to reach individual children who respond differently to the demands of school than the children with whom they worked in the past. For instance, sometimes, when an educator calls home to alert parents to a problem, the reaction may be unexpected—no one is at home and the phone call is not returned because the parents do not speak English, the respondent is a sibling scarcely older than the struggling student, or the teacher's concerns are met with indifference, perplexed defeat, or even hostility. It is not surprising that some educators locate the educational problems outside of the school and attribute school failure to the student and family. Yet, these deficiency models are too simplistic and potentially defeating for educators and students alike. This chapter explores the complex interplay between factors that can lead to school success or failure, which include the psychological variables within the child and their development vis-à-vis the family, community, and peer group. It begins to explain how these factors intersect with the school program and how to create a learning environment in which school science achievement is valued, supported, and placed within the grasp of the individual students. Yet, there are no simple answers to questions of school achievement and group differences.

ATTRIBUTION THEORY: A MODEL THAT EXPLAINS GENDER DIFFERENCES IN GENERAL

There is one area of inquiry into achievement patterns among groups that stands out in both the amount and quality of research that has gone into understanding the issues involved. Researchers who study gender differences in achievement in science and mathematics have developed an impressive literature on the relation between the individual student and school science attainment as it is affected by the family, community and society, and peer groups. Because, since the 1970s, girls have steadily narrowed the gender gap in achievement and women have increasingly become more equitably represented in science and mathematics careers, this research has a great deal of explanatory power. It can also contribute to an understanding of other group differences in science achievement that stem from ethnicity, SES, or even the presence of a disability.

Eccles (1995) and her colleagues at the University of Michigan developed and tested a model to explain how social forces act on young women's decisions to study science and mathematics. This model includes the psychological and social factors that influence long- and short-range achievement goals and behaviors such as career aspirations, course selections, persistence on difficult tasks, and how hard a student works on achievement-related activities. Drawing on the theoretical and empirical work associated with decision making, achievement theory, and attribution theory (see Atkinson, 1964; Crandall, 1969; Weiner, 1974), Eccles and her colleagues created a model for achievement-related choices. This model, depicted in Fig. 10.1, links choices to two sets of beliefs: the individual's expectations of success and the importance, or subjective task value, that the individual attaches to the various options perceived to be available, leading to achievement related choices. Although many Americans believe that an individual's choices are entirely his or her own and that society should not be held responsible for poor decisions, Eccles' model assumes that the individual's beliefs are formed by cultural norms, experiences, and attitudes (following Fig. 10.1 from left to right). The psychological processes underlying individual choice are constructed from years of experiences at home, in one's community, and at school.

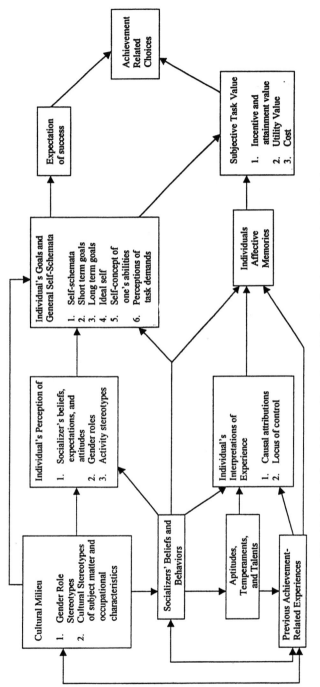

FIG. 10.1. Eccles' model. *Note.* From *Issues Related to Gender Equity*, by J. S. Eccles, 1995.

For example, consider a student's decision to enroll in advanced science and mathematics courses. Eccles' (1995) model predicts that students are most likely to enroll in science courses if they think they will do well in them and value the courses highly. Expectations for success depend on the confidence the student has in his or her intellectual abilities and on the student's estimations of the difficulty of the course (see box labeled *Individual's goals . . .* in Fig. 10.1). These beliefs have been shaped by past experiences with the subject matter, by the student's interpretation of those experiences (e.g., does the student think that past successes are a consequence of high ability or hard work?), and by the interpretation of these experiences provided by all the significant actors (i.e., family, peers, teachers) in the student's life (see bottom portion of Fig. 10.1, working from left to right). The value that person attaches to a science or mathematics course is influenced by responses to questions such as: Do I like doing the subject? Is the course required? Is the course instrumental in meeting my long or short range goals? Have my parents or counselors insisted that the course be taken or, conversely, have other people tried to discourage me from taking the course? Am I afraid of the material to be covered in the course?

These questions and the student's responses to them are useful in understanding both gender or group differences in participation in mathematics, physical science, computer science, and technology courses. Eccles' (1995) model, derived from several longitudinal studies, predicts that females will be less likely to participate in math and science if:

1. They express less confidence than males in their abilities to master mathematics and science and to succeed in careers requiring these skills than in other subject areas and careers.
2. They value success and participation in these fields less than they value success and participation in other fields.
3. They enjoy math and science less than they enjoy other subjects.
4. They experience an unsupportive environment in connection with math and science, either in school or at home.

Expectations for Success/Confidence in One's Ability

Expectations for success is the first important component of Eccles' model. It leads to confidence in one's abilities to succeed, influencing educational and vocational choices (e.g., Atkinson, 1964; Bandura, 1977; Weiner, 1974). The more confident a person is in his or her abilities related to a certain area, the more likely he or she is to chose it as a career. From about the ages of 10 to 12 years, females report lower expectations for their performance and less confidence in their ability in mathematics and physical science than boys. Yet, at the same time, they also express increasing confidence in their abilities in other areas such as language arts and social studies. Consequently, they are more likely to choose conditions that bolster their confidence and avoid situations that they perceive as being risky and unrewarding, resulting in a movement away from science and mathematics.

Values as Mediators of Achievement-Related Choices

Subjective task value is the second major component of Eccles' expectancy/value model of achievement-related choices. *Value* is defined in terms of the importance one attaches to being good at the subject area, the fit between the characteristics associated with the activity and the individual's personal values and self-concept, and the intrinsic enjoyment one gets out of doing the subject. The model predicts that decisions regarding course enrollments, college majors, and occupational choices are influenced by the value individuals attach to the various achievement-related options (e.g., careers) that they believe are available to them.

In a longitudinal study of the math course enrollment decisions of high aptitude, college-bound students, Eccles and her colleagues found that gender differences in students' decisions to enroll in advanced mathematics were determined primarily by gender differences in the value students' attached to mathematics (Eccles, Adler, & Meece, 1984). Girls were less likely than were boys to enroll in advanced mathematics, primarily because they felt that mathematics was less important, less useful for their longer term goals, and less enjoyable than did boys.

How Gender Roles Influence Values

Personal values that are acquired through gender-stereotyped socialization (via parents, peers, educators, and the media) can affect educational and vocational choices in several ways. Studies documented that females and males value different personal characteristics and behaviors. For example, females seem to be more interested than males in social relationships and people-related issues, whereas males tend to be more interested in things and abstract manipulation of information (see Eccles, 1992; Eccles & Harold, 1990). Females are also more concerned with how to integrate intensive family responsibilities with work demands. Occupations consistent with these goals and values have greater appeal to women than do occupations that conflict with the fulfillment of these goals and values or that are perceived as such. Because both boys and girls stereotype mathematicians and scientists as loners who have little time for their families or friends (Boswell, 1979), such professions hold little appeal to someone who rates social values high and wants to devote time and energy to family as well as work. Yet, real scientists have little in common with the prevalent stereotype, and science is an endeavor carried out by human beings, not depersonalized robots. If science were viewed and experienced by students as an activity in which teams of people work closely together on interesting problems, or if its definition was expanded in the minds of students to include the social sciences, its appeal might be broadened (Cleminson, 1990).

Gender Differences and Parents' Influence

Because some parents socialize their sons in a different way than their daughters, parents can create unfortunate gender differences resulting in disadvantages in science for their daughters. Parents may subtly or overtly influence their daughters' skill levels (in mechanics, mathematics, and computers), interest patterns, and self-perceptions. In a longitudinal study, Eccles (1992) has showed that parents of elementary school students have gender-role biased perceptions of their children's competencies. Parents tended to believe that boys are both better and more interested than girls in sports and mathematics, whereas girls are better and more interested in language arts and instrumental music. These parental perceptions exist despite very little actual gender differences in the children's aptitudes and interests (Eccles, 1992) and may set in motion events that ultimately create the very differences that the parents originally believed to be present. If parents think that boys are naturally better at math than girls, they may have lower estimates of their daughters' math ability than is warranted by the girls' actual level of competence. These perceptions affect the kinds of experiences parents provide for their children, giving boys more opportunities to do math-related activities than girls.

Parents' gender-role stereotypes, in interaction with their child's sex, contribute to their causal attributions for and emotional reaction to their child's performance; the importance they attach to their child acquiring various skills; the advice they give regarding school subjects; and their choice of activities and toys for their child. In turn, these subtle or explicit parental responses influence their children's confidence in their abilities, interests in mastering various skills, and, affective reactions to participating in various activities. These factors influence the amount of time and type of effort children devote to mastering skills related to science and mathematics. This model (Fig. 10.1) of the effects of gender-typed social influences on the psychological development of girls and its subsequent effects on science and mathematics participation is compelling because it is consistent with much of the research base, but also rings true for many adult women who retrospectively examine similar choices that they have made.

OTHER MODELS, OTHER INTERPRETATIONS

It is legitimate to ask if this broad and encompassing model that accounts for the course-taking pattern and choices made by large samples of subjects, the majority of whom were middle class and White, can explain achievement patterns among other ethnic and socioeconomic groups. Donna Ford Harris, a professor currently at the University of Virginia, responded to this explanation for gender differences in science achievement with the following comments:

> While it is common knowledge that this is a male-dominated society, it is not dominated by minority males. Males of color face racism, lower teacher expectations, greater under-representation in the sciences and related fields, greater under-representations in gifted programs, greater under-achievement and greater drop-out rates, over-representation in special education . . . , and different cultural and socialization patterns than White and/or middle class males. Minority males are also more likely to be of low socioeconomic status. These are all issues related to gender equity. . . . Minority females share equity issues with White females, but they have additional burdens to overcome in the sciences (and school at large)—racism, sexism, lower teacher expectations, different socialization and cultural practices . . . (personal communication, July, 1994)

Ford-Harris' comments are important for a number of reasons, not the least of which is the reminder that assumptions about the role of gender in relation to achievement in science must be tempered with the knowledge that both ethnicity and SES can affect trends in gender differences. Moreover, results from large samples of students may mask important variations among subgroups. For instance, a huge longitudinal study showed that parents of children of color are more likely to expect their daughters rather than their sons to attend college (Peng, 1995). In chapter 3 of this volume, we discussed some interesting and perhaps unexpected trends in gender and achievement in science among the various ethnic and socioeconomic groups in Hawaii. Although Eccles' model is sufficiently comprehensive to account for results like these, the gender difference data in her research point in a different direction.

Also implicit in Ford-Harris' remarks is a sentiment raised by other scholars who happen to be persons of color: There is a visceral distrust of a model based on choice, given experiences with racial segregation (historical and current through de facto measures), prejudice, and the constriction of choices for students of color who attend dysfunctional schools. The indisputable historical evidence that some groups have systematically been denied opportunities to learn, as well as current practices such as tracking and inequitable funding of schools, leads some to question a model based on achievement-related choice. Although Eccles' model could be extended to students who attend high-poverty schools, the gross lack of resources and support can circumscribe choice so severely that the fine points raised at many stages of the model seem rather academic. Although Eccles' model is a convincing explanation for the experiences of the primarily White middle-class families and their children, there may be other models that help to explain achievement patterns and the concomitant barriers for people of color, students from low-income families, students with disabilities, and English language learners.

The Family's Role in Achievement by Ethnicity and SES

We know that parents' education level is strongly associated with student achievement in science and mathematics and that the dropout rate for students who speak a language other than English at home is much higher than for those without difficulties with English, 44% versus 12%, respectively (The Findings From the Condition of Education, 1997). Parental income and educational levels affect the amounts and kind of learning opportunities provided for their children, who, for instance, less frequently attend outside-of-school classes, museums, zoos, art galleries, concerts, or libraries under their parents direction. Children who live in low-income neighborhoods find fewer mentors or role models related to science and math careers or have fewer learning materials within the home. Breaking this down by ethnicity, regression analysis and between-group comparisons suggest that Black American, Hispanic, and American Indian children have fewer learning opportunities through the home than do Whites or Asian Americans (Peng, 1995). Of course, in the direst of circumstances, a family structure may be too fractured to supply even the necessities of life, never mind a trip to the local aquarium. Yet, the study also suggests that if parents' educational expectations are high and there is good communication among parent, child, and school, what the family does is more important than what the family has. In the United States, neither social class nor ethnicity is destiny.

Although teachers in high-poverty schools are more likely than their counterparts in more affluent areas to report a lack of parental involvement, such schools may also be making less of an effort to contact parents regarding the child's academic performance, school program, or posthigh-school plans (The Findings From the Condition of Education, 1997). Contrary to the opinions held by some, because low SES parents cannot provide the support for learning that one expects from middle-class parents, this does not mean that they do not care about their children's performance in school.

In a study designed to examine how high school students from different ethnic and income groups manage the different expectations made of them by parents, peers, and the school (Phelan, Yu, & Davidson, 1994), researchers found that 78% of the students they interviewed said that their parents pressured them to do well in school, regardless of whether the student was highly successful or struggling. However, there was a clear difference in the type of support parents were able to provide and this seemed related to school success. Parents of high-achieving students were able to help their children negotiate the demands of school (dealing with teachers, helping with homework, and assisting their children in making academic decisions), whereas parents of children who had difficulties in school or were at risk of failure were unable to help or were unsure about what to do.

Language and culture also affect communication among parents, school, and students. For example, I was a member of the PTA group for our local elementary school, which has a ethnically, linguistically, and socioeconomically diverse population. This diversity was not reflected in the PTA membership, which was mostly White and middle class. Many of the PTA activists seemed to subscribe to the belief that the missing parents did not care. To counter this perception and provide a more welcoming atmosphere for parents newly immigrated to the United States, we launched a special PTA meeting for the parents of students in the ESL program, about one quarter of the student body. We found interpreters for three main language groups represented, arranged for buses to pick up parents without cars, hired two babysitters to assist parents who needed to bring their young children with them, and arranged for food and a movie for the children. The turnout was phenomenal and took on a festival-like atmosphere. About 45 parents attended and even more young children (the babysitters were nearly overwhelmed, but older siblings pitched in to help). Although it was not clear how much parents learned from this one event, they expressed a great deal of enthusiastic approval, and it was now indisputably obvious to the PTA and the school administration that these parents cared a great deal, but that other factors interfered with their involvement with school.

A qualitative study of the parental involvement within three Latino families (i.e., Nicaraguan, Colombian, and Cuban) and their children's school program (especially in science) revealed that language, transportation problems, long work hours, and a different set of expectations of the role of parents were the main barriers to school–family communications (Casal, 1998). Because the three students in this study were all doing well in school, the Latino parents depended on the school to reach out to them. Yet, they often felt that they were rebuffed by English-speaking parents in PTA groups. Casal admonished the assumption that parental involvement programs constructed for a stable middle-class community will be effective for all ethnic minority groups. As a science teacher, she learned that her parent communications and the many home projects that she assigned her students helped to establish active links between the home and the classroom: "Parents can feel empowered if they are valued and involved in the educational process . . . by including them as effective mentors of science at home . . ." (p. 27). This is consistent with Ladson-Billings (1995) view of culturally consistent pedagogy. In her study, one of the important characteristics of the effective teachers of African American students was the teachers' ability to convey their respect to the students' parents.

There is an expectation in U.S. education that good parents are advocates for their children. In other countries and cultures, however, parents believe that the teachers' judgments are to be respected without question, that the school knows best, and that the good parents' role is to support the school. This notion of parental advocacy (lobbying on your child's behalf) is contrary to these beliefs. Consequently, American educators have an additional professional obligation to look out for the needs of children new to the country or whose parents are uninvolved in school because these parents may not understand this advocacy role or may not be able to provide it for any number of reasons.

Although parents of immigrant children may have difficulty communicating with the school, they may be very effective in supporting their children's academic progress at home. In 1992, *Scientific American* published a study of children who are successful in science and mathematics, poverty and language differences notwithstanding. This study focused on the children of boat people, refugees from Indochina who arrived in the

United States in the early 1980s. These children have done well in American schools in a relatively short period of time, despite their status as recent immigrants to the United States, whose first language is not English (Caplan, Choy, & Whitmore, 1992). They also suffered the trauma of the war and dislocation and had their formal schooling interrupted for months and years. About 4 years after having arrived in the United States, the 536 children from 200 nuclear families were scoring slightly better than the national average on standardized achievement tests. The majority was earning As and Bs in school mathematics and science, but was doing less well in English and the humanities. This was despite the fact that most attended schools in low-income metropolitan areas, schools notorious for their problems. How did these children achieve such success in a relatively short time?

The study showed the family structure to be the pivotal factor in these children's school achievement. Contrary to the general trend often observed in social science research, for the boat people, the larger the family the higher the children's grades. The Indochinese students spent long hours every evening doing homework with their families. The older siblings often helped the younger, facilitated by parents who did the chores so that their children could study without interruption. The children learned not only content, but also how to study, internalizing values from their culture that support success in education settings—love of learning, intrinsic motivation, persistence in problem solving, the importance of effort as opposed to perceived ability, and the setting of realistic goals.

The finding that it was the family that supplied both the means and incentives for its children to succeed is somewhat contrary to common American notions of efficacy, which hold that the individual is responsible for his or her success. For the boat people, their sense of control over their lives was traced to familial identity and efficacy. Caplan et al. (1992) concluded that "Although different in origins, both traditional Indochinese and middle class American values emphasize education, achievement, hard work, autonomy, perseverance and pride . . . (but the American mores) encourage independence and individual achievement, whereas Indochinese values foster interdependence and family-based orientation" (p. 41).

This interesting study shows that group (family) efforts rather than individual ones can spur high achievement, even in the urban school environment. If these Indochinese children could get up to speed in U.S. schools despite poverty, school delays, and their non-English-speaking immigrant status, then certainly effective interventions can be found for other groups, such as the children of poor Black Americans, Hispanics, or Native Americans. However, the boat people seem to be an unusual group—immigrants who had extricated themselves from a dire situation. Family connections were strengthened through the years of delays and refugee camps. Because education was restricted in Indochina, the future of the children and their families in the United States was seen as inextricably linked to school success, which was connected to both social acceptance and economic progress. This is why the parents were so completely committed to the education of their children.

On the other hand, one wonders if the result would be very different if any ethnic group with a similar profile—intact nuclear families with many siblings that had fled from a life-threatening environment to a new situation that promises better economic rewards and freedom—was selected for study. This study could be interpreted simply as meaning that children can get a decent education in American schools if their parents try hard enough to provide support for the children. Yet, this interpretation lets schools and the social support systems off the hook. Other explanations are also possible. These families were, in a sense, a select group who had bonded under the most trying physical and psychological conditions and survived intact, while instilling a message that the children were responsible for the families' future. The parents required that the siblings join in family study groups instead of joining typical peer groups and their activities, avoiding negative influences of American society. The political realities of the families' lives were crucial to the attitudes developed by the children. The exceptional conditions do not make the children's achievements any less impressive or the efforts of the parents to provide safe and productive learning environments for their children any less admirable. However, although these circumstances are probably nearly impossible to replicate, the lessons learned—focus at home on education; peer, sibling, and parental support of study; and group effort attributed to achievement rather than individual effort or innate ability—provide some interesting openings for interventions either within the home or at afterschool homework centers. The peer group's attitudes toward school is a significant predictor of achievement and all the student study skills and attitudes that go along with it (Wang, Haertel, & Walberg, 1995).

Voluntary and Involuntary Minorities: John Ogbu's Theory

John Ogbu, an anthropologist originally from West Africa, developed a theory for interpreting the differing achievement patterns of various immigrant groups entering the United States versus those others who had a longer and more difficult history in an American society. Ogbu's work, which included observations within U.S. schools and international data comparing the school achievement of immigrant groups, provides a powerful and provocative framework for understanding the achievement gaps between various ethnic groups (Ogbu, 1992).

Ogbu made the distinction between two groups: voluntary and involuntary minorities. *Voluntary minorities* are people who immigrate to a new country voluntarily because they desire a better life, more economic opportunities, and/or more political freedom. Their positive expectations influence how they perceive and respond to schooling. Over time, they do well in school, despite initial difficulties with language and cultural differences. They would not, for instance, perceive learning the attitudes and behaviors necessary for science achievement as a threat to their own cultural identity. This is because their cultural identity remains strong through activities involving home life, peer groups, and many ties to their own ethnic community (e.g., churches, social events, language classes, or business ties). The academic success of the children of the boat people in American schools (previously recounted) is a good example of voluntary minorities and their accomplishments, but others abound.

In contrast, involuntary minorities are people brought to a country against their wills as slaves or as forced labor (e.g., African Americans), or who were involuntarily colonized (e.g., American Indians and early Mexican Americans). As such, they have been historically denied true assimilation and usually experience greater difficulties in school. This is because, over time, they develop what Ogbu called *secondary cultural characteristics*, traits developed in opposition to the mainstream culture. These secondary cultural characteristics (developed after immigration) serve as both boundary-maintaining mechanisms (for solidarity within the group in response to an unwelcoming or even hostile dominant culture) and as coping strategies. For African Americans vis-à-vis the White dominant culture of schools, these secondary cultural characteristics may include differences in linguistic, cognitive, learning, and communication styles. Ogbu (1992) said, "Among involuntary minorities, school learning tends to be equated with the learning of the culture and language of White Americans, that is . . . the frames of reference of the 'enemy' or 'oppressors' . . . Thus, involuntary minorities may . . . interpret school learning as a process . . . detrimental to their social identity, sense of security, and self-worth" (p. 10). This may be summarized as acting White, which can result in perceived (or real) conflicts between the community and the peer group on one hand, and the culture of school achievement on the other (Fordham & Ogbu, 1986). For example, consider the following statements made by students who are involuntary minorities by Ogbu's definition: " 'I wouldn't let them put me in a higher track because I wanted to be with my friends.' 'Being Mexican means being popular, cutting classes, acting crazy' " (from Phelan et al., 1994, p. 420).

Ogbu (1988) did not shy away from recognizing that such student attitudes and behaviors work against achievement:

> Black youths do not consciously reject school meanings and knowledge. In fact, they say emphatically that schooling is important to them and they want to get an education in order to escape from poverty and other problems in their ghetto community. But although they verbalize a strong desire for education, black youths tend to behave in ways that will not necessarily lead to school success. For example, they tend to be excessively tardy, lack serious attitude toward their schoolwork, and do not persevere in doing their schoolwork. . . . Consequently, many do not do well enough in school to obtain the credentials they need for employment in mainstream economy. (p. 170)

In this view, students' lack of attentiveness in science and mathematics classes and other behaviors perceived as negative by teachers can be interpreted as byproducts of these important psychological–social conflicts of students of color. Ogbu listed coping strategies that he believed to be effective for involuntary minorities striving for school success (i.e., private schools, involvement in church activities, intervention programs, and mentors), but ultimately suggested that voluntary minorities must come to understand and use the pattern of "accommodation without assimilation." This is the alternation model common among voluntary minorities, who learn that it is possible to participate in two languages and two cultural frames of reference without undermining their loyalty to their minority community.

Ogbu also suggested a shared response to this situation. Certainly, the schools and dominant culture have a responsibility to wipe out the barriers that make the American Dream less obtainable for some groups than others due to racism and policies and practices that stack the deck against the less powerful. Yet, he also suggested that the effort needs to be conjoined by forces within the minority community, which must teach children to recognize and accept responsibility for school adjustment and academic performance. This means that in order for science educators (especially those who are members of the dominant culture, statistically the majority of science teachers) to be successful, they need to create welcoming and accessible science classrooms. They must help students cross the boundaries from the world of their homes, peer groups, and communities (friendly to the student but sometimes suspicious of science) to the world of school, and, for some, to science-related careers. Certainly, if science teachers ever needed a rationale for consciously providing their students with role models who "look like them," or for family science programs or approaches that link the community to the school science programs, Ogbu's theory provides it.

What About the Student's Role in Science Achievement? Discipline and Behavior

This chapter explored research that attempts to account for the differential performance of students in science, including factors such as parental expectations and support, attitudes of teachers, peer groups, culture, and societal legacies, all of which, alone or in combination, can impede a student's academic progress in science. Yet, what of the individual student himself or herself? Doesn't each person bear responsibility for learning? What of free will? Is it not the individual's choice to misbehave, cut classes, neglect study? The goal of a large-scale, longitudinal study using High School and Beyond data commissioned by the U.S. Department of Education (Peng, 1995) was to ask if some groups have generally less positive attitudes toward science and mathematics and if attitudes and behaviors are at the heart of the achievement gap. A summary of the literature showed that Black and Hispanic students have positive attitudes toward science and mathematics and that there are no differences among the various ethnic groups (with the exception of Asian Americans, who have somewhat more positive attitudes than all other groups). Black and Hispanic students more frequently report that they look forward to these classes than do White students. A majority of all students in all ethnic groups expect to have some higher education beyond high school, but there is a decrease in expectations for college graduation from 8th to 10th grade for all groups. Similarly, for all groups, attitudes toward science and mathematics steadily decline from 4th to 12th grade. This may be due to the complexity of the subject matter, the quality of instruction, school facilities and the curriculum, and to the cumulative school experiences of students in both mathematics and science (Peng, 1995).

Peng's (1995) study shows that teachers perceive Hispanic and Black students as being more disinterested in their work and less attentive and more disruptive than other groups, despite expressed enthusiasm for math and science:

> Overall, the findings show that career aspirations and enjoyment of science and mathematics did not differ by racial-ethnic groups. However, there are group differences in classroom behavior and the number of advanced sci-

ence and mathematics courses taken. While many Hispanic, black, and American Indian students like science and mathematics and aspire at a young age to science and mathematics careers, they are reported by teachers to be less likely to exhibit the kind of classroom behavior that is conducive to learning. In addition, they are not enrolled in the type of courses that will prepare them for postsecondary science and mathematics studies. (p. 30)

Rather, students of color are likely to find themselves in low-track, noncollege preparatory classes, so that regardless of their attitude, motivation, or ability, they are shut out of the opportunity to pursue higher level science and mathematics in college and placed in classes where the pervasive atmosphere is frequently one of disinterest and nonachievement (discussed in chap. 7). Because of these factors, they leave school unprepared to enter undergraduate science and mathematics or they become disinterested in these fields as they eventually fall behind (Peng, 1995).

Social Class and Cultural Capital

Although it is clear that students' gender and ethnicity affect attitudes and opportunities in science education and achievement differences cannot be explained by social class alone, class differences play a part in school achievement. As one visits schools that are characterized by differences in the income levels of the children's families regardless of the students' ethnicity, one can observe three different trends in students' approach to science learning as one moves from schools with students from high-income levels to those with low-income levels. The following generalizations are gross, and certainly, there are many exceptions. The first difference is the students' background knowledge and experiences related to school science, which we discussed in this chapter and in chapter 4. Consider the 6-year-old child on a family outing whose exasperated father gripes, "Jason, if you didn't constantly accelerate and decelerate, but kept a steady pace, you wouldn't want to sit down and rest so often." Although the parental sentiment expressed here is probably universal, the way the father has chosen to communicate it bespeaks a person who has some passing formal knowledge of physics. The cumulative effect of hundreds of comments like this, made each day over the course of 10 or 15 years, is that Jason may find himself in science classes for the gifted and talented in secondary school. The propensity for middle-class parents to impart verbal information that will be useful in school, as they perform mundane parenting tasks, has been well-established.

The second difference has to do with off-task behavior, disruptive to teaching. Teachers in high-poverty schools report that student misbehavior, absenteeism and tardiness, verbal abuse and disrespect of teachers, and physical conflicts and weapons possession are serious problems (The Findings From the Condition of Education, 1997). The differences in behavior seem to be more of quantity than of quality. In low-income schools, there is more behavior designed to delay, disrupt, or derail a lesson. Effective teachers must take more care to bring the class into the context of the lesson, and sometimes need to cajole students into participation. Individual students must be personally invited (or told) to go to work by the teacher. In contrast, at affluent schools, students seem to approach the work more or less automatically, whether the lesson is well-crafted and interesting, or banal. It is not so much that they are docile as they do not seem to question the connection between schoolwork and the rewards they believe it will bring them, just as schooling has brought rewards to their parents, neighbors, and older siblings.

This is the third difference, one that has a substantial effect on the students' behavior and attitudes in school. The ability to connect a serious productive school behavior with personal goals is probably more a function of the educational background of the student's parents than parental income, but it still comes down to class differences. The child who regularly sees adults engaged in activities such as reading, writing, or working at a computer as an intrinsic part of their well-paying jobs is undoubtedly more clear about school expectations and rewards than are children who do not often see such examples. Middle-class children are more likely to have role models for study and scholarship that are congruent with the kinds of activities that schools ask of them and see the possible benefits, both economic and personal.

Ogbu (1988) addressed this issue in the context of the economics and politics of the opportunity structure in the United States over the last 30 years. Through government policies and encouragement of the private sector, college-educated or middle-class Black Americans have benefited by having the glass ceiling raised (although certainly not by any means eliminated). This has the effect of establishing the linkage between making it in school and in the job market, between school credentials and postschool rewards.

A recent study by Jencks and Phillips (reported in Dionne, 1998) showed that the earnings of Black men, who scored above the 50th percentile on national tests, were 96% of that of the White average, nearly equal. Earnings have greatly increased from 1964, when Jencks collected data showing that the earning power of Blacks was only 66% of that of Whites. This earlier study caused Jencks to conclude that education did not make much difference in the earning power of Blacks, and that the only way to provide an equal opportunity was to redistribute wealth. The new data establish the link between schooling and rewards for the middle class, but the problem remains for lower classes. Ogbu (1988) pointed out that, "For the working-class, lower-class, and under-class blacks, there has been no comparable official policies to increase their employment opportunities ... and most of them continue their traditional marginal participation (in the job market) in which the linkage between schooling, work, and earnings is relatively weak" (p. 168).

With variation in SES comes variations in *cultural capital,* a term coined by Boudieu (as cited in Daugherty, 1996), which refers to a complex of skills and attitudes including verbal facility, general cultural awareness, and knowledge about how the school system and society work. Daugherty (1996) pointed out that, ". . . Students who are endowed with cultural capital are more likely to know—when faced with a variety of curricular choices—which one are the best avenues to success. They have a better understanding of which courses, tracks, and schools help them get accepted to college and are less likely to go 'off-track' " (p. 49). A study by Hoffer et al. (1995), based on NELS-88 data (a 5-year longitudinal study with a large national database), showed that course-taking patterns in science and math are largely a function of SES. SES is the strongest correlate of persistence within these curricula—the higher a student's SES, the more science and mathematics courses taken, and the higher the achievement. Students with more cultural capital are more likely to understand the importance of these courses to long-term goals. In the context of science education reform, increasing the number of science and mathematics courses required for high school graduation should help equalize cultural capital (provided such requirements do not wash students out of school altogether).

Negative Mutual Accommodation: Building Potemkin Schools

Working class or poor children who find themselves in schools that are socioeconomically diverse can learn how to play the school success game from peers and others in the community (build cultural capital), especially if the school requires students to engage in the kind of learning that requires reasoning, writing, and discourse about ideas. Yet, if children of modest means go to schools that are predominantly low SES, unless the school has worked hard to create a learning community that provides for the development of academic values and scholarly accomplishments, then something else, something insidious, can occur. Educators and students begin a process of what might be called *negative mutual accommodation.* This occurs when some children behave in ways that signal teachers that they do not want to learn. They do not do their assigned homework, for instance, and eventually, the teacher accommodates them by assigning less homework because it is difficult to teach a class where some students have done the preparation and others have not. Less homework results in a slower learning pace. Reading normally assigned for home is done in class, the instruction becomes more passive. As the instruction bogs down, the more enthusiastic and willing students become bored and are soon drawn into the syndrome of reduced expectations for learning. Teachers, under pressure to give decent grades despite declining classroom standards, accommodate again by providing high grades. Because report card grades are good, parents are lulled into thinking that their children are learning—until the standardized test scores come in, or high school graduates return from their colleges in distress, having reaped the rewards of having attended a "Potemkin High School."

The irony is that the affective atmosphere in such schools can be quite positive—we all read the articles about schools where students have high self-esteem and low achievement. Human beings respond positively to one another, negotiating behaviors to reduce stress. Teachers do not set out to intentionally provide students with an inferior education, nor would students say that they want one. Yet, over time, this is what evolves. Within such an environment, it is very difficult for an individual teacher to maintain high goals. Shutting the door of the classroom and ignoring what goes on in the rest of the school is eventually self-defeating. That is why the current movement for school-based reform focused on academics and involving the parents and community in pursuit of these goals makes so much sense.

Although the student behaviors and teacher responses previously described can occur anywhere, regardless of the SES level of the community, if this type of negative mutual accommodation begins to occur in affluent schools, there is soon a great hue and cry raised by the parents, some students, and some teachers. Standards are upheld or affluent parents choose private schools for their children.

An exception to this trend, however, can be seen in some special education classrooms, in which accommodations are supposed to occur, regardless of the SES of the students. Unfortunately, sometimes the results are misguided and students who need more help in learning actually have less opportunity to learn because of reduced class requirements (see chap. 7). For example, I once met a college professor whose adult son had mild Down's Syndrome. Although he was proud that his son had successfully made the transition to a job and independent living, he was also dismayed to report that the only activity in which the young man was involved in high school that remotely matched the demands of the outside world was his job as manager of the high school football team. There, he simply could not mess up and he did not. Yet, in his classes, all failure was excused, even for those activities well within his ability. Of course, the accommodation line is an incredibly difficult one for educators to walk. Determining what is reasonable to ask of each student who has been identified as having disabilities, in all academic areas, is probably impossible. If a teacher adheres bull-headedly to one standard for all, irrespective of disability, then students may find learning impossible and failure imminent. Yet, accommodations that require too little of students can also lead to eventual failure. The inclusion movement holds some promise for higher standards for students with disabilities because students in heterogeneous classrooms generally try to work to the level of their peers. Moreover, teams of special education and general education science teachers working together may be better equipped to determine what constitutes reasonable accommodations rather than either working alone.

RESILIENT CHILDREN: RESILIENT SCHOOLS

This chapter explored several of the theories that provide complex explanations of the achievement gaps in science. Science teachers could respond to these ideas, quite rightly, by observing that their jobs are to teach science well and that they cannot solve all of the social problems that have been plaguing America for centuries. However, it seems that educators may have to grapple with the problems of the world outside the science classroom in order to reach those within it. Effective educators seeking explanations for their students' learning patterns ineluctably seek to understand the barriers (e.g., physical, psychological, sociological and political, alone or in combination) that stand in the way of science attainment, especially for those in underrepresented groups.

The theories presented here rest, at least to some extent, on the choices made by the individual student, which are influenced by environmental factors. Some students seem to make more of educational opportunities than do others, no matter how dire their personal circumstances or demoralizing the educational environment. Resilient students are those who have made it academically, despite odds not in their favor. They are the exceptions to the rule. They have a heightened likelihood of success despite environmental adversities brought on by early conditions and experiences.

A brief synthesis of the literature summarizing the research comparing resilient, high-achieving students with nonresilient comparison groups shows that the resilient groups tended to have higher self-concepts and educational aspirations and felt more internally controlled. They had stronger interpersonal skills and were more responsive to others. They were autonomous and good problem solvers and set realistic personal goals. They planned and changed their environment to alter their lives in successful ways (Freiberg, 1993; Wang et al., 1995). In a study of 180 resilient and 180 nonresilient low-SES students attending five urban middle schools, Huang and Waxman (1996) found that resilient students had fewer absences, spent more time per day on homework, did additional unassigned reading, and watched television less during the week than did the nonresilient group. In the context of their mathematics classrooms, the resilient students differed from the nonresilient group in that they reported higher motivation to achieve and more involvement in their mathematics classes and felt more affiliation with peers and teachers. They participated more often, did their homework, and were attentive. The researchers examined the results by ethnic group and found that Asian American students seemed more motivated than the other two groups, with a greater intrinsic desire to succeed and earn good grades. They expected to do well and saw mathematics as more satisfying than did the Hispanic students, who in this study, reported lower parent involvement and academic self-concept. There were no differences (by ethnicity) in students' sense of affiliation with the mathematics, other students, and the teacher. Resilient students' propensity to see themselves as belonging in mathematics and as being attached to their classmates may lie at the heart of the achievement issue. When students feel disengaged and alienated, they are at risk for failure and dropping out of school. Despite coming from the same schools and classrooms, some students perceive themselves as belonging whereas others do not, and an array of personal responses, such as inattentiveness, low participation rates, and absences, only exacerbate the sense that mathematics is not for them. (This is a reason why caring science teachers seem to be so important to students in underrepresented groups—they seem to broker students' interactions with material that may seem strange, unfamiliar, or even threatening.)

Although this notion of resiliency is most often applied to individuals, it may also be applied to groups. Indeed, a goal of educators working with urban youth may be to establish zones of resilience, including families, students, peers, and communities, that can provide youngsters with protective factors as well as interventions as necessary (Freiberg, 1993).

Aspects of these zones of resilience crucial to school success include: administrative direction that fosters an orderly and safe school environment where academics are highly valued, the quality of the curriculum and instruction, peer networks that back achievement, supportive families, and bringing the community itself into the schooling process (Wang et al., 1995). The latter is often promoted by a school leader who wants to break the isolation of the school and create contextualized learning experiences. These qualities can be nurtured in any school, no matter what the income level of the students, and demonstrated by well-documented projects such as the Comer Schools, the Coalition for Successful Schools, the Accelerated Schools Project, and CRESPAR.

Science teachers dedicated to education reform and science for all have to look beyond their classroom walls in order to grapple with the complex array of factors affecting student achievement in science. Still, despite the many reasons for low achievement, there is probably no substitute for outstanding instruction as the cure.

11

Policy, Research, and Practice in Science Education Reform

I believe
fate smiled & destiny
laughed as she came to my cradle
"know this child will be able"
laughed as she came to my mother
"know this child will not suffer"
laughed as my body she lifted
"know this child will be gifted
with love, with patience
and with faith
she'll make her way"
— "Wonder," a song by Natalie Merchant (1995)

WHAT EVER HAPPENED TO ELENA?

This volume opened with a melodramatic fictitious event involving the reader and Elena. The purpose was not to inspire pity for Elena. Indeed, save for the rather outlandish circumstances by which Elena is orphaned and imaginary responsibility is transferred to the reader, Elena's situation is neither particularly bad nor unrealistic. She is healthy, happy, and loved. She is living above the poverty level, a circumstance not enjoyed by about 25% of the nation's children. She attends schools that are well-funded and generally highly regarded.

Rather, the purpose of the Elena scenario was to create a situation in which the reader, as a responsible, moral person, must come to grips with the fact that the school system, in general, and the science education program, in particular, simply does not work well for this child. If Elena's welfare was truly everyone's responsibility, then the tendency toward satisfaction with a system that we acknowledge as flawed (although it may work well for some students), would be replaced by frustration and the desire to create something better.

The Elena scenario and other situations presented throughout this volume ask us to imagine how schools might be changed if the obligation for the education of each child in America was given to each responsible adult. Yet, schools cannot be changed in a haphazard way and should not be altered so that the needs of a few children prevail over all. The equity schema introduced in chapter 1 and refined in chapter 6 provides a framework to examine the equity of science education within a school or school district by looking first at outcomes (achievement). If outcomes are unsatisfactory, especially for groups of diverse learners, then an examination of inputs (resources, very broadly defined) is logical. This volume argued that for many low SES students, students of color, English language learners, students with disabilities, and girls, the conditions for learning science are so unequal, that gaps in science achievement are hardly surprising. Furthermore, systematically examining opportunity to learn factors is the obvious and rational approach for improvement.

If students have been provided a reasonable decent floor of resources for learning science, and outcomes are still low for some groups, then interventions should be considered. This will cost money and necessitate trade-offs. The argument made in this volume, however, is that if a decent basic floor of resources were in place (and it often is not), the amount and extent of interventions necessary are likely to shrink substantially. However, getting the basic floor of resources in place also costs money. For instance, if a goal is to provide all U.S. high school students with certified science teachers who have substantial background knowledge in their science subject areas (at least undergraduate majors), then this would likely entail substantial costs, despite the fact that most states have this on the books as a requirement for teacher licensure. Due to the number of uncertified and unqualified teachers currently teaching science, correcting the situation would be expensive (e.g., higher salaries to attract people with this expertise or funds for educating new science teachers).

The science education reform movement with its high standards linked to promising practices for teaching and learning holds a great deal of promise for underserved students because it includes all students, is systemic, and provides accountability through measures of success. Moreover, many state and local systems of education demonstrated their willingness to back the reform with serious efforts at school improvement when achievement falls short of the goals. Increasingly, states are willing to disaggregate data in order to better understand and respond to the needs of various groups of learners, and to evaluate school programs via assessment systems that include those who have been exempted in the past, such as students with disabilities and English language learners.

Thus, systemic reform has built the foundation for improved science education for all by providing worthy goals (the standards), aligned assessment systems (in progress), and the will and funding (in some situations) to achieve them. However, the goal of high standards achieved by all is bound to be far more difficult than anyone imagined. Given the unprecedented diversity within our schools, coupled with the objective of providing every child with an education characterized by a level of learning expected of only a few in the past, it is crucial to examine critically every aspect of the reform. First and foremost, is there a danger of increasing the gaps between the haves and have nots in science?

For policymakers, administrators, and science educators who make systemic decisions (from national leaders to science department chairs), attention to equity issues is critical. Some of these big decisions can be colorblind and still benefit students who have been underserved in the past. Decisions to provide better curriculum materials, aligned with science standards, or to promote curriculum-based professional development are two examples. Yet, in addition to the colorblind approach, the willingness to examine the effects of new curricula on specific groups of diverse learners using sound research methods, or to create more effective learning environments for students who are not flourishing under mainstream conditions, must also be part of equitable systemic reform.

For individual classroom science teachers, the challenge is, perhaps, even greater. Teachers are in the positions not only to make important decisions about how the science learning environment will be structured for their students as groups, but they also have the power to directly influence the lives of individual students. Although this has always been the challenge that teachers face, the diversity within American schools, coupled with the increasingly high stakes for all involved with the educational enterprise, makes a teacher's job harder, if not heroic. The movements toward involving teachers in important curricular decisions, continuous in-house professional development, and teacher action research are all positive signs that those who are working directly with students can influence the reform from the bottom–up, as policymakers make congruent top–down decisions. We need more teachers with the ability to understand how to best reach diverse learners as we aim for science for all and to communicate their knowledge and practice to the field.

This volume has taken a positive and optimistic approach toward systemic reform, while bringing to light the equity issues involved. It focuses primarily on the within-schools factors that can be influenced by science educators and policymakers. Yet, also acknowledged are the social, cultural, economic, and political factors outside of schools that impinge on the success of our students. Economic inequities and social problems are seldom left at the school or science classroom door. Due to its necessarily limited scope, this volume has only touched on some of these issues and has not critically examined the stubborn substructural inequities that threaten to topple any systemic improvements made in the educational arena.

We offer a response that is more ethical than political because it ought to cross political lines—informed, compassionate commitment. What if each citizen felt a compelling moral responsibility for a child like Elena? In advocating for Elena's best interests in education, one would soon discover the inadequacies of a system characterized by more student diversity, increased academic demands through standards-based reform, limited and unequal resources, and meager research and development efforts that are often metaphorically color-blind. In the United States, parents (especially middle class, well-situated parents) tend to defend the interests of the individual child in school. Educators often consider needs common to all children. Because, as we reform science education, the current system has not been effective for Elena and many of her peers, we must find a way to do both.

References

Adenika-Morrow, T. J. (1996, May). A lifeline to science careers for African-American females. *Educational Leadership, 53,* 80–83.

Alexie, S. (1999, June 21/28). The toughest Indian in the world. *The New Yorker,* pp. 96, 98, 100–102, 104–106.

Allen, N. J. (1995, April). *"Voices from the bridge" Kickapoo Indian students and science education: A worldview comparison.* Paper presented at the annual meeting of the National Association for Research in Science Teaching, San Francisco, CA.

Alsalam, N., Fischer, G. E., Ogle, L. T., & Smith, T. M. (1993). *The condition of education 1993.* Washington, DC: U.S. Government Printing Office.

American Association for the Advancement of Science. (1992). *Benchmarks for Science Literacy.* New York: Oxford University Press.

American Association for the Advancement of Science (1998). *Blueprints for reform.* New York: Oxford University Press.

American Association for the Advancement of Science, Project 2061. (1989). *Science for all Americans.* New York: Oxford University Press.

American Association of University Women. (1992). *How schools shortchange girls.* Washington, DC: Author.

American Chemical Society. (1996). *Chemcom: Chemistry in the community.* Dubuque, IA: Kendall-Hunt.

American Indian Science and Engineering Society. (1995). *Educating American Indian/Alaska Native elementary and secondary students.* Boulder, CO: Author.

Anderson, R. (1996, April). *Putting the National Science Education Standards into practice: Needed research.* Paper presented at the annual convention of the National Association for Research in Science Teaching, St. Louis, MO.

Apple, M. W. (1995). Taking power seriously: New directions in mathematics education and beyond. In W. G. Secada, E. Fennema, & L. B. Adajian (Eds.), *New directions for equity in mathematics education* (pp. 329–348). Cambridge University Press.

Arnold, C. L., & Kaufman, P. D. (1992). *School effects on educational achievement in mathematics and science: 1985–86.* National Assessment of Educational Progress. Research and Development Report. (ERIC Document Reproduction Service No. ED 345 951)

Atkinson, J. W. (1964). *An Introduction to motivation*. Princeton, NJ: Van Nostrand.

Atwater, M. (1995). *Equity for Black Americans in science education*. Background paper prepared for Equity Blueprint Committee. Washington, DC: American Association for the Advancement of Science Project 2061.

Atwater, M. M. (1996, October). Social constructivism: Infusion into the multicultural science education research agenda. *Journal of Research in Science Teaching, 33*, 821–838.

Ausubel, D. P. (1960). The use of advance organizers in the learning and retention of meaningful verbal material. *Journal of Educational Psychology, 51*, 267–272.

Bach, R. L. (1984). *Labor for participation and employment of Southeast Asian refugees in the United States*. Washington, DC: Office of Refugee Resettlement (DHHS).

Baird, B. (1995). Status of science education in rural schools. In P. B. Otto (Ed.), *Science education in the rural United States* (pp. 15–30). Washington, DC: Office of Educational Research and Improvement (ED).

Ball, D. L., & Cohen, D. K. (1996, December). Reform by the book: What is—or might be—the role of curriculum materials in teacher learning and instruction reform? *Educational Researcher, 25*, 6–8.

Bandura, A. (1977). Self-efficacy: Toward a unifying theory of behavior change. *Psychological Review, 84*, 191–215.

Banks, J. A. (1994). *Multiethnic education: Theory and practice*. Needham Heights, MA: Allyn & Bacon.

Barba, R. H. (1995). *Science in the multicultural classroom*. Needham Heights, MA: Allyn & Bacon.

Barth, P. (1994). *Curriculum Connections Blueprint*. Washington, DC: American Association for the Advancement of Science.

Bass, G. M., & Reis, R. R. (1995, April). *Scientific understanding in high ability high school students: Concepts and process skills*. Paper presented at the annual meeting of the American Educational Researchers Association, San Francisco, CA.

Batey, A., & Hart-Landsberg, S. (1993). *Riding the wind: Rural leadership in science and mathematics education*. Portland, OR: Northwest Regional Lab. (ERIC Document Reproduction Service No. ED 365 481)

Becker, J. R. (1981). Differential treatment of females and males in mathematics classes. *Journal of Research in Mathematics Education 72*, 119–132.

Bell, M., Bell, J., & Hartfield, R. (1993). *Everyday mathematics*. Evanston, IL: Everyday Learning Corporation.

Benbow, C. P., & Stanley, J. C. (1996). Inequity in equity: How "equity" can lead to inequity for high potential students. *Psychology, Public Policy and Law, 2*, 249–292.

Benning, V. (1998a, October 21). Alexandria lags on state tests. *The Washington Post*, p. B4.

Benning, V. (1998b, October 22). Hearing is set on state tests. *The Washington Post*, p. B01.

Benning, V. (1998c, October 30). Board eyes setting high standard on Va. exams. *The Washington Post*, p. B01.

Bernhardt, E. B. (1995, April). *A content analysis of science methods texts: What are we told about the bilingual learner?* Paper presented at the annual meeting of the American Educational Research Association, San Francisco, CA.

Bishop, J. H., Moriarty, J. Y., & Mane, F. (1998). Diplomas for learning not seat time: The impacts of New York Regents Examinations. In *Educational finance to support high learning standards: Final report* (pp. 56–77). New York: New York State Board of Regents.

Bobo, L. (1988). Group conflict, prejudice, and the paradox of contemporary racial attitudes. In P. Katz & D. Taylor (Eds.), *Eliminating racism: Profiles in controversy*. New York: Plenum.

Booth, W. (1995, July 21). University of California ends racial preferences. *The Washington Post*, pp. A1, A13.

Borland, J. H., & Wright, L. (1994). Identifying young, potentially gifted, economically disadvantaged students. *The Gifted Child Quarterly, 38*, 164–171.

Boswell, S. (1979, April). *Nice girls don't study mathematics: The perspective from elementary school*. Paper presented at the annual meeting of the American Educational Research Association, San Francisco.

Bourdieu, P. (1977). Cultural reproduction and social reproduction. In J. Karabel & A. H. Halsey (Eds.), *Power and ideology in education*. New York: Oxford University Press.

Bowles, S., & Gintes, H. (1976). *Schooling in capitalist America: Educational reform and the contradictions of economic life*. New York: Basic Books.

Boykin, A. W. (1986). The triple quandary and the schooling of Afro-American children. In U. Neisser (Ed.), *The school achievement of minority children* (pp. 57–92). Hillsdale, NJ: Lawrence Erlbaum Associates.

Boykin, A. W. (1994). Harvesting talent and culture: African-American children and educational reform. In R. Rossi (Ed.), *Schools and students at risk: Context and framework for positive change* (pp. 116–138). New York: Teachers College Press.

Breckenridge, J. S., Goldstein, D. S., & Zucker, A. A. (1996). *The impact on students of the SSI program: A pilot study of the impacts of the Louisiana and Montana SSIs*. Menlo Park, CA: SRI International.

Broder, D., & Morin, R. (1998, December 27). Struggle over new standards. *The Washington Post*, pp. A-1 & A-18.

Brosnan, F. L. (1983). Overrepresentation of low-socioeconomic minority students in special education programs in California. *Learning disability quarterly, 6*, 517–25.

Bruckerhoff, C. (1997, March). *Lessons learned in the evaluation of statewide systemic initiatives*. Paper presented to the Evaluation and Policy Studies Team at the National Institute for Science Education, University of Wisconsin, Madison.

Burbridge, L. (1991). *The Interaction of race, gender and status in education outcomes*. MA: Center for Research on Women, Wellesley College. (ERIC Document Reproduction Service No. ED 360243)

Burkham, D. T., Lee, V. E., & Smeardon, B. A. (1997). Gender and science learning early in high school: Subject matter and laboratory experiences. *American Educational Research Journal, 34*(2), 297–332.

Caplan, N., Choy, M. H., & Whitmore, J. (1992). Indochinese refugee families and academic achievement. *Scientific American, 266*(2), 36–42.

Carroll, L. G. (1946). *Alice's adventures in Wonderland*. New York: Random House.

Casal, T. (1998, April). Parental involvement of Latino families. Paper presented at the annual meeting of the National Association for Research on Science Teaching in San Diego, CA.

Casserly, P. L. (1979). *Helping able young women take math and science seriously in school*. New York: The College Board.

Cawley, J. (1994). *Equity in science education: A perspective on students with disabilities*. Background paper prepared for Equity Blueprint Committee. Washington, DC: American Association for the Advancement of Science Project 2061.

Cawley, J. F., Kahn, H., & Tedesco, A. (1989). Vocational education and students with learning disabilities. *Journal of Learning Disabilities, 22,* 630–634.

Ceci, S. J. (1991). How much does schooling influence general intelligence and its cognitive components? A reassessment of the evidence. *Developmental Psychology, 27,* 703–722.

Center for the Study of Social Policy. (1992). *The challenge of change—What the 1990 Census tells us about children.* St. Paul, MN: University of Minnesota.

Chaney, B., Burgdorf, K., & Atash, N. (1997, Fall). Influencing achievement through high school graduation requirements. *Educational evaluation and policy analysis, 19*(3), 229–244.

Charles A. Dana Center, The University of Texas at Austin (1996a, October). *Successful Texas schoolwide programs: Research study results.* Austin, TX: Author.

Charles A. Dana Center, The University of Texas at Austin (1996b, October). *Successful Texas schoolwide programs: School Profiles.* Austin, TX: Author.

Charles A. Dana Center, The University of Texas at Austin (1996c, October). *Successful Texas schoolwide programs: Voices of practitioners and parents.* Austin, TX: Author.

Chipman, S., & Thomas, V. G. (1987). The participation of women and minorities in mathematical, scientific, and technical fields. *Review of Research in Education, 14,* 387–430.

Cleminson, A. (1990). Establishing an epistemological base for science teaching in the light of contemporary notions of the nature of science and of how children learn science. *Journal for Research in Science Teaching, 27,* 429–445.

Clewell, B. C., Thorpe, M. E., & Anderson, B. T. (1987). *Intervention programs in math, science, and computer science for minority and female students in grades four through eight.* Princeton, NJ: Educational Testing Service.

Clune, W. (1993). *2061 and educational equity. Background paper prepared for the Project 2061.* Washington, DC: American Association for the Advancement of Science, Project 2061.

Cobern, W. W. (1988, April). *World view theory and misconceptions research.* Paper presented at the annual conference for the National Association of Science Teachers, Lake of the Ozarks, MO.

Cobern, W. W. (1991). *Worldview theory and science education research.* National Association of Research on Science Teaching, Monograph #3.

Cobern, W. W. (1993a, January). *A cooperative research group for the study of culture and science education in developing countries.* Paper presented at the UNESCO International Conference on Science Education in Developing Countries, Jerusalem, Israel.

Cobern, W. W. (1993b, April). *Worldview, metaphysics, and epistemology.* Paper presented at the annual conference for the National Association of Science Teachers, Atlanta, GA.

Cochron-Smith, M. (1995). Color blindness and basket making are not the answers: Confronting the dilemmas of race, culture, and language diversity in teacher education. *American Educational Research Journal, 32*(3), 493–522.

Cohen, D. K., & Hill, H. C. (1998, January). State policy and classroom performance: Mathematics reform in California. *CPRE Policy Briefs,* RB-23-January 1998, 1–13.

Colburn, A. (1997, April). *Beliefs driving the behaviors of an exemplary urban science teacher.* Paper presented at the 1997 Annual Conference of the National Association of Research Science Teaching.

Colvin, R. (1988, November 30). California researchers "accelerate" activities to replace remediation. *Education Week,* 106–107.

Consortium for Policy Research in Education. (1995, July). Tracking student achievement in science and math: The promise of state assessment programs. *CPRE Policy Briefs*, 1–12.

Corcoran, T. B. (1997, February). *Evaluating systemic reform*. Paper presented at the NISE Forum, Washington, DC.

Crandall, V. C. (1969). Sex differences in expectancy of intellectual and academic reinforcement. In C. P. Smith (Ed.), *Achievement-related behaviors in children* (pp. 11–45). New York: Russell Sage Foundation.

Czerniak, C. M., & Lumpe, A. T. (1996). Relationship between teacher beliefs and science education reform. *Journal of Research in Science Teaching*, 7(4), 247–266.

Darling-Hammond, L. (1994). Performance-based assessment and educational equity. *Harvard Educational Review*, 64(1), 5–30.

Daugherty, K. J. (1996). Opportunity-to-learn standards: A sociological critique. *Sociology of Education, Extra Issue*, 40–65.

Davidson, M. (1990). *Northwest ESD 189 special education equity project: Final report. July 1, 1989 to June 30, 1990*. Seattle, WA: Washington Research Institute. (ERIC Document Reproduction Service No. ED 332 443).

Delpit, L. (1988). The silenced dialogue: Power and pedagogy in educating other people's children. *Harvard Educational Review*, 58, 280–898.

Dionne, E. J., Jr. (1998, August 11). Good teachers do make a difference. *The Washington Post*, p. A21.

Dresselhaus, M. S., Franz, J. R., & Clark, B. C. (1994, March 11). Interventions to increase the participation of women in physics. *Science*, 263, 1392–1393.

Driver, R., Asoko, H., Leach, J., Mortimer, E., & Scott, P. (1994, October). *Constructing scientific knowledge in the classroom*. 5–12.

Eccles, J. S. (1992). School and family effects on the ontogeny of children's interests, self-perceptions, and activity choice. In J. Jacobs (Ed.), *Nebraska Symposium on Motivation, 1992*. Lincoln: University of Nebraska Press.

Eccles, J. S. (1995). *Issues related to gender equity*. Background paper prepared for Equity Blueprint Committee. Washington, DC: American Association for the Advancement of Science Project 2061.

Eccles, J. S., Adler, T. F., & Meece, J. L. (1984). Sex differences in achievement: a test of alternate theories. *Journal of Personality and Social Psychology*, 46, 26–43.

Eccles, J. S., & Blumenfeld, P. C. (1985). Classroom experiences and student gender: Are there differences and do they matter? In L. C. Wilkinson & C. Marrett (Ed.), *Gender influences in classroom interaction* (pp. 79–114). Hillsdale, NJ: Lawrence Erlbaum Associates.

Eccles, J. S., & Harold, R. D. (1990). Gender differences in educational and occupational patterns among the gifted. In N. Colangelo, S. G. Assouline, & D. L. Amronson (Eds.), *Talent development: Proceedings from the 1991 Henry B. and Jocelyn Wallace National Research Symposium on Talent Development*. Unionville, NY: Trillium Press.

Educational Equity Project. (1989). *Our voices, our vision: American Indians speak our for educational excellence*. New York: The College Board. Boulder, CO: American Indian Science and Engineering Society.

Eisenhart, M., Finkel, E., & Marion, S. F. (1996, Summer). Creating the conditions for scientific literacy: A re-examination. *American Educational Research Journal*, 33, 261–295.

Entwisle, D. R., & Alexander, K. L. (1992, February). Summer setback: Race, poverty, school composition, and mathematics achievement in the first two years of school. *American Sociological Review*, 57, 72–84.

Fennema, E., Carpenter, T. P., Jacobs, V. R., Franke, M. L., & Levi, L. W. (1998a). A longitudinal study of gender differences in young children's mathematical thinking. *Educational Researcher, 27*(5), 6–11.

Fennema, E., Carpenter, T. P., Jacobs, V. R., Franke, M. L., & Levi, L. W. (1998b). New perspectives in gender differences in mathematics: A reprise. *Educational Researcher, 27*(5), 19–21.

Feyerabend, P. K. (1976). On the critique of scientific reason. In R. S. Cohen, P. K. Feyerabend, & M. W. Wartofsky (Eds.), *Essays in memory of Imre Lakatos: Boston studies in the philosophy of science.* Dordrecht, The Netherlands: Reidel.

Findings From The Condition of Education. (1997). Washington, DC: U.S. Department of Education, National Center for Educational Statistics.

Firestone, W. A., Mayrowetz, D., & Fairman, J. (1998). Performance-based assessment and instructional change: The effects of testing in Maine and Maryland. *Education Evaluation and Policy Analysis, 20*(2), 95–113.

Fisher, J. B., Schumaker, J. B., & Deshler, D. D. (in press). Searching for validated inclusive practices: A review of the literature. *FOCUS on Exceptional Children.*

Fordham, S., & Ogbu, J. U. (1986). Black students' school success: Coping with the "burden of 'acting white.'" *The Urban Review, 18*(3), 176–206.

Fraser, J. W., & Irvine, J. J. (1998, May 13). "Warm demanders." *Education Week on the Web.* http://www.edweek.com

Freiberg, H. J. (1993). A school that fosters resilience in inner-city youth. *Journal of Negro Education, 62*(3).

Friedman, A. J., & Donley, C. C. (1985). *Einstein as myth and muse.* Cambridge, England: Cambridge University Press.

Gamoran, A. (1989). *Instructional organization and educational equity* (OERI Grant G00869007). Madison, WI: National Center on Effective Secondary Schools. (ERIC Document Reproduction Services No. ED 318 125)

Gamoran, A. (1992). Access to excellence: Assignment to honors English classes in the transition from middle to high school. *Education evaluation and policy analysis, 14,* 185–204.

Gamoran, A., & Berends, M. (1987). The effects of stratification in secondary schools: Synthesis of survey and ethnographic research. *Review of Educational Research, 57,* 415–435.

Gamoran, A., & Weinstein, M. (1995). *Differentiation and opportunity in restructured schools.* Madison, WI: Center on Organization and Restructuring Schools. (ERIC Document Reproduction Service No. ED 386 828)

Gardner, H. (1983). *Frames of mind.* New York: Basic Books.

Geary, R. (1997, April 21). Class conflict. *The New Republic, 12,* 14.

George, Y. S., & Van Horne, V. V. (1996). *Science education for all (SERA).* Washington, DC: American Association for the Advancement of Science.

Gibbons, A. (1992). Minority programs that get high marks. *Science, 258,* 1190–1196.

Gilliam, D. (1997, January 18). Clinton plan could cure a sick city. *The Washington Post,* pp. C1, C3.

Grasmick, N. (1998, March). *Letter from the Superintendent: High School Assessments.* [Online]. Available: http://www.msde.state.md.us/R&D/hsimprovement/supt-5th-6thgrade-letter.html

Green, T. F. (1980). *Predicting the behavior of the educational system.* Syracuse, NY: Syracuse University Press.

Green, T. F. (1983). Excellence, equity and equality. In L. S. Shulman & G. Sykes (Eds.), *Handbook of teaching and policy* (pp. 318–341). New York: Longman.

Greene, M. S. (1995, June 25). Daily struggles, distant dreams. *The Washington Post*, pp. A1, A16–A18.

Greenfield, T. A. (1996). Gender, ethnicity, science achievement and attitutudes. *Journal of Research in Science Teaching, 33*(8), 901–933.

Greeno, J. G. (1997, January/February). On claims that answer the wrong questions. *Educational Researcher, 26*, 5–17.

Gregory, J., Shanahan, T., & Walberg, H. (1985). Learning disabled 10th graders in main streamed settings: A descriptive analysis. *Remedial and Special Education, 6*(4), 25–33.

Grossen, B. (1995, July). *What works in middle school: Teaching big ideas in science.* Paper presented at NSF/AAAS conference on science and learning disabilities, Washington, DC.

Grossen, B., Romance, N. R., & Vitale, M. R. (1994). Science: Educational tools for diverse learners. *School Psychology Review, 23*, 442–463.

Haberman, M. (1995, June). Selecting "star" teachers for children and youth in urban poverty. *Phi Delta Kappan, 76*, 777–781.

Hamilton, L. S. (1998). Gender differences on high school science achievement tests: Do format and content matter? *Educational Evaluation and Policy Analysis, 20*(3), 179–195.

Hampton, E. (1991). Toward a redefinition of American Indian/Alaska native education. *Canadian Journal of Native Education, 20*, 261–309.

Harnisch, D., & Wilkinson, I. (1989, April). *Cognitive return of schooling for the handicapped: Preliminary findings from high school and beyond.* Paper presented at the annual meeting of the American Educational Research Association, San Francisco, CA.

Harvard-Smithsonian Center for Astrophysics (Producer). (1993). *A private universe* [Film]. (Available from the Annenberg/CPB Math and Science Collection, P.O. Box 2345, S. Burlington, VT, 05407-2345)

Heilbrunn, J. (1997, January 20). Speech therapy. *The New Republic, 4*, 17–19.

Heller, K. A. (1982). *Placing children in special education: Equity through valid educational practices.* Washington, DC: National Academy Press. (ERIC Document Reproduction Service No. 217 618)

Henig, J. R. (1997, March). *Building confidence for sustainable school reform in the District of Columbia.* Paper prepared for the seminar on "Education Reform in the District of Columbia: Lessons from Other Cities," organized jointly by the Woodrow Wilson International Center for Scholars' Comparative Urban Studies Project and the George Washington University Center for Washington Area Studies.

Hilton, T. L., Hsia, J., Solorzano, D. G., & Benton, N. L. (1988). *Persistence in science of high ability minority students.* Princeton, NJ: Educational Testing Service.

Hodgkinson, H. L. (1990). *The demographics of American Indians: One percent of the people, fifty percent of the diversity.* Washington, DC: Institute for Educational Leadership Publications.

Hodgkinson, H. L. (1995, October). What should we call people? Race, class and the Census for 2000. *Phi Delta Kappan, 77*(2), 173–179.

Hoffer, T. (1992). Middle school ability grouping and student achievement in science and mathematics. *Educational Evaluation and Policy Analysis, 14*, 205–227.

Hoffer, T. B., et al. (1995). *Social background differences in high school mathematics and science coursetaking and achievement. Statistics in brief.* Chicago, IL: National Opinion Research Center. (ERIC Document Reproduction Service No. ED 389 533)

Hofmeister, A., Carnine, D., & Clark, R. (1994). *A Blueprint for action: Technology, media and materials*. Washington, DC: American Association for the Advancement of Science, Project 2061.

Holzer, J. (1989). Untitled. From *The Living Series*. Cincinnati, OH: Cincinnati Art Museum.

Horn, J. G. (1995). What is rural education? In P. B. Otto (Ed.), *Science education in the rural United States* (pp. 15–30). Washington, DC: Office of Educational Research and Improvement (ED).

Horwitz, S., & Strauss, V. (1997, February 16). A well-financed failure: System protects jobs while shortchanging classrooms. *The Washington Post*, pp. A1, A24–25.

Huang, S. L., & Waxman, H. C. (1996, April). *Learning environment differences between high- and low-achieving minority students in urban middle schools*. Paper presented at the Annual Meeting of the American Educational Research Association.

Jencks, C. (1972). *Inequality: A reassessment of the effect of family and schooling in America*. New York: Basic Books.

Jencks, C. (1979). *Who gets ahead?: The determinants of economic success in America*. New York: Basic Books.

Kahle, J. B. (1996). *Thinking about equity in a different way*. Washington DC: The American Association for the Advancement of Science.

Kahlenberg, R. (1995a, April 3). Class, not race. *The New Republic*, 21, 24–27.

Kahlenberg, R. (1995b, July 17 & 24). Equal opportunity critics. *The New Republic*, 20, 22, 24–25.

Kantowitz, B., & Springen, K. (1997, October 6). Why Johnny stayed home. *Newsweek*, p. 60.

Kidsnet. [On-line]. (1998). Available: http://www.kidsnet.org. Washington, DC: Author.

Kluegel, J., & Smith, E. (1986). *Beliefs about inequality: Americans' views about what ought to be*. New York: de Gruyter.

Kohr, R. L., Masters, J. R., Coldiron, J. R., Blust, R. S., & Skiffington, E. (1991). The relationship of race, class, and gender with mathematics achievement for fifth-, eighth-, and eleventh-grade students in Pennsylvania schools. *Peabody Journal of Education*, 66, 147–171.

Kozol, J. (1991). *Savage inequalities*. New York: Crown Publishers.

Kuhn, T. S. (1962). *The structure of scientific revolutions*. Chicago: University of Chicago Press.

Kulik, J. A., & Kulik, C. L. C. (1991). Ability grouping and gifted students. In N. Colangelo & G. Davis (Eds.), *Handbook of Gifted Education* (pp. 178–196). Boston: Allyn & Bacon.

Lacelle-Peterson, M., & Rivera, C. (1993). *Will the national educational goals improve the progress of English language learners?* Washington, DC: Clearinghouse on Language and Linguistics. (ERIC Document Reproduction Service No. ED 362 073)

Ladson-Billings, G. (1995). Toward a theory of culturally relevant pedagogy. *Journal of Educational Research*, 32, 465–491.

Laguarda, K. G. (1998, March). *Assessing SSIs impacts on student achievement: An imperfect science*. Menlo Park, CA: SRI Associates.

Laguarda, K. G., Breckenridge, J. S., & Hightower, A. M. (1994, September). *Assessment programs in the Statewide Systemic Initiatives (SSI) states: Using student achievement data to evaluate the SSI*. Washington, DC: Policy Studies Associates, Inc.

Land, R. (1997). Moving up to complex assessment systems. *Evaluation Comment, 7*(1), 1–21.

Lee, O. (1995). *Asian American students in science education.* Background paper prepared for Equity Blueprint Committee. Washington, DC: American Association for the Advancement of Science Project 2061.

Lee, O. (1997). Diversity and equity for Asian American students in science education. *Science education, 81*(1), 107–122.

Lee, O. (1998). *Current conceptions of science achievement in major reform documents and implications for equity and assessment.* (Research Monograph #12). Madison, WI: University of Wisconsin, National Institute for Science Education.

Lee, O. (in press). Science knowledge, world views, and information sources in social and cultural contexts: Making sense after a natural disaster. *American Educational Research Journal.*

Lee, O., & Anderson, C. W. (1993). Task engagement and conceptual change in middle school science classrooms. *American Educational Research Journal, 30,* 585–610.

Lee, O., & Fradd, S. H. (1996a). Interactional patterns of linguistically diverse students and teachers: Insights for promoting science learning. *Linguistics and Education: An International Research Journal, 8,* 269–297.

Lee, O., & Fradd, S. H. (1996b). Literacy skills in science performance among culturally and linguistically diverse students. *Science Education, 80,* 651–671.

Lee, O., & Fradd, S. H. (1998). Science for all, including students from non-English-language backgrounds. *Educational Researcher, 27*(4), 12–21.

Lee, O., Fradd, S. H., & Sutman, F. X. (1995). Science knowledge and cognitive strategy use among culturally and linguistically diverse students. *Journal of Research in Science Teaching, 32,* 797–816.

Leinhardt, G., Seeward, A. M., & Engel, M. (1979). Learning what's taught: Sex differences in instruction. *Journal of Educational Psychology, 71,* 432–439.

Lenz, B. K., Schumaker, J. B., & Deschler, D. (1995). *Planning for academic diversity in America's classrooms: Windows on reality, research, change and practice.* Lawrence, KS: The University of Kansas Center for Research on Learning.

Linn, R. L. (1994, December). Performance assessment: Policy promises and technical measurement standards. *Educational Researcher, 23,* 4–14.

Linn, R. L., & Herman, J. L. (1997, February). *A policymaker's guide to standards-led assessment.* Denver, CO: Education Commission of the States.

Lipton, E. (1995, June 25). In Fairfax high tech equals power. *The Washington Post,* pp. A1, A11.

Lorde, A. (1996). Our difference is our strength. *Ms., 7*(1), 61–64.

Loucks-Horsley, S., et al. (1998). *Designing professional development for teachers of mathematics and science.* Thousand Oaks, CA: Corwin Press.

Loveless, T. (1995). *Parents, professionals, and the politics of tracking policy.* Cambridge, MA: Harvard University, Kennedy School of Government. (ERIC Document Reproduction Service No. ED 390121)

Luft, J., da Cunha, T., & Allison, A. (1998, April). *Increasing the participation of minority students in science: A study of two teachers.* Paper presented at the annual meeting of the National Association for Research in Science Teaching, San Diego, CA.

Lynch, S. (1990). Fast-paced science for the academically talented: Issues of age and competence. *Science Education, 74*(6), 585–596.

Lynch, S. (1991). Untangling the bilingual education controversy. *Studia Anglica Posnaniensia: An International Review of English Studies*, 25–27.

Lynch, S. (1992, Summer). Fast-paced high school science for the academically talented: A six-year perspective. *The Gifted Child Quarterly*, 36, 147–154.

Lynch, S. (1993, April). *The gifted and talented at Walbrook High, a restructured school in Baltimore, Maryland: Alika's story.* Paper presented at the annual conference of the American Educational Research Association. (ERIC Document Reproduction Services Number ED 360 784).

Lynch, S. (1994). Ability grouping and science education reform: Policy and research base. *Journal of Research in Science Teaching*, 31(2), 105–128.

Lynch, S. (1995, April). *The missing link: The pre-implemented curriculum in Project 2061.* Paper presented at the annual meeting of the National Association for Research in Science Teaching, San Francisco, CA.

Lynch, S. (1997). Novice teachers' encounters with national science education reform: Entanglements or intelligent interconnections? *Journal for Research in Science Teaching*, 34(1), 3–17.

Lynch, S. (1998, March). An equity schema for science education reform: Listening to our better angels. In *Educational finance to support high learning standards: Final report.* New York: New York State Board of Regents.

Lynch, S., Atwater, M., Cawley, J., Eccles, J., Lee, O., Marrett, C., Rojas-Medlin, D., Secada, W., Stefanich, G., & Wiletto, A. (1996). *An Equity Blueprint for Project 2061 science education reform: Second draft.* Washington DC: American Association for the Advancement of Science, Project 2061.

Lynch, S., & Mills, C. A. (1993). Identifying and preparing disadvantaged and minority youth for high-level academic achievement. *Contemporary Educational Psychology*, 18, 66–76.

Lynch, S., & Mills, C. J. (1990). The skills reinforcement project: An academic program for high potential minority youth. *Journal for the Education of the Gifted*, 13, 364–379.

Lynch, S., & Taymans, J. (1998, January). *Novice teachers' implementation of the Unit Organizer: Theory meets practice in the real world.* Paper presented at the Annual Conference of the Association for the Education of Teachers in Science, Minneapolis, MN.

Lynch, S., & Thomas, G. (1995). Hands-On Universe at Robinson Secondary School. In S. Rockman (Ed.), *Evaluation of the Hands-On Universe project for the 1994–1995 academic year* (pp.). San Francisco: Lawrence Berkeley Laboratory.

Madaus, G. F. (1994, Spring). A technological and historical consideration of equity issues associated with proposals to change the nation's testing policy. *Harvard Educational Review*, 64(1), 5–30.

Maker, C. J. (1996). Identification of gifted minority students: A national problem, needed changes and a promising solution. *Gifted Child Quarterly*, 40, 41–50.

Malloy, C. (1996, November 17). Glimmers of hope amid clouds. *The Washington Post*, pp. B1, B7.

Marrett, C., & Ziege, A. (1995). *Towards an equity agenda.* Background paper prepared for Equity Blueprint Committee. Washington, DC: American Association for the Advancement of Science Project 2061.

Martinez, D. (1996, December). First People, firsthand knowledge. *Sierra*, 81(6), 50–51, 70–71.

Maryland schools: Who's paying? (1997, April 18). *The Washington Post*, p. A23.

Maryland State Department of Education (1997). *Maryland school performance report 1997.* Baltimore, MD: Author.

Massell, D. (1998, July). State strategies for building local capacity: Addressing the needs of standards-based reform. *CPRE Policy Briefs,* 1–15.

Massell, D., & Goertz, M. (1994, August). *2061 POLICY Blueprint.* Paper prepared for the American Association for the Advancement of Science Project 2061, Washington, DC.

Mathematical Sciences Education Board National Research Council. (1990). *Reshaping school mathematics: A philosophy and framework for curriculum.* Washington, DC: National Academy Press.

Matthew, K. L. (1995). Teaching and learning science in the rural setting. In P. B. Otto (Ed.), *Science education in the rural United States* (pp. 15–30). Washington, DC: Office of Educational Research and Improvement (ED).

Matthews, J. (1998, November 8). Take out your no. 2 pencils. *The Washington Post Magazine,* pp. 11–13, 25–31.

Matyas, M. L., & Malcom, S. M. (1991). *Investing in human potential: Science and engineering at the crossroads.* Washington, DC: American Association for the Advancement of Science.

Meadows, L. (1998, January). *Effective teaching in an urban middle school.* Paper presented at the annual meeting of the Association for the Education of Teachers in Science, Minneapolis, MN.

Medlin, D. R. (1995). *Meeting the Challenge of Equity in Science Education in Rural Schools.* Background paper prepared for Equity Blueprint Committee. Washington, DC: American Association for the Advancement of Science Project 2061.

Merchant, N. (1995). Wonder. On *Tigerlily* [CD]. NY: Electra Entertainment Group, Warner Communications.

Mid-Atlantic Eisenhower Consortium for Mathematics and Science Education. (1997). *TIMSS: A sourcebook of eighth grade findings.* Philadelphia: Author.

Monk, D. (1994, November). *Fiscal Implications of Project 2061: A Finance Blueprint for reform.* Paper prepared for the American Association for the Advancement of Science Project 2061, Washington, DC.

Morning, C. (1988). *Final report to the Exxon Foundation: Improving the response capabilities of educational programs for minorities.*

Murphy, N. (1996, March). *Multicultural Mathematics and Science: Effective K–12 practices for equity.* (ERIC Document Reproduction Services Number EDO-SE-96-1)

Nakashima, E. (1998, May 26). New school of thought on tests. *The Washington Post,* pp. B1, B5.

National Center for Educational Statistics. (1992a). *Language characteristics and academic achievement: A look at Asian and Hispanic eighth graders in NELS: 1988.* Washington, DC: U.S. Department of Education, Office of Educational Research and Improvement.

National Center for Educational Statistics. (1992b, March). *The 1990 science report card.* Washington, DC: U.S. Department of Education, Office of Educational Research and Improvement.

National Center for Educational Statistics (1996, July). Increasing the inclusion of students with disabilities and limited English proficient students in NAEP. *Focus on NAEP, 2,* 1–5.

National Center for Research on Teacher Learning. (1994). *A Blueprint for the education of Project 2061 teachers.* East Lansing: Michigan State University.

National Center for Science Teaching and Learning. (1994). *School Organization Blueprint.* Paper prepared for the American Association for the Advancement of Science Project 2061, Washington, DC.

National Commission on Teaching and America's Future. (1996). *What matters most: Teaching for America's future.* New York, NY: Author.

National Council of Teachers of Mathematics. (1989). *Curriculum and evaluation standards for school mathematics.* Reston, VA: Author.

National Council of Teachers of Mathematics. (1991). *Professional standards for teaching mathematics.* Reston, VA: Author.

National Council of Teachers of Mathematics. (1995). *Assessment Standards for School Mathematics.* Reston, VA: Author.

National Education Goals Panel. (1994). *Data volume for the National Education Goals Report* (Vol. 1). Washington, DC: Author.

National Research Council. (1989). *Everybody counts.* Washington, DC: National Academy Press.

National Research Council. (1995). *National science education standards.* Washington, DC: National Academy Press.

National Research Council. (1996). *National science education standards.* Washington, DC: National Academy Press.

National Science Board. (1996). *Science & engineering indicators—1996.* Washington, DC: U.S. Government Printing Office. (NSB 96-21)

National Science Board. (1998). *Science & engineering indicators—1998.* Arlington, VA: National Science Foundation.

National Science Foundation. (1992). *Indicators of science and mathematics education 1992.* Washington DC: Author.

National Science Foundation. (1994). *Women, minorities, and persons with disabilities in science and engineering.* Arlington, VA: Author.

National Science Foundation. (1996a). *Indicators of science and mathematics education, 1995* (1996 ed.). Arlington, VA: Author.

National Science Foundation, (1996b). *Indicators of science and mathematics education, 1996.* Arlington, VA: Author.

National Science Foundation, (1996c). *Women, minorities and persons with disabilities in science and engineering: 1996.* Arlington, VA: Author.

National Science Foundation, (1996d, March). Student Achievement through USI on urban systemic initiatives 1996. *Synergy,* 1–6.

National Science Foundation, (1998, January). *Infusing equity in systemic reform: An implementation scheme.* Arlington, VA: Author.

National Science Foundation Directorate for Education and Human Resources. (1996, October). *Review of instructional materials for middle school science.* Washington, DC: Author.

National Science Foundation, Division of Research, Evaluation, and Dissemination, Directorate for Education and Human Resources. (1992). *Indicators of science and mathematics education 1992.* Washington, DC: Author.

National Science Teachers' Association. (1996). *Pathways to science standards: High school level.* Arlington, VA: Author.

National Science Teachers' Association. (1998). *Standards for Science Teacher Education.* Arlington, VA: Author.

Newmann, F., Brandt, R., & Wiggins, G. (1998, August–September). An exchange of views on "Semantics, psychometrics, and assessment reform: A close look at 'Authentic' assessments." *Educational Researcher, 27*(6), 19–20.

Nieto, S. (1996). *Affirming diversity: The sociopolitical context of multicultural education.* New York: Longman.

Nitko, A. J. (1995, Fall). Is the curriculum a reasonable basis for assessment reform? *Educational measurement: Issues and Practice,* 5–10, 35.

Oakes, J. (1985). *Keeping track.* New Haven, CT: Yale University Press.

Oakes, J. (1986). Keeping track, Part 1: The policy and practice of curriculum inequality. *Phi Delta Kappan, 68,* 148–153.

Oakes, J. (1990a). *Lost talent: The underparticipation of women, minorities, and disabled persons in science.* Santa Monica, CA: The Rand Corporation.

Oakes, J. (1990b). *Multiplying inequalities: The effects of race, social class, and tracking on opportunities to learn mathematics and science.* Santa Monica, CA: The Rand Corporation.

Oakes, J., & Wells, A. S. (1996). *Beyond the technicalities of school reform.* Los Angeles: UCLA Graduate School of Education and Information Studies.

Odden, A., & Clune, W. (1995). Improving educational productivity and school finance. *Educational Researcher, 24*(9), 24–30.

Ogbu, J. U. (1988). Class stratification, racial stratification, and schooling. In L. Weis (Ed.), *Class, race and gender in American education* (pp. 163–182). Albany: State University of New York Press.

Ogbu, J. U. (1992, November). Understanding cultural diversity and learning. *Educational Researcher, 21,* 5–14, 24.

O'Sullivan, C. Y., Reese, C. M., & Mazzeo, J. (1997). *NAEP science report card of rthe nation and the states.* Washington, DC: U.S. Department of Education.

O'Sullivan, C. Y., Weiss, A. R., & Askew, J. M. (1998). *Students learning science: A report on policies and practices in U.S. schools.* Washington, DC: U.S. Department of Education.

Parmar, R., & Cawley, J. (1993). Analysis of science textbook recommendations to meet the needs of students with disabilities. *Exceptional Children, 59,* 518–531.

Parsons, J. S., Kaczala, C., & Meece, J. L. (1982). Socialization of achievement attitudes and beliefs: Classroom influences. *Child Development, 53,* 322–339.

Pellegrino, J. W., Jones, L. R., & Mitchell, K. J. (1998). *Grading the Nation's Report Card: Evaluating the NAEP and transforming the assessment of educational progress.* Washington, DC: National Academy Press.

Peng, S. (1995). *Understanding racial-ethnic differences in secondary school science and mathematics achievement.* Research and development report. Washington, DC: Nation Center for Educational Statistics. (ED381342)

Phelan, P., Yu, H. C., & Davidson, A. L. (1994). Navigating the psychosocial pressures of adolescence: The voices and experiences of high school youth. *American Educational Research Journal, 31,* 415–447.

Phillips, D. C. (1995, October). The good, the bad, and the ugly: The many faces of constructivism. *Educational Researcher, 24,* 5–12.

Porter, A. C. (1993, June–July). School delivery standards. *Educational Researcher, 22,* 24–30.

Portz, J. (1997, March). *External Actors and the Boston Public Schools: The Courts, Business Community, and the Mayor.* Paper prepared for the seminar on "Education Reform in the District of Columbia: Lessons from Other Cities," organized jointly by the Woodrow

Wilson International Center for Scholars' Comparative Urban Studies Project and the George Washington University Center for Washington Area Studies, Washington, DC.

Powell, M., & Loeb, V. (1997a, February 18). In lieu of planning, patchwork. *The Washington Post*, pp. A1, A8–A9.

Powell, M., & Loeb, V. (1997b, February 18). For reformers, fire code law suit brought dismaying side effects. *The Washington Post*, p. A9.

Project 2061. (1996, Fall). Project 2061's influence on reform. *Project 2061 Today*, 6, 1–2.

Proulx, L. G. (1997, February 4). To each his zone? *The Washington Post*, Health, 13, p. 16.

Raspberry, W. (1997, March 7). Sermon on a bus. *The Washington Post*, p. A21.

Raudenbush, S. W., Rowan, B., & Cheong, Y. F. (1993). Higher order instructional goals in secondary schools: Class, teacher, and school influences. *American Educational Research Journal*, 30, 523–553.

Rawls, J. (1971). *A theory of justice*. Cambridge, MA: Belknap Press.

Redden, M. R. (1978). What is the state of the art? In H. Hofman (Ed.), *Science education for handicapped students*. Washington, DC: National Science Teachers Association.

Reyes, L. H., & Stanic, G. M. A. (1988). Race, sex, socioeconomic status and mathematics. *Journal for Research in Mathematics Education*, 19, 26–43.

Rivera, C., & Vincent, C. (1997). High school graduation testing: Policies and practices in the assessment of English Language Learners. *Educational Assessment*, 4(4), 335–355.

Rivera, C., Vincent, C., Hafner, A., & LaCelle-Peterson, M. (1997). *Statewide assessment programs: Policies and practices for the inclusion of limited English proficient students*. Washington, DC: ERIC Clearinghouse on Assessment and Evaluation. (ERIC Document Reproduction Service # ED421484)

Rockman, S. (1995). In school or out: Technology, equity, and the future of our kids. *Communications of the ACM*, 38, 25–29.

Rodriguez, A. J. (1997). The dangerous discourse of invisibility: A critique of the National Research Council's National Science Education Standards. *Journal of Research in Science Teaching*, 34, 19–38.

Rodriguez, A. J. (1998). Busting open the Meritocracy Myth: Rethinking equity and student achievement in science education. *Journal of Women and Minorities in Science and Engineering*, 4, 195–216.

Rogers, P., & Kaiser, G. (1985). *Equity in mathematics education: Influences of feminism and culture*. London: Falmer Press.

Rojas-Medlin, D. (1994). *Meeting the challenge of equity in science education in rural schools*. Background paper prepared for Equity Blueprint Committee. Washington, DC: American Association for the Advancement of Science Project 2061.

Rosebery, A. S., Warren, B., & Conant, F. R. (1992). Appropriating scientific discourse: Findings from language minority classrooms. *Journal of the Learning Sciences*, 2, 61–94.

Roseman, J. E., Kesidou, S., & Stern, L. (1996, November). *Identifying curriculum materials for science literacy: A Project 2061 evaluation tool*. Paper presented for the National Research Council's Colloquium "Using the National Science Education Standards to Guide the Evaluation, Selection, and Adaptation of Instructional Materials," Washington, DC.

Rosser, S. V. (1989). Feminist scholarship in the sciences: Where are we now and when can we expect a breakthrough? In N. Tuana (Ed.), *Feminism and science*. Bloomington: Indiana University Press.

Rosser, S. V. (1993). Female friendly science: Including women in curricular content and pedagogy in science. *Journal of General Education, 42,* 191–220.

Rucker, W., Dilley, C., & Lowry, D. (1988). *Heath mathematics.* Lexington, MA: Heath.

Salinger, G. L. (1991). The materials of physics instruction. *Physics Today, 44,* 39–45.

Sanchez, R. (1996, September 6). Blacks, whites finish high school at same rate. *The Washington Post,* p. A3.

Sanders, W. L., & Horn, S. P. (1995, March 3). Education assessment reassessed: The usefulness of standardized and alternative measures of student achievement as indicators for the assessment of educational outcomes. *Education policy analysis archives, 3*(6), 1–13.

Scantleberry, K., & Kahle, J. B. (1993). The implementation of equitable teaching strategies by high school biology student teachers. *Journal of Research in Science Teaching, 30,* 537–546.

Schmidt, W. H., et al. (1996). *Characterizing pedagogical flow: An investigation of mathematics and science teaching in six countries.* Dordrect, The Netherlands: Kluwer.

Secada, W. G. (1989). Educational equity versus equality of education: An alternative conception. In W. G. Secada (Ed.), *Equity in education.* Philadelphia: The Falmer Press.

Secada, W. G. (1991–1992). Agenda setting, enlightened self-interest, and equity in mathematics education. *Peabody Journal of Education, 66*(2), 22–56.

Secada, W. G. (1994a). Equity and the teaching of mathematics. In M. Atwater (Ed.), *Proceedings of a seminar on multi-cultural education in mathematics education* (pp.). Athens: Department of Science: University of Georgia.

Secada, W. G. (1994b). Equity and the teaching of mathematics. In M. M. Atwater, K. Radzik-Marsh, & M. Strutchens (Eds.), *Multicultural education: Inclusion for all* (pp. 19–38). Athens: The University of Georgia.

Secada, W. G. (1994c). Equity in restructured schools. *NCSMSE Research Review, 3*(3), 11–13.

Secada, W. G. (1995). *Recommendations for the science education of Hispanic students.* Background paper prepared for Equity Blueprint Committee. Washington, DC: American Association for the Advancement of Science Project 2061.

Shavelson, R. J., Baxter, G. P., & Pine, J. (1992). Performance assessments: Political rhetoric and measurement reality. *Educational Researcher, 21*(4), 22–27.

Shields, P. M., Corcoran, T. B., & Zucker, A. A. (1994, June). *Evaluation of NSF's Statewide Systemic Initiatives (SSI) Program: First-year report.* Prepared for the National Science Foundation. Menlo Park, CA: SRI International.

Shulman, L. S. (1986). Those who understand: Knowledge growth in teaching. *Educational Researcher, 15*(2), 4–14.

Slavin, R. E. (1990). Achievement effects of ability grouping in secondary schools: A best-evidence synthesis. *Review of Educational Research, 60,* 471–499.

Sleeter, C. E., & Grant, C. A. (1991). Mapping terrains of power: Student cultural knowledge versus classroom knowledge. In C. E. Sleeter (Ed.), *Empowerment through multi-cultural education* (pp. 49–68). New York: State University of New York Press.

Spillane, J. P., & Reimann, C. B. (1995, November). Local Educational Agencies and scientific literacy. *MSSI Policy & Practice Brief, Number 4,* Michigan Department of Education.

Spurlin, Q. (1995). Making science comprehensible for language minority students. *Science Teacher Education, 6*(2), 71–78.

Stake, R. E., & Raizen, S. A. (1997). Underplayed issues. In S. A. Raizen & E. D. Britton (Eds.), *Bold Ventures: Vol. 1.* Boston, MA: Kluwer.

Stecher, B. M., & Klein, S. P. (1997). The cost of science assessments in large-scale programs. *Educational Evaluation and Policy Analysis, 19*(1), 1–14.

Stefanich, G. (1994). *A blueprint on science for students with disabilities.* Background paper prepared for Equity Blueprint Committee. Washington, DC: American Association for the Advancement of Science Project 2061.

Stein, M., Norman, J., & Chambers, J. C. (1998, January). *Scaling up support in urban school districts: Using summer institutes to support change.* Paper presented at the annual meeting of the Association for the Education of Teachers in Science; Minneapolis, MN.

Subotnik, R. (1997). Teaching gifted students in a multicultural world. In J. A. Banks & C. A. McGee Banks (Eds.), *Multicultural Education: Issues and perspectives* (pp. 361–382). Boston, MA: Allyn & Bacon.

Sunburst Communications. (1998). *Voyage of the Mimi.* [On-line]. Available: http://www. nysunburst.com/mimi.html

Terwilliger, J. (1997, November). Semantics, psychometrics, and assessment reform: A close look at "authentic" assessments. *Educational Researcher, 26*(8), 24–27.

Texas Educational Agency. (1997, May 1). *Student performance results.* [On-line]. Available: www.tea.state.tx.us/student....smet/results/swreport/passelthn.htm

Thernstrom, S. (1993, Summer). The declining significance of race. *The American Experience,* p. 6.

Thompson, C. L., & Zeuli, J. S. (1997, May). The frame and the tapestry: Standards-based reform and professional development. In G. Sykes (Ed.), *The Heart of the Matter: Teaching as the Learning Profession* (pp. 1–52). San Francisco: Jossey-Bass.

Tidball, M., & Kistiakowsky, B. (1976). Baccalaureate origins of American scientists and scholars. *Science, 193,* 747–752.

Traub, J. (1995, July 17). It's elementary. *The New Yorker,* 74–79.

Treisman, E. U. (1990, March). *Academic peristroika: Teaching, learning and the faculty's role in turbulent times.* FIPSE Lecture at California State, San Bernadino.

United States Commission on Civil Rights. (1992). *Civil rights issues facing Asian Americans in the 1990s.* Washington, DC: U.S. Government Printing Office.

U.S. Department of Education, National Center for Education Statistics. (1996a, February). *High school seniors' instructional experiences in science and mathematics* (NCES 95-278). Washington, DC: U.S. Government Printing Office.

U.S. Department of Education, National Center for Education Statistics. (1996b, November). *Pursuing excellence* (NCES 97-198). Washington, DC: U.S. Government Printing Office.

United States Department of Education, National Center for Education Statistics. (1996c). *Urban Schools: The challenge and location of poverty* (NCES 96-184). Washington, DC: Author.

United States Department of Education, Office of Educational Research and Improvement. (1993). *National excellence: A case for developing America's talent.* Washington, DC: Author.

United States National Research Center for TIMSS. (1996, September). *A splintered vision: An investigation of U.S. science and mathematics education.* Dordrect, The Netherlands: Kluwer.

Van Sickle, M., & Spector, B. (1996). Caring relationships in science classrooms: A symbolic interaction study. *Journal of Research in Science Teaching, 33*(4), 433–454.

Vasquez, J. A. (1988). Contexts for learning for minority students. *The Educational Forum, 52*(3), 243–253.

Vetter, B. M. (1995). *Status of Hispanics in science and engineering in the United States.* Washington DC: American Association for the Advancement of Science.

Vobejda, B., & Pearlstein, S. (1996, September 27). Household income climbs. *The Washington Post*, pp. A1, A22.

Waldrip, B., & Taylor, C. S. (1994, March). *Permeability of students' world views to their school views.* Paper presented at the Annual Meeting of the National Association for Research in Science Teaching, Anaheim, CA.

Wang, M. C., Haertel, G. D., & Walberg, H. J. (1995, April). *Educational resilience: An emergent construct.* Paper presented at the Annual Meeting of the American Educational Research Association, San Francisco.

Webster's encyclopedic unabridged dictionary of the English language. (1989). New York: Gramercy Books.

Weiner, B. (1974). *Achievement motivation and attribution theory.* Morristown, NJ: General Learning Press.

Weiss, I. (1993). *National survey of science and mathematics education.* Unpublished tabulations.

Weiss, I. R. (1997, June). The status of science and mathematics teaching in the United States: Comparing teacher views and classroom practice to National Standards. *NISE Brief, 1*(3), 1–7.

Weissbourd, R. (1998). *The vulnerable child: What really hurts America's children and what we can do about it.* Reading, MA: Addison-Wesley.

Weldon, S. (1995, July 12). Magnet schools saved, but at what cost to system? *The Silver Spring Gazette*, p. A13.

White, P. A., Porter, A. C., Gamoran, A., & Smithson, J. (1996, June). Upgrading high school math: A look at three transition courses. *CPRE Policy Briefs*, 1–8.

Willetto, A. (1995). *Blueprint for the science education of American Indian/Alaskan Native K–12 students.* Washington, DC: American Association for the Advancement of Science Project 2061.

Wilson, H. C., & James, R. K. (1995). Serving the needs of minority students in rural settings. In P. B. Otto (Ed.), *Science education in the rural United States* (pp. 15–30). Washington, DC: Office of Educational Research and Improvement (ED).

Wilson, W. J. (1996). *When work disappears.* New York: Knopf.

Wolin, R. (1998, August 17 & 24). Reconstructing America: The symbol of America in modern thought by James W. Ceaser. *The New Republic*, 35–41.

Woodward, J., & Baxter, J. (1997). The effects of an innovative approach to mathematics on academically low-achieving students in mainstream settings. *Exceptional children, 63*(3), 373–388.

Wright, L. (1994, July 25). One drop of blood. *The New Yorker*, 46–55.

Wright, P., & Santa-Cruz, R. (1983). Ethnic composition of special education programs in California. *Learning Disability Quarterly, 6*(4), 387–394.

Wyckoff, J. H., & Naples, M. (1998). Educational finance to support high learning standards: A synthesis. In (Ed.), *Educational finance to support high learning standards: Final report* (pp. 1–25). New York: New York State Board of Regents.

Author Index

A

Adenika-Morrow, T. J., 121
Adler, T. F., 251
Alexander, K. L., 153
Alexie, S., 21
Allen, N. J., 68, 70, 75, 76, 77, 78
Allison, A., 198
Alsalam, N., 31
American Association for the Advancement
    of Science, Project 2061, 1, 13, 85,
    104, 133, 135, 170, 180, 209, 217
American Association of University Women,
    118, 121, 198–199
American Indian Science and Engineering
    Society, 120–121
Anderson, B. T., 91
Anderson, C. W., 11
Anderson, R., 118
Apple, M. W. 10
Arnold, C. L., 50
Askew, J. M., 133
Asoko, H., 117
Atash, N., 233, 234
Atkinson, J. W., 248, 250
Atwater, M., 11, 16, 17, 30, 117
Ausubel, D. P., 204

B

Bach, R. L., 51
Baird, B., 59, 60
Ball, D. L., 108, 109
Bandura, A., 250
Banks, J. A., 88, 196
Barba, R. H., 121, 203
Barth, P., 182,, 199
Bass, G. M., 180, 181
Batey, A., 59
Baxter, G. P., 225
Baxter, J., 116, 117
Becker, J. R,
Bell, J., 116
Bell, M., 116
Benbow, C. P., 184
Benning, V., 221, 233, 235, 237
Benton, N. L., 90
Berends, M., 161
Bernhardt, E. B., 63, 202
Bishop, J. H., 234
Blumenfeld, P. C., 199
Blust, R. S., 53
Bobo, L., 88
Booth, W., 88
Borland, J. H., 177, 178, 181

Subject Index

A

Ability Grouping, 89, 156–184
  competing mandates, 165–169
  and gifted/talented, 175–183
  history of, 156–157
  policy positions, 158–159
  politics, 177–179
  research on, 158–161
  and resources, 157–158
  restructured schools, 161–165
  school organization, 169–175
  talent development, 155–156, 183–184
Accountability, *see also* Assessment; Evaluation
Achievement, *see also* Assessment; TIMSS
  attitudes toward, 261–264
  and diverse groups, 21–46, 47–66
  gaps, 21–66, *see also* specific groups
  parental influence on, 51–52
  participation rates in science, 21–66
  programs that promote, 89–91
  and SES, 48–54
  and school type, 52–54, 61
  tests, 21–24
American Indians/Alaskan Natives, 28, 37–43, 120–121
  achievement, 32, 40–42,
  and curricula, 120–121
  demographics, 37–40
  and disadvantaged schools, 52
  as English language learners, 40
  and ethnicity/SES, 30, 40–42
  graduation rates, 40
  and gender, 35
  participation rates in science and math, 33, 35, 38–39, 42–43
  and worldview, 75–78
American Association for the Advancement of Science Directorate of Education and Human Resources Programs, 49
Asian Americans, 28–29, 43–45, 76–77, 256–258
  achievement, 32, 43–44
  attitudes of, 262–262, 267
  demographics, 43, 38–39
  as English language learners, 44, 63–64
  and ethnicity/SES, 30, 43–45, 36, 49–51
  families, 256–258
  and gender, 35
  graduation rates, 63–64
  participation rates in science and math, 33, 38–39, 43, 44, 63–64
  and worldview, 67–68
Assessment, *see also* Evaluation; NAEP; TIMSS
  accommodations, 219–220